THE METAPHYSICS

• THE BARNES & NOBLE LIBRARY OF ESSENTIAL READING •

THE METAPHYSICS

Aristotle

Translated by John H. McMahon

Introduction by Michael P. Levine

BARNES & NOBLE

NEW YORK

THE BARNES & NOBLE
LIBRARY OF ESSENTIAL READING

CONTENTS

INTRODUCTION

OPEN Aristotle's *Metaphysics* to any page and find yourself among the philosophers. Many of the great and perennial problems in philosophy are to be found here, and it continues to be one of the most widely discussed philosophy texts ever. As W. D. Ross says, "The motive which inspires Aristotle throughout the *Metaphysics* is the wish to acquire that form of knowledge which is most worthy of the name of wisdom."[1] Aristotle thought that wonder at the world around us was the beginning of philosophy. However, in a less romantic vein he also thought that the task of philosophy was, in a sense, to extinguish wonder by offering complete explanations of all there was to wonder about.

Whether one is new to philosophy, interested in intellectual history, or curious about the man whom Plato—in reference to his own great Academy—nicknamed "the mind of the school," the *Metaphysics* can be extraordinarily rewarding. Like the rest of the extant Aristotelian corpus, the *Metaphysics* constitutes a significant and influential part of the history of philosophy, and intellectual history generally. Remarkably, its influence—both religious and secular—has been virtually continuous over nearly two thousand five hundred years. Greek, Jewish, Arabic, and especially Christian philosophy are all Aristotelian to a degree. The *Metaphysics* in particular was central to the thought of Aquinas (1224-1274) and medieval philosophy, as well as to

Dante. The issues examined include the nature of metaphysics and philosophical method; reality; substance and attribute; form and matter and their relation of opposition; the existence and nature of a Prime Mover or an Unmoved Mover; essence; potentiality and actuality; truth; causation; unity; theology; the nature of numbers; sameness and difference; fact and value; the relationship between mind and matter; and criticism of other schools of thought—including important Pre-Socratics as well as that of Socrates and Plato. Of the approximately one hundred fifty treatises that Aristotle allegedly wrote, only thirty survive and luckily the *Metaphysics* is among them.

Aristotle was born at Stagira in Chalcidice, now part of Northern Greece, in 384 BC. His father, Nicomachus, was the physician to Amyntas II of Macedonia. The *Nichomachean Ethics* however are named after Aristotle's son, also named Nicomachus, who edited the *Ethics*. In 343 BC, Philip of Macedon chose Aristotle to supervise the education of his young son, Alexander (later to be the "Great"), and Aristotle taught Alexander for the next three years. In the school at Mieza, near modern Naousa, which can still be visited, Aristotle taught Alexander physics, meteorology, geography, morals, politics, and theology. They apparently had an amicable relationship and remained in contact, though the fondness Alexander at one time felt for Aristotle may have waned. Just how influential a figure Aristotle was over the ruthless Alexander, and in what ways he was most influential is unclear. Alexander did like to read and learn, but it would be difficult to imagine that Aristotle shaped Alexander's character in ways that he would have much approved of. (Aristotle did endorse slavery as a natural institution in the first book of the *Politics*.) Alexander wrote one letter to Aristotle in which he complained about his teacher writing his lecture notes down in the form of a treatise. Alexander must have liked the idea of relatively secret or private teachings—wanting to know things others did not. In reply, Aristotle said that most people would understand what he wrote anyway.

Soon after Alexander succeeded to the throne in 336 BC, Aristotle returned to Athens. It had been about twelve years after he left Plato's Academy, and he must have missed philosophizing and aspects of the Academy no matter how much he disagreed with the theories taught there. After being passed over to head the Academy in favor of Xenocrates, Aristotle established the Lyceum—his own school for philosophy. At the Lyceum, in the grove of Apollo Lyceius at the outskirts of Athens, Aristotle had philosophical discussions while walking in its shaded colonnades. It is from these walks and way of conducting philosophy that *Peripatetic* came to be the term relating to the philosophy or teaching methods of Aristotle. Following Alexander's death and the ensuing violent anti-Macedonian riots, he left Athens in 323 BC to avoid being put on trial for "impiety"—one of the stock charges at the time and one brought earlier against Socrates. He resigned the presidency of the Lyceum and died aged 62 in Chalcis on Euboea (the largest island of the Grecian archipelago) in 322 BC. Aristotle was alleged to be good natured, good humoured, witty, "handsome, but with small eyes," bald, and he liked to dress "distinctively."[2] Virtually all of Aristotle's treatises are versions of lecture notes he delivered to his students at the Lyceum. Thus Aristotle was among the first to start the popular practice of turning lecture notes into books that remains common with university lecturers to this day.

After Aristotle's death, his manuscripts were arranged and ordered by others. Metaphysics means "after the *Physics*," and it received its name simply because it was the group of manuscripts placed directly after the *Physics*. The term then became known as the branch of philosophy in which the kinds of topics Aristotle discusses in those treatises are examined—for example: substance, form, cause, and God. Metaphysics is sometimes called *first philosophy*. It is fundamentally concerned with the foundations and basic principles of philosophy as well as of other disciplines. Basic principles are those that cannot be inferred from or supported by anything more basic. They are supported by methods—usually not empirical—suitable to the subjects being investigated. In the *Metaphysics*, basic principles are often argued for by showing the paradoxical consequences of their denial. *Metaphysics* also refers to the theoretical and the a priori (non-empirical) investigation of questions regarded outside the scope of ordinary empirical science.

The traditional ordering of the treatises or books that make up the *Metaphysics* may not be random but it makes little sense, rendering the work as whole and the connections between its parts unclear and difficult to follow. (Different lists and translations of Aristotle's writings, and different arrangements of the work itself, vary as to the number of books they assign to the *Metaphysics*. The number, in line with the last of the ancient lists, is thirteen.) A number of scholars however, most notably Wilhelm Jaeger in 1912, and later W. D. Ross, sorted out a more logical sequence.[3] Those manuscripts revised and delivered by Aristotle, in the order he gave them, have been distinguished from student notes and editors' insertions. Additionally, sections of chapters that follow discussions of problems in earlier chapters in different books have been grouped together in later translations. One of the treatises is actually more of a lexicon that can be treated as either an appendix or a preliminary.

The significance of language and the importance of defining key terms for philosophy is also something that, while not new to Western philosophy since such concerns are clearly present in Socrates and Plato, nevertheless becomes even more crucial in Aristotle's writing. The fact that he includes a lexicon of key terms and concepts in the *Metaphysics*, along with the time he devotes to further explaining terms throughout the work, is evidence of the importance he attributed to this kind of linguistic analysis. Without these concerns about language and meaning, philosophy as Aristotle conceived it would not have been possible. Here too, his influence has been constant and never more so than in the twentieth century.

As with the *Physics* and *De Anima*, Aristotle began the *Metaphysics* with a historical survey—a style of philosophizing that remains prevalent in which one's own philosophical views are contextualized and compared with those of others. Although Aristotle became dissatisfied with aspects of Plato's philosophy in the Academy well before he left it to start his own, just how indebted he is to what he learned from Plato is apparent in his own writing. Without Plato it is difficult to imagine Aristotle. Nevertheless, in several places in the *Metaphysics* he critiques a centerpiece of Plato's best known philosophy—his theory of the Ideal (also known as the theory of the Forms or of Ideas).

Plato's theory of Ideas maintains that a Universal—a Universal (like "roundness") being anything that can be predicated of a particular (a ball, or planet)—exists independently of particular things that instantiate them. This view concerning the relation between Universals and particulars became known as Platonism or Realism. For example, there is a Form of the Good that exists independently of any good thing, and an ideal Form of "chair" (and all other things) that exists independently of all actual particular chairs, but that all such chairs instantiate. Particulars participate in or partake of the ideal Form "chair" that exists as a Universal in the realm of the Forms. It is a kind of abstraction from, or archetype of, all instances of all kinds of chairs—but an archetype that any particular chair has to partake of or participate in if it is to be a chair. Furthermore, it is the Forms rather than the Particulars that are, in a sense, most real. Thus, Plato's idealism, as illustrated most famously in his allegory of the cave in *The Republic*, maintains that the reality of the things we perceive is only a rather pale reflection of a higher realm of reality and truth—that of the Forms. That is the simplest explanation of what is arguably a more complex theory.

Nominalism (of or pertaining to names) is the view that denies objectivity to Universals or the Platonic Forms. It denies Platonism, or Realism as it is sometime called, which maintains that the Forms objectively exist even apart from being instantiated in any particular things. (Roundness, for example, exists apart from any round things.) Nominalists believe that words and concepts are Universal, but only concrete, individual things exist objectively. It is called nominalism because it maintains that Universals are merely names for abstractions like house, tree, or circle. They do not have real existence. Nothing with a separate essence of any of these Universals exists. Nominalism claims that there is no universality or objective existence to mental concepts or ideas existing in the mind. Nor is there any objective existence to these concepts and ideas as they exist in particular things that are similar in terms of class or species. Redness and roundness do not exist apart from red and round things. Thus, the philosophy of William of Ockham (1285?-1349?), George Berkeley (1685-1753), David Hume (1711-1776), and most contemporary philosophy influenced by linguistic analysis is nominalistic. Modern nominalistic theories include logical positivism, pragmatism, instrumentalism, and semantic accounts.

As expected, there are important variants—moderate to extreme—on nominalist and Platonist (Realist) positions. Some versions of nominalism are seen as opposed to Aristotle's and Aquinas' views as well as Plato's, even though nominalism is a position grounded in Aristotle's objection in the Metaphysics to Plato's Ideal theory. In contemporary terms, Aristotle and Aquinas are seen as moderate Realists. Moderate realism takes Universals to be located in the mind, but regards them as having a real and objective basis in particular things.

Plato's Ideal theory was itself developed in reaction to Pythagorean mysticism, the Heraclitean doctrine of continuous change, Socrates' views, and undoubtedly other sources as well. Aristotle's discussion of form and matter was an extension of Plato's more diffuse discussion of what he termed the principles of Unity and Dyad, and also of the Pythagorean principles of Limited and Unlimited. Matter, for Aristotle, is not necessarily something that we could know by means of our senses—the way it is thought of today. It was not necessarily "sensible." It could also be that which we come to know through our understanding instead of our senses. Matter could be "intelligible" through understanding without being "sensible." He also thought that there were different kinds or grades of sensible matter. Some, but not all matter, for example, could be generated (brought into existence) and destroyed (made to pass out of existence).[4]

For Aristotle, the explanation of why something exists must refer not only to its matter and form, but also to the four kinds of causes that bring it about. Aristotle's four kinds of cause are very different from, and cannot be subsumed under, the contemporary ordinary concept of a cause as an event temporally antecedent to its effect—an event that (somehow) brings about its effect. This ordinary concept is philosophically problematic and highly contested in contemporary philosophical thought. According to Aristotle, there are Material, Formal, Efficient and Final causes. The Material Cause is the matter that is changing. Aristotle says, "In one sense, what is described as a cause is that material out of which a thing comes into being and which remains present in it. Such, for instance, is bronze in the case of a statue, or silver in the case of a cup . . ." (*Physics* II.3). Since bronze and silver are both types of metal, metal is also seen as the Material Cause of the statue or cup. The Formal Cause is the form taken by the matter. The form that a statue or a cup will take is itself a cause of these things. The Efficient Cause is the primary source of change—the "maker" or "doer"—that which brings about the change in introducing form to matter. The sculptor would be the efficient cause of the statue. The Final Cause is the goal or purpose of the change. Aquinas employs this Aristotelian schema of causes in his various proofs for the existence of God. In Aristotelian terms, only the Material Cause can be said to be antecedent. Even the Final Cause operates during the change. Originally Aristotle thought that all of the kinds of causes were necessary and operative in all cases, but he probably changed his view on this.

In commenting on his philosophical predecessors, and using them as the foil for his own ideas, Aristotle was among the first—in Western Philosophy at any rate–to institute a method of philosophizing that lasted through the Middle Ages and is almost universally employed today. There is no completely original philosophy if that means a philosophy with no historical predecessors or intellectual influences and stimuli. For all its originality, Aristotle's writing is a continuation of the problems and philosophical and quasi-scientific investigations of his predecessors—beginning with the Milesian (from the city of Miletus) Pre-Socratics in the sixth century BC—Thales, Anaximander, and Anaximenes. These are the most prominent of the early thinkers Aristotle calls the Physicists since they were concerned with explaining the natural world.

Medieval Scholasticism resulted from the blending of Christian doctrine with Aristotelian philosophy—metaphysics in particular. It became the official philosophy of Roman Catholicism. Aristotle's most significant objection to Plato's Ideal theory is one that had repercussions throughout Scholastic philosophy when the so-called nominalist and realist (the Aristotelian and Platonic positions respectively) controversy became prominent in the late eleventh and twelfth centuries. The dispute had theological as well as philosophical implications. The Church was opposed to nominalism (the view that denies objectivity to universals) because it took it to be incompatible with the triune nature of God—three distinct persons but essentially one divine person. (The Church maintained that each distinct aspect or person of the trinity partook of the universal or essence of the one God.) Nominalism also had implications for the doctrine of natural law. It was thought that if there was no common human nature there could be no natural law. Apart from alleged theological consequences, it continues to be a significant source of philosophical dispute today. Aristotle rejected Plato's account of the relation between Universals and Particulars—a disagreement that also extended to, among other things, metaphysical conceptions of substance, accident, essence, and categories. But the significance of the objection, in the first instance, was that it struck at the core of Plato's view of reality—denying in fact that the realm of ideal Forms (kinds of archetypes) as conceived by Plato existed at all.

It took the fluid imagination and wishful thinking of the early church, medieval Scholastic, and other philosophers—mostly Christian but also Arabic and Jewish—to see a theistic God in Aristotle's theology of the Unmoved or Prime Mover; and then to develop it in line with his views on potentiality, actuality, substance, form, and causation. Aristotle, after all, believed the universe to be eternal. God is not the creator of the universe, as in scripture, but is its final cause—the reason behind its existence—and the physical universe depends upon God for its existence and motion at every moment. In his *Summa Theologiae* (1267-73), Aquinas develops these aspects of Aristotle's thought into a more complete theology. However, it is not easily apparent how or why Aquinas and others could use Aristotle's *Metaphysics* as a basis for developing a theistic account of God compatible with their respective scriptures. A novice can see that the God of the philosophers (based on Aristotle's *Metaphysics*) is not merely different, but significantly at odds with God as depicted in scripture. Athens is not Jerusalem. This adaptation of Aristotle's theology for their own religious ends and purposes is arguably not merely unsuccessful, but also one of the oddest developments in the history of philosophy. It is an extended and grand legacy that although dominant in contemporary analytic philosophy of religion—most of which is Christian and scholastically influenced or closely connected—some would see as both religiously and philosophically undesirable.

There is an enduring view, a received position, that interprets and regards metaphysics as primary not only in the sense of it being concerned with first principles and basic notions of substance or being, essence, and reality as such; but also as the most significant of all the various fields of philosophy. This view is often attributed to Aristotle and no doubt there is some textual support for it in the *Metaphysics*. Furthermore, contemporary philosophy has seen a grafting of many of Aristotle's traditional metaphysical issues onto philosophy of language and logic, so that the primacy and importance once attributed only to metaphysics—the idea that it is the ultimate or supreme branch of philosophy, the one more concerned with truth and wisdom than any other—is now sometimes applied to both—especially of course by some contemporary metaphysicians and philosophers of language.

While not disputing the significance Aristotle attributes to metaphysics, it is probably a mistake to regard him as considering it as unsurpassed in importance. If anything, Aristotle was clear that various branches of philosophy and the natural sciences were concerned with investigating different aspects of reality. To attribute supremacy—whether epistemic or evaluative in some other way—to one branch as opposed to another would be to draw faulty comparisons—not unlike perhaps trying to measure the value of one kind of virtue against another. It was Aristotle who said that one should not expect to find all virtues in a single individual, and it is implausible to suppose that he would have thought that the value and utility of one branch of philosophy could intelligibly be measured against some other. In practical or utilitarian terms, however, it is more likely Aristotle would have regarded, or have been committed to regarding, ethics as the most significant—concerned as it is with individuals' well-being and happiness.

One thing that, although not absent in the *Metaphysics*, is less evident than in some of his other works, is Aristotle's greatness as a humanist and as a moral philosopher with a practical and this-worldly focus—one that however realistic remains, in many ways, idealistic. This side of Aristotle is most obvious in the *Nichomachean Ethics* and his two other ethical treatises, but it is also evident in parts of the *Poetics, Rhetoric, Politics* and elsewhere. He not only cared deeply about questions like character and virtue in relation to human happiness, friendship, and love—he also had insightful things to say about them. For all of his technical ability, colossal intelligence, and interest in science, Aristotle was among the very first of the practical or applied philosophers—one who saw the significance of philosophy and philosophers as lying in their service to humankind. As a great moral psychologist; one who studied the nature of the virtues and vices; who was interested and dissected how and why people succeeded and failed to succeed morally and as human beings (to succeed morally is to succeed as a human being for Aristotle); and as an enemy of superstition, religious fanaticism, and moral turpitude, Aristotle might well have wished he could have been more influential, in real terms, than seems to be the case.

The *Metaphysics* is an original and standard work in philosophy. Although it is often difficult and does not read as easily as Plato's *Dialogues*, it is an indispensable and influential part of Western philosophy and intellectual history, and a work whose ideas are still much discussed in contemporary metaphysics.

Michael P. Levine is Professor of Philosophy at the University of Western Australia. Recent publications include *Integrity and the Fragile Self* (2003, co-authored); *The Analytic Freud* (ed); *Racism in Mind* (2004, *co-editor*) and articles on moral psychology, social and political philosophy, metaphysics, architecture and ethics, and film.

BOOK I

1. ALL men by nature are actuated with the desire of knowledge, 980a and an indication of this is the love of the senses; for even, irrespective of their utility, are they loved for their own sakes; and preeminently above the rest, the sense of sight. For not only for practical purposes, but also when not intent on doing anything, we choose the power of vision in preference, so to say, to all the rest of the senses. And a cause of this is the following,—that this one of the senses particularly enables us to apprehend whatever knowledge it is the inlet of, and that it makes many distinctive qualities manifest.

By nature then, indeed, are animals formed endowed with sense; but in some of them memory is not innate from sense, and in others it is. And for this reason are these possessed of 980b more foresight, as well as a greater aptitude for discipline, than those which are wanting in this faculty of memory. Those furnished with foresight, indeed, are yet without the capability of receiving instruction, whatever amongst them are unable to understand the sounds they hear; as, for instance, bees, and other similar tribes of animals; but those are capable of receiving instruction as many as, in addition to memory, are provided with this sense also.

The rest, indeed, subsist then through impressions and the operations of memory, but share experience in a slight degree; whereas the human race exists by means of art also and the powers of reasoning.

Now, experience accrues to men from memory; for repeated acts of memory about the same thing done constitute the force of a single experience: and experience seems to be a thing almost similar to science and art.

But science and art result unto men by means of experience; for experience, indeed, as Polus saith, and correctly so, has produced art, but inexperience, chance. But an art comes into being when, out of many conceptions of experience, one universal opinion is evolved with respect to similar cases. For, indeed, to entertain the opinion that this particular remedy has been of service to Callias, while laboring under this particular disease, as well as to Socrates, and so individually to many, this is an inference of experience; but that it has been conducive to the health of all,—such as have been defined according to one species,—while laboring under this disease, as, for instance, to the phlegmatic, or the choleric, or those sick of a burning fever, this belongs to the province of art.

As regards, indeed, practical purposes, therefore, experience seems in no wise to differ from art; nay, even we see the experienced compassing their objects more effectually than those who possess a theory, without the experience. But a cause of this is the following—that experience, indeed, is a knowledge of singulars, whereas art, of universals; but all things in the doing, and all generations, are concerned about the singular: for he whose profession it is to practice medicine, does not restore man to health save by accident, but Callias, or Socrates, or any of the rest so designated, to whom it happens to be a man. If, therefore, anyone without the experience is furnished with the principle, and is acquainted with the universal, but is ignorant of the singular that is involved therein, he will frequently fall into error in the case of his medical treatment; for that which is capable of cure is rather the singular.

But, nevertheless, we are of opinion that, at least, knowledge and understanding appertain to art rather than experience; and we reckon artists more wise than the experienced, inasmuch as wisdom is the concomitant of all philosophers rather in proportion to their knowledge.

But this is so because some, indeed, are aware of the cause, and some are not. For the experienced, indeed, know that a thing is so, but they do not know wherefore it is so; but others— I mean the scientific—are acquainted with the wherefore and the cause. Therefore, also, we reckon the chief artificers in each case to be entitled to more dignity, and to the reputation of superior knowledge, and to be more wise than the handicrafts- men, because the former are acquainted with the causes of the 981b things that are being constructed; whereas the latter produce things, as certain inanimate things do, indeed; yet these perform their functions unconsciously,—as the fire when it burns. Things indeed, therefore, that are inanimate, by a certain constitution of nature, perform each of these their functions, but the handicrafts- men through habit; inasmuch as it is not according as men are practical that they are more wise, but according as they possess the reason of a thing, and understand causes.

And, upon the whole, a proof of a person's having knowledge is even the ability to reach; and for this reason we consider art, rather than experience, to be a science; for artists can, whereas the handicraftsmen cannot, convey instruction.

And further, we regard none of the senses to be wisdom, although, at least, these are the most decisive sources of knowl- edge about singulars; but they make no affirmation of the wherefore in regard of anything,—as, for example, why fire is hot, but only the fact that it is hot.

Therefore, indeed, is it natural for the person who first discovers any art whatsoever, beyond the ordinary power of the senses, to be the object of human admiration, not only on account of something of the things that have been discovered being useful, but as one that is wise and superior to the rest of men. But when more arts are being discovered—both some, indeed, in relation to things that are necessary, and others for pastime—we invariably regard such more wise than those, on account of their sciences not being for bare utility. Whence all things of such a sort having been already procured, those sciences have been invented which were pursued neither for purposes of pleasure nor necessity, and first in those places where the inhabitants enjoyed leisure: wherefore, in the neighborhood of Egypt the mathematical arts were first established; for there leisure was spared unto the sacerdotal caste. It has then, indeed, been declared in the Ethics what is the difference between an art and a science, and the rest of the things of the same description.

But, at present, the reason of our producing this treatise is the fact, that all consider what is termed wisdom to be conversant about first causes and principles; so that—as has been said on a former occasion—the experienced seem to be more wise than those possessing any sense whatsoever, and the artificer than the experienced, and the master-artist than the handicraftsman, and the speculative rather than those that are productive. 982a That, indeed, wisdom, therefore, is a science conversant about certain causes and first principles is obvious.

2. Now, since we are engaged in investigating this science, the following must form a subject for our consideration; namely, about what kind of causes, and what kind of first principles, is this science—I mean wisdom—conversant. If, doubtless, one would receive the opinions which we entertain concerning the wise man, perhaps from this our proposed inquiry would be evident the more.

Now, in the first place, indeed, we go on the supposition that the wise man, especially, is acquainted with all things scientifically, as far as this is possible, not, however, having a scientific knowledge of them singly. In the next place, a person who is capable of knowing things that are difficult, and not easy for a man to understand, such a one we deem wise (for perception by the senses is common to all, wherefore it is a thing that is easy, and by no means wise). Further, one who is more accurate, and more competent to give instruction in the causes of things, we regard more wise about every science. And of the sciences, also, that which is desirable for its own account, and for the sake of knowledge, we consider to be wisdom in preference to that which is eligible on account of its probable results, and that which is more qualified for preeminence we regard as wisdom, rather than that which is subordinate,—for that the wise man ought not to be dictated to, but should dictate unto others; and that this person ought not to be swayed in his opinions by another, but one less wise by this man. Respecting this wisdom and wise men do we entertain such and so many suppositions.

But of these characteristics the scientific knowledge of all things must needs be found in him most especially who possesses the universal science; for this person, in a manner, knows all things that are subjects of it. But, also, the most difficult nearly for men to know are the things that are especially universal, for they are most remote from the senses. But the most accurate of the sciences are those respecting things that are primary, in the most eminent sense of the word; for those from fewer principles are more accurate than those said to be from addition, as arithmetic than geometry. But, also, that science, without doubt, is more adapted towards giving instruction, at least, which speculates about causes; for those do afford instruction who assign the causes in regard of each individual thing. Now, understanding and scientific knowledge, for their own sakes, most especially reside in the science of that which is most particularly fitted for being scientifically known. For he who selects scientific knowledge, for its own sake, will especially choose that which is preeminently science; but such is that which is the science of that which is particularly fitting as an object of scientific knowledge, and particularly fitting as objects of scientific knowledge are first principles and causes; for on account of these, and by means of these, are the other objects of knowledge capable of being made known: but not these by means of those things that are subordinate to them. Most fit for preeminence likewise amongst the sciences, and fit for preeminence in preference to that which is subservient, is the science which communicates the knowledge of that on account of which each thing is to be done; but this constitutes the good in each particular, but, in general, that which is the best in every nature.

982b

From all, therefore, that has been stated, the sought-for appellation lights upon the same science; for it is necessary that this be a science speculative of first principles and of causes, for the good, also, viewed as a final cause, is one from amongst our classified list of causes.

But that the science under investigation is not a science employed in producing, is evident from the case of those who formed systems of philosophy in the earliest ages. For from wonder men, both now and at the first, began to philosophize, having felt astonishment originally at the things which were more obvious, indeed, amongst those that were doubtful; then, by degrees, in this way having advanced onwards, and, in process of time, having started difficulties about more important subjects,—as, for example, respecting the passive conditions of the moon, and those brought to pass about the sun and stars, and respecting the generation of the universe. But he that labors under perplexity and wonder thinks that he is involved in ignorance. Therefore, also, the philosopher—that is, the lover of wisdom—is somehow a lover of fables, for the fable is made up of the things that are marvelous. Wherefore, if, for the avoidance of ignorance, men from time to time have been induced to form systems of philosophy, it is manifest that they went in pursuit of scientific knowledge for the sake of understanding it, and not on account of any utility that it might possess. But the event itself also bears witness to the truth of this statement; for on the supposition of almost all those things being in existence that are requisite towards both ease and the management of life, prudence of such a sort as this began to be in requisition. Therefore is it evident that we seek scientific knowledge from no other actual ground of utility save what springs from itself.

But as we say a free man exists who is such for his own sake, and not for the sake of another, so, also, this alone of the sciences is free, for this alone subsists for its own sake.

Wherefore, also, the acquisition of this science may be justly regarded as not human, for, in many instances, human nature is servile.

So that, according to Simonides, the deity only should enjoy this prerogative; yet that it is unworthy for a man not to investigate the knowledge that is in conformity with his own condition. But if, in reality, the poets make any such assertion, and if the Godhead is in its nature constituted so as to envy, in this respect it is especially natural that it should happen, and that all those that are over-subtle should be unfortunate: but neither does the divine essence admit of being affected by envy, but—according to the proverb—the bards utter many falsehoods. 983a

Nor ought we to consider any other science more entitled to honor than such as that under investigation at present. For that which is most divine is also most worthy of honor. But such will be so in only two ways; for that which the deity would especially possess is a divine one amongst the sciences; and if there is any such science, this would be the case with the science of things divine. But this science, such as we have described it, alone is possessed of both of these characteristics; for to all speculators doth the deity appear as a cause, and a certain first principle; and such a science as this, either God alone, or he principally, would possess. Therefore, indeed, may all sciences else be more requisite than this one; but none is more excellent.

It is, indeed, necessary, in a manner, to establish the order of this science, in its development, in a direction contrary to the speculations that have been carried on from the beginning. For, indeed—as we have remarked—all men commence their inquiries from wonder whether a thing be so,—as in the case of the spontaneous movements of jugglers' figures to those who have not as yet speculated into their cause; or respecting the solstices, or the incommensurability of the diameter; for it seems to be a thing astonishing to all, if any quantity of those that are the smallest is not capable of being measured. But it is necessary to draw our inquiry to a close in a direction the contrary to this, and towards what is better, according to the proverb. As also happens in the case of these, when they succeed in learning those points; for nothing would a geometrician so wonder at, as if the diameter of a square should be commensurable with its side. What, therefore, is the nature of the science under investigation has been declared; as, also, what the aim should be which the present inquiry and the entire treatise should strive and attain.

3. But since it is manifest that one ought to be in possession of a science of primary causes (for then we say that we know each individual thing when we think that we are acquainted with the first cause); and since causes are denominated under four different heads, the first of which we assert to be the substance and the essence of a thing (for the inquiry of the wherefore, in the first instance of a thing, is referred to the last reason, but the first wherefore of a thing is a cause and first principle); and the second cause we affirm to be the matter and the subject; and the third is the source of the first principle of motion; and the fourth, the cause that is in opposition to this,—namely, both the final cause 983b and the good; for such is an end of every generation.

Therefore, although there has been a sufficient amount of speculation concerning these in our treatise on Physics, let us, however, bring forward those who before our time have approached to an examination of entities, and have formed systems of philosophy respecting truth. For it is obvious that they also affirm that there are in existence certain first principles and causes; therefore will it, at any rate, be of service to our present treatise should we take a review of these philosophers; for either we shall thereby discover a certain different description of cause, or we shall, in preference, repose our confidence in those that have been already enumerated.

Now, the majority of those who first formed systems of philosophy consider those that subsist in a form of matter to be alone the principles of all things; for wherefrom all entities arise, and wherefrom they are generated, as from an original, and whereto they are corrupted,—ultimately the substance, indeed, remaining permanent, but in its passive states undergoing a change,—this they assert to be an element, and this a first principle of all things.

And for this reason they are of opinion that nothing is either produced or destroyed, inasmuch as such a constitution of nature is always in a state of conservation; as we say, that Socrates neither is absolutely brought into being when he may become handsome or musical, nor that he is destroyed when he may throw aside these habits on account of the fact of the subject,— namely, Socrates himself remaining permanent; so neither is it the case with anything else that it is either generated or corrupted anew. For it is necessary that there should be a certain nature— either one or more than one—from which the other entities are produced, that remaining in a state of conservation. The plurality, indeed, and the species of such a first principle, all do not affirm to be the same.

But Thales, indeed,—the founder of this kind of philosophy,— affirms the nature just mentioned to be water (wherefore, also, he declared the earth to be superimposed upon water), probably deriving his opinion from observing that the nutriment of all things is moist, and that even actual heat is therefrom generated, and that animal life is sustained by this (but that wherefrom a thing is produced, this is a first principle of all things); and doubtless for this reason, likewise, holding such a theory, both from the fact of the seeds of all things possessing a moist nature, and of water being a first principle of their nature to things that are humid.

But there are some who suppose those who lived in the most ancient times, and far previous to the present generation, and who first formed schemes of theology, to have also entertained opinions after this manner concerning Nature; for these philosophers constituted both Oceanus and Tethys as the parents of generation, and water as the object of adjuration amongst the gods,—called Styx by the poets themselves; for most entitled to respect is that which is most ancient,—now an object of adjuration is a thing most entitled to respect. Whether, 984a therefore, there is this certain early and ancient opinion concerning Nature, in all likelihood would be an obscure point to decide. Thales, indeed, is said to have declared his sentiments in this manner concerning the first cause; for no one would deign to place Hippo along with these, on account of the meanness of his intellect.

But Anaximenes and Diogenes placed air before water, and especially as a cause of simple bodies; whereas, Hippasus of Metapontum, and Heraclitus of Ephesus, fire; but Empedocles introduced four bodies,—that is, one in addition to those three already mentioned,—adding earth as a fourth; for that these ever continued permanent; and further, that they are not produced, save that, either in plurality or in paucity, they are compounded together, or dissolved into one and from one component element.

But Anaxagoras of Clazomenae—in age, indeed, being prior to this speculator, but in his works subsequent to him— maintains that first principles are infinite. For he asserts that almost all things being homogeneous—as water or fire—in this way are produced and destroyed by concretion and dissolution merely; but that, in other respects, no entities were either brought into existence, or caused to cease to exist, but continued as things that are everlasting.

From these things, indeed, therefore, one would suppose that the only cause with these philosophers was that said to exist in a form of matter.

But as these speculators advanced in this way, the thing itself guided them, and constrained them to investigate further; for though every possible corruption and generation is from something subsisting, as one or more, yet why does this happen, and what is the cause of this,—for undoubtedly the subject, at least, itself is in no wise instrumental in making itself undergo a change? Now, I say, for example, that neither the wood nor the brass is the cause of either of these bodies undergoing a change; neither does the wood, indeed, produce a bed, and the brass a statue; but there is something else that is a cause of change. But the investigation of this is the investigation of a different principle, that is, the second cause,—as we have stated,—the principle of the origin of motion.

Those, indeed, therefore, who from the earliest times have altogether adopted such a method as this, and affirm the subject to be one, have created no difficulty for themselves; but some of these, at least, who say that it is one, as if overpowered by this investigation, assert that the one is immoveable, and the entire of nature, not only according to generation and corruption,—for this is an ancient dogma, and one which all acknowledge,—but also according to every other change, whatever; and this a tenet peculiar to themselves. Of those, indeed, therefore, who affirm 984b the universe to be one merely, to none has it occurred to see clearly into a cause of such a kind, unless, perhaps, to Parmenides, and to him so far as that he lays down not one merely, but, somehow, even two causes to exist. And for those, truly, who make them more numerous is it allowable rather to assert the existence of such a cause as the efficient cause,—I mean those who make causes to be the hot and the cold or fire and earth; for they employ the fire as possessing a motive nature, but water and earth, and such like, as something that is contrary to this.

But after these philosophers, and after the assertion of principles of this sort,—as if on the grounds of their insufficiency to generate the nature of entities,—again constrained by actual truth, as we have said, they investigated the principle next following, in the way of a consequence. For of the excellent and beautiful order of some things, and of the production of others of the entities, it is not natural to assign, perhaps, either earth or anything of this kind as a cause; nor is it natural that they should think that it is; nor was it seemly, on the other hand, to attribute so important a part to chance and fortune.

Now, whosoever affirmed mind, as in animals so also in nature, to be the cause of the system of the world, and of the entire harmony of it, the same appeared, as it were, of sober temperament, in comparison with the vain theorists of the earlier ages. Indeed, then, we know that Anaxagoras openly adopted these principles. Hermotimus of Clazomenae, however, has the credit assigned him of having put forward a similar theory of causation at an earlier period.

Those, indeed, therefore, who have entertained these opinions have laid down as a first principle of entities, at the same time the cause of their orderly arrangement, with such a one as that of the origin of motion in things.

4. Someone, however, might indulge in the surmise that Hesiod was the first to broach such a description of cause as the above; and that this is the case with whatsoever other speculator, if any, that may have placed love or desire as a first principle in entities; as, for instance, also Parmenides: for this philosopher, likewise, in drawing up his scheme of the generation of the universe says,

The first thing of all the gods, indeed, plann'd he Love.

But Hesiod's words are,

First, indeed, of all was Chaos; but next in order,
Earth with her spacious bosom. Then
Love, who is preeminent amongst all the Immortals;

just as if it were necessary that in entities there should subsist some cause which will impart motion, and hold bodies in union together. How, indeed, then, in regard of these, one ought to distribute them, as to their order of priority, can be decided afterwards.

But, also, since things contrary to those that are good appeared inherent in Nature, and not only order and the beautiful, but also disorder and what is base; and since the evil things were more numerous than the good, and the worthless than the fair, 985a accordingly, someone else introduced harmony and discord, as a cause severally of each of these. For if anyone would follow the subject up, and form his opinion according to the faculty of thought, and not according to the obscure assertions of Empedocles, he will find harmony, indeed, to be a cause of the things that are good, and discord of those that are evil. Wherefore, if any should say that Empedocles both, in a certain sense, affirms, and that he was the first to affirm, that the evil and the good are first principles, perhaps he would make such an assertion correctly, if the cause of all things that are good be the good itself, and of those that are evil the evil.

These persons, indeed, therefore, as we have said, even thus far have adopted into their systems two causes, as we have defined them in our Physics,—I mean the material cause, and the principle of the origin of motion; that is, the efficient cause: obscurely, no doubt, and by no means clearly, but, in a manner, like the conduct of those who are unexercised in battles; for these latter, also, advancing forwards against their adversaries, strike frequently skillful blows: but neither do those combatants act thus from a scientific system, nor do these early speculators appear like men who understand that they are making the assertions which they actually are; for in no respect, almost, do they appear to employ these first principles, save to a small extent.

For Anaxagoras, also, employs mind as a machine for the production of the orderly system of the world; and when he finds himself in perplexity as to the cause of its being necessarily so, he then drags it in by force to his assistance; but, in the other instances, he assigns, as a cause of the things that are being produced, everything else in preference to mind.

And Empedocles, to an extent further than this last-named philosopher, employs his causes, however, neither adequately, nor does he discover in them that which confessedly is involved in them. Frequently, at least, in his system the harmony indeed separates, and the discord unites things together. For when the universe may be dissolved into its component elements, by reason of discord, then fire is commingled into one and each of the rest of the elements; but when all things, by reason of harmony, may unite into one, it is necessary that the parts from each undergo separation again.

Empedocles then, indeed,—in contradistinction to the early speculators,—first introduced this cause, having divided it, not having constituted, as single, the first principle of motion, but first principles thereof which are different and opposite. But, moreover, the reputed elements, in form of matter, he was the first to assert the existence of as being four in number; he did 985b not, doubtless, employ at least four, but regarded them as if there were only two; fire by itself, and those things that are opposed to this, as one nature,—namely, both earth, and air, and water. But one may acquire this information by drawing the speculation itself from his poetry. This philosopher, indeed, therefore, as we have stated, enumerated his first principles in this way, and affirmed them to be so many in number.

But Leucippus, and his companion Democritus, assert that the full and the empty are elements; terming, for instance, the one, indeed, an entity, and the other a nonentity; and of these, the full and solid they call an entity, and the empty and the attenuated, a nonentity. Wherefore, they say that entity, in no respect less than nonentity, has an existence, because neither has the vacuum a being more than corporeity, and that these are the causes of entities as material causes.

And as they who make the substance, which is the subject, one, generate all things else by means of the passive conditions of this substance, assigning the rare and the dense as first principles of these affections, in the same manner these also affirm that differences are causes of the other things. They, indeed, say that these are three, even figure, and order, and position; for they affirm that entity differs merely in rhythm, and diathege, and trope; out of these the rhythm is figure, and the diathege order, and the trope position. For, indeed, the letter A differs from the letter N in figure, and AN from NA in order, and Z from N in position. But respecting motion, whence or how it exists in entities, in like manner, with the rest of the early speculators, have these carelessly neglected such inquiries.

Respecting, then, two causes of the four, according to the statements we have just made, so far has it appeared that an inquiry has been prosecuted by our predecessors.

5. But amongst these, and prior to them, those called Pythagoreans, applying themselves to the study of the mathematical sciences, first advanced these views; and having been nurtured

therein, they considered the first principles of these to be the first principles of all entities. But since, among these, numbers by nature are the first, and in numbers they fancied they beheld many resemblances for entities and things that are being produced, rather than in fire, and earth, and water; because, to give an instance, such a particular property of numbers is justice, and such soul and mind; and another different one is opportunity; and it is the case, so to speak, in like manner with each of the other things.

Moreover, also, in numbers discerning the passive conditions and reasons of harmonies, since it was apparent that, indeed, other things in their nature were in all points assimilated unto numbers, and that the numbers were the first of the entire of Nature, hence they supposed the elements of numbers to be the 986a elements of all entities, and the whole heaven to be an harmony and number. And as many phenomena as they could demonstrate to be conformable, both in their numbers and harmonies, with the passive conditions and parts of the heaven, and with its entire arrangement, these they collected and adapted to their philosophy: and if there was any interval left anywhere, they supplied the deficiency, in order that there might be a chain of connection running through their entire system. Now, I say, as an illustration, since the decade seems to be a thing that is perfect, and to have comprised the entire nature of numbers, hence they also assert that the bodies that are borne through the heaven are truly ten in number; and whereas nine only are apparent, on this account they constitute the confronting earth tenth. But respecting these theorists, we have arrived at more accurate decisions in other parts of our works.

But the reason why we have gone in review through these philosophers is this, in order that we may receive also from them what they have already laid down as being first principles, and in what manner they fall in with the causes just enumerated. Undoubtedly do these appear to consider number to be a first principle, and, as it were, a material cause of entities, and as both their passive conditions and habits, and that the even and the odd are elements of number; and of these, that the one is finite and the other infinite, and that unity, doubtless, is composed of both of these, for that it is both even and odd, and that number is composed of unity, and that, as has been stated, the entire heaven is composed of numbers.

But others of these very philosophers affirm that first principles are ten in number, denominated in accordance with the following coordinate series, namely:

Bound	Infinity	Rest	Motion
Odd	Even	Straight	Crooked
Unity	Plurality	Light	Darkness
Right	Left	Good	Bad
Male	Female	Square	Oblong

In the same manner seems Alcmaeon of Croton to have formed his opinion; and this philosopher certainly, either from those just named, or they from this person, have derived this their theory; for Alcmaeon had reached the age of manhood when Pythagoras was an old man; but he enumerated his sentiments in a manner similar with the Pythagoreans. For he affirms that the greater portion of things human may be reduced to two classes, calling them contrarieties; not distinguished as these had distinguished them, but such as were of any casual sort whatever, as for example:

White	Black	Good	Bad
Sweet	Bitter	Small	Great

This philosopher, indeed, then, has indefinitely thrown out his opinions about the rest; but the Pythagoreans have declared 986b both how numerous, and which these contrarieties are.

From both of these, therefore, it is possible to acquire thus much information,—that contraries are first principles of entities; but how numerous, and which these are, may be ascertained only from other speculators. How, indeed, in respect of the causes enumerated, it is possible to draw up a compendious application of their principles has not, in distinct terms, been clearly declared by them; but they seem to arrange the elements as in a form of matter: for of these, as inherent, they say that the substance consists, and has been molded.

Of the ancients, therefore, indeed,—even of those who assert the elements of Nature to be many,—it is sufficient from these statements to examine into their intention.

But there are some who have declared their opinions about the universe as though it were one Nature; but all have not put forward their theories in the same manner, either in regard of that which is constituted in an orderly way, or of that which is in accordance with the course of Nature. With, indeed, then, the present investigation of causes does this theory regarding them by no means adapt itself. For they do not,—as some of the physiologers who supposed entity to be one,—nevertheless, generate them from unity as from matter; but these, who say that entity and unity are the same, assert their production to take place after a different manner; for those, indeed, have added motion, at least, in their generation of the universe; but these say that it is immovable.

Of a truth, however, so far at least the theory of this school is akin to our present investigation; for Parmenides, indeed, appears to adopt a system of unity in accordance with reason: whereas Melissus, a theory of it according to matter. Wherefore, also, indeed, one says that the universe is finite, and the other that it is infinite. Xenophanes, first of these, however, having introduced this system of unity (for Parmenides is said to have been his pupil), made nothing plain, neither did he seem to have apprehended the nature of either of these; but looking wistfully upon the whole heaven, he affirms that unity is God.

These, indeed, therefore, as we have stated, must be omitted in regard of our present investigation,—two of them entirely,— even as being a little too uncivilized; namely, Xenophanes and Melissus. Parmenides, however, appears to express himself, in some passages, with more circumspection; for, with the exception of entity—considering nonentity to have no existence—he thinks entity to be necessarily one, and nothing else. Concerning which philosopher, we have spoken with more clearness in our Physics. Yet, compelled to follow the phenomena, and supposing unity to subsist according to reason, but plurality according to sense, he again lays down two causes, and two first principles,— heat and cold; as, for example, in other words, he means fire 987a and earth; but of these he arranges the one under the category of entity, that is, the hot, and the other under that of nonentity, viz. the cold.

From the statements, indeed, therefore, that have been made, and from those who have already devoted themselves to rational speculations, and are wise men, we have derived these views; from the earliest philosophers have we appropriated, indeed, both the corporeal first principle (for water and fire, and such like, are bodies), and from some of these one such, and from others many corporeal principles; both, however, agreeing in classing them as forms of matter. But from certain amongst these early speculators,—who at the same time establish both this cause, and along with this that of the origin of motion,—we have appropriated even this very efficient cause; from some, indeed, as a single principle, but from others, as one that is twofold. Up to the period of the Italic sects, and independent of them, the rest of the investigators have spoken with more modera-tion regarding these first principles, except, as we have said, in the case of those who happen to have employed two causes; and one of these, the second cause—namely, the origin of motion— some, indeed, make single, and others twofold.

But the Pythagoreans, in the same manner, have spoken of two first principles; but thus much have they added,—which, also, is peculiar to themselves,—namely, that they do not regard the finite, and the infinite, and the one, to be certain different natures; as, for instance, fire, or earth, or any other such thing: but that the infinite itself, and the one itself, constitute the substance of those things of which they are predicated. Wherefore, also, they affirmed that number is the substance of all things. Respecting, then, these points, likewise, in this manner have they declared their opinions; and respecting quiddity they began, indeed, to make assertions and to frame definitions; but they treated of matters with great simplicity. For they both framed their definitions superficially, and in whatever first an alleged definition should be inherent, this they considered to be the substance of the thing; as if anyone should think that twofold is the same thing with the dyad, since the twofold first is inherent in the two; yet perhaps the being in what is twofold is not the same thing as being in a dyad; but if not, unity will be plurality, which also was the result with them.

From our predecessors, indeed, therefore, and from the rest, it is possible for us to acquire thus much information.

6. After the schools of philosophy enumerated, supervenes the system of Plato; in most points treading on the heels of these Pythagoreans: but also having peculiar tenets of its own, differing from the philosophy of the Italics. For from a young man having at the first been associatd with Cratylus, and being conversant with the opinions of Heraclitus,—that all sensible objects are in a state of continual flux, and that scientific knowledge concerning them had no existence,—he, indeed, subsequently in this way came to entertain these suppositions. But while Socrates was 987b engaged about the formation of systems of Ethics, indeed, and that he broached no theory as regards the entire of Nature, seeing that he was searching, doubtless, in morals for the universal, and that he was the first to apply his understanding to the subject of definitions, Plato, having applauded him on account of this his investigation of universals, was led to entertain thus much of his supposition,—as that this took place in regard of other things, and not in regard of certain of the objects that are cognizant by the senses; for it is impossible, in his opinion, that there should be a common definition of any of the sensible natures, seeing that they are continually in a state of undergoing a change. This philosopher, indeed, therefore, termed such things amongst entities, ideas; and asserted that all things are styled sensible according as they were different from these, or as

they subsisted in accordance with these: for his theory was this,—that, according to participation, the most of things synonymous are homonymous with the forms. Employing, however, the import of the term participation, he changed the name merely; for the Pythagoreans, indeed, affirm that entities subsist by an imitation of numbers: but, Plato, by a participation of them, changing the name. At all events, as to participating at least, or imitation, what it may be, in the case of forms, they both in common omitted to investigate.

But, moreover, besides sensibles and forms, he affirms that mathematical entities are things of an intermediate nature; differing, on the one hand, from sensibles in being eternal and immovable; but, on the other, from forms, in the fact that the most of such are similar, but that every form itself constituted one thing merely.

But since the forms are causes of other things, the elements of all these he supposed to be elements of entities. Therefore, indeed, he regarded the great and the little to be first principles as matter, but unity as substance; for from these, by participation of unity, that the forms are numbers. That, doubtless, unity at least is as substance, and that not any other entity is denominated so, Plato affirmed, similarly with the Pythagorics; and the dogma, that numbers are causes to other things of their substance, he in like manner asserted with them.

But, in place of the infinite considered as one, the having made a dyad, and the having made the infinite, out of the great and the small, this was peculiar to him: and, moreover, Plato affirmed the existence of numbers independent of sensibles; whereas the Pythagoreans say that numbers constitute the things themselves, and they do not set down mathematical entities as intermediate between these.

The principle of his having made unity, therefore, and numbers, as different from things, and not as the Pythagoreans, who regarded them the same, as well as the introduction of forms, ensued on account of his logical investigations; for his predecessors took no share in dialectical science. But the constituting a dyad, as a different nature from the one, arose from the fact that the numbers, with the exception of those that are first, are suitably generated from this as from a certain express image.

And yet it happens in a contrary way; for it would not be 988a reasonable that it should take place thus: for, indeed, at present, from matter they make many things, whereas form generates only once. And from one matter there appears to be produced one table; but he who introduces form, though being one, makes many tables. In like manner, also, the male stands in relation to the female; for the one is impregnated from a single copulation, whereas the male impregnates many. These, however, are imitations of those first principles. Plato, indeed, therefore, respecting these objects of investigation, laid down distinctions in this way.

But it is manifest, from the things that have been stated, that Plato only employed two causes; namely, both the formal cause and the material cause: for, according to him forms are the causes of what anything is to the rest of the entities, and unity to the forms; and that there is a certain cause which subsists according to matter, which is that subject through which the forms have a subsistence that are resident in sensibles, and through which unity is said to be in the forms, because the actual dyad constitutes the great and the small. Further, the cause of "the well and the ill" he ascribed severally to the several elements; which particular point we affirm certain philosophers—such as Empedocles and Anaxagoras—to have investigated more elaborately than the early speculators.

7. Concisely, indeed, therefore, and by way of summary, we have recounted both who they are that have declared their opinions, and in what manner they happen to have spoken concerning both first principles and truth. Nevertheless, however, we have received thus much information from them,—that no one of those who have declared their sentiments, concerning a first principle and a cause, has made any assertion beyond those definitions that have been set down in our Physics; but notwithstanding that all

of them have unfolded their views with obscurity, indeed, yet in a manner they appear as persons engaged in cursorily treating those four causes enumerated above and elsewhere.

For, indeed, some speculators speak of the first principle as matter, whether they may suppose one principle or more to exist, and whether they consider it as body, and whether as a thing that is incorporeal: as, for instance, Plato, indeed, in his mention of the great and the small; and the Italics, in their theory of the infinite; and Empedocles, in that of fire, and earth, and water, and air; and Anaxagoras, in his system of the infinity of homogeneous things. Now, truly, all these touched upon a cause of this kind: and, further, as many as affirmed the existence, as a first principle, of air, or fire, or water, or a substance of greater density than fire, but of greater rarity than air; for certain philosophers have also declared a thing of this sort to be the first element. All these, indeed, therefore, adopted this cause merely in a superficial way.

But certain others introduce the second cause; namely, the origin of the principle of motion: as, for instance, as many as make a first principle of harmony and discord, or mind or love. But of the essence and the substance—that is, of the formal cause—not one, indeed, has rendered a clear account: most especially do those make assertions respecting it who adopt the hypothesis of forms, and the things inherent in forms; for neither do they suppose that forms, and the things inherent in forms, 988b subsist as matter to sensibles; nor, as though from thence were derived the principle of motion (for, in preference, they assert them to be causes of immobility, and of things being in a state of rest); but, in regard of the essence, to each of the other things do forms supply this, and unity imparts it to the forms.

But the final cause of actions, and changes, and motions, in a certain manner, they assert to be a cause: yet in this way they do not assert it to be a cause; nor do they speak of it in a way conformably to what it naturally is. For they, indeed, who assign mind or harmony as such, have laid down these causes as, doubtless, a something that is good; they do not, however, affirm that from these, as final causes, anything amongst entities either is in existence, or is being produced, but that, as it were, from these the Emotions of these things were derived. So, also, in like manner, they who say that either unity or entity is such a nature of this kind, affirm it to be a cause of substance, indeed; yet they do not, for a certainty, affirm that anything either exists or is produced from this as a final cause. Wherefore, it happens unto them, in a manner, both to affirm, and not to affirm, that the good is a cause of this sort; for they do not make the assertion absolutely, but by accident.

That, therefore, our distinctions have been laid down correctly respecting causes, both as to how numerous and what sort they are, do even all these early philosophers appear to us to bear witness, in not being able to fix upon any other cause. And, in addition to the testimony of these speculators, it is evident that first principles must be investigated, either all in this way, or in some such mode as has been adopted by these philosophers. Now, how each of these has declared his opinions, and how the case stands, in regard of the possible doubts respecting first principles, let us, after this, proceed to pass through a review of such points.

8. As many, indeed, therefore, as set down the universe as both one and a certain single nature, as matter, and this such as is corporeal and involving magnitude, it is obvious that they labor under manifold errors. For they have established the elements of bodies merely, but not of incorporeals, when even there are in existence, I mean, things that are incorporeal. And in endeavoring to assign causes of generation and corruption, and drawing up, concerning all bodies in nature, systems of physiology, they take away the cause of motion. Further, the not positing also the substance as a cause of anything, nor as such the formal principle, or the very essence of a thing, this was erroneous.

And, in addition to the foregoing, the assertion that anything whatsoever might readily be a first principle of simple bodies, except earth, but at the same time not examining into their mode of generation one from another, how they are produced,—

now I mean fire and water, and earth and air, for partly by concretion, and partly by separation, are things produced from one another,—this was an error of theirs. But this, in regard of the being prior and posterior, will involve the greatest difference; for, indeed, earth would appear to be a thing most elementary of all, from which, as a first principle, elements are produced by 989a concretion: but a thing of this kind would be most minute in its parts, and a thing most refined amongst bodies. Wherefore, as many as establish fire as a first principle would make assertions particularly in consonance with this theory. But each philosopher also acknowledges something of this sort to be an element of other things,—I mean an element of bodies.

No one, at least of subsequent speculators, even of those who assert the universe to be one, has thought fit to maintain earth to be an element, doubtless, on account of the size of the component particles, but each of the three elements has obtained a certain umpire; for, indeed, some assert fire to be this, but others, water, and some, air. Although why, pray, do they not assert this of earth, as the majority of men do? For they say that earth constitutes all things. But Hesiod, also, says that earth was the first produced amongst bodies: thus it has happened that the supposition is an ancient and vulgar one. According, indeed, therefore, to this account, if one affirms to be this either any one thing belonging to these save fire, or if one lays down, as such, a thing denser than air, indeed, but more refined than water, he would not make such an assertion as this correctly. But if that which is subsequent in generation be prior in Nature, and if that which has been digested and compounded together be a thing that is subsequent in its production, there would take place that which is the contrary of these,—water, for instance, would be a thing prior to air, and earth, to water. With regard to those who are for establishing one such cause as we have declared, let these remarks be sufficient.

But the same assertion may be made even if any one posits these corporeal principles as being many in number; as, for example, Empedocles, who says that four bodies, elementarily, constitute matter. For, likewise, to this philosopher partly, indeed, the same consequences, but partly those that are peculiar to his own system, must needs happen. For, also, we see, in the case of things that are being produced one from another, that the fire and earth do not always continue as of the same body. But we have spoken on these subjects in our Physics. And respecting the cause of things that are being moved, whether we must assign one or two such, we should be inclined to think that we have not expressed ourselves either correctly or altogether irrationally. And, in short, must the principle of alteration be overturned by those who make assertions in this way; for not from heat will arise cold, nor from cold, heat. For what change the contraries themselves would undergo, and what would be the one nature which should become fire and water, that very philosopher (I mean Empedocles) does not declare.

But if anyone should suppose that Anaxagoras mentions two elements, he would form his opinion most especially in accordance with a theory which, although that philosopher himself did not enunciate distinctly, yet, indeed, would, as a necessary consequence, follow in the footsteps of those who introduced this dogma. For, otherwise, would even the assertion be absurd,— that all things from the beginning have been in a state of mixture; both on account of its happening that all things prior to this should preexist in an unmixed state, and on account of 989b its not being consonant to Nature, that anything at random should be mingled with anything at random too; and, in addition to these reasons, we may add, that, according to this doctrine, their passive states and accidents would be separated from substances (for to the same things belong mixture and separation). If anyone, however, follows up the subject, arranging into clauses together those statements which he wishes to make, he would, in all probability, utter assertions that would assume an air of novelty. For when there was nothing in existence that has been separated, it is obvious that no true assertion could be put forward in regard of that substance; now, I say, for instance, that it would not necessarily be a thing either white, or black, or darkish, or any other color, but a thing necessarily colorless, for otherwise it would possess some one of these colors. In like manner would it be with that which is insipid, according to this same mode of reasoning: nor could it be so with anything else of those things that are similar; for neither is it possible that it could possess any actual thing of a certain quality or quantity, or that anything else be so. For therein would be inherent something of those termed partial forms; yet this is impossible when all things have been in his system mingled together, for already it would subsist in a state of separation: but, with the exception of mind, he affirms all things to be mingled, and that mind only is unmixed and pure. Now, from these statements it is consequential with him that he should denominate, as the first principles, both unity (for this is simple and unmixed) and another thing, as if it were an entity such as we are for establishing—viz., the indefinite prior to its having been defined, and to partaking of a certain form. Therefore, the assertion is made neither correctly nor clearly, notwithstanding that he intends something similar with both those who subsequently make statements to this effect, and more in harmony with the present phenomena. For these, however, happen only to be familiar with the theories appertaining to generation, and corruption, and motion: for, also, with regard to such a substance, they investigate almost only both the first principles and the causes.

But as many as frame their speculation respecting all entities, but of entities have set down some, indeed, as being cognizant by sense, and others as not being sensibles, it is manifest that they institute for themselves an inquiry concerning both kinds. Wherefore, one might be induced, in preference, to linger upon an investigation respecting these, as to what they say, well or not well, in regard of the examination of those speculations now proposed by us.

Those, indeed, called Pythagoreans in a far more outlandish manner employ their first principles and elements than the physiologist. But the cause is, because they have not derived them from sensibles; for those natures that are mathematical amongst entities are without motion, except those pertaining to astrology. They, however, discuss and treat of all points concerning Nature; for they both generate the heaven, and respecting the parts thereof, and the passive conditions and the operations 990a thereof, they closely observe that which takes place; and upon these they lavish their first principles and causes, as if acknowledging to the rest of the natural philosophers that whatsoever thing is such as is cognizant by the senses, that this constitutes entity, and such as that which is called heaven comprises. But the causes and the first principles—as we have said—they affirm are sufficient both to secure a transition even to a higher order of entities, and that they are more sufficient than those that are in harmony with physical theories.

From what mode, however, there will be motion, merely on the supposition of the existence of the subjects of finite and infinite, and odd and even, they in no wise declare; or how it may be possible, without motion and change, that there should be generation and corruption, or the operations of those bodies that are whirled along the heaven.

But further, whether one grants to them that from these results magnitude, or whether this should require to be demonstrated, nevertheless, in a certain manner, some bodies will be light, indeed, and some involving weight; for the things from which they adopt for themselves their theories, and make assertions, they in no respect affirm in regard of sensibles in preference to mathematical bodies. Therefore, concerning fire or earth, or the other bodies of such a kind, they have declared nothing whatsoever, inasmuch as affirming, in my opinion, nothing that is peculiar to them concerning sensible natures.

But further, how must we receive as causes the passive conditions of number, and the number itself as the cause of entities which subsist in the heaven, and of things that are being produced there both from the beginning and at present, and at the same time allow that there is no other number save this number from which the order of the universe consists? For since, indeed, in this portion of the creation (according to these philosophers) there may be in existence opinion and opportunity, but a little above, or a little below, injustice and separation, or mixture; and since they may adduce a demonstration that each one of these is number, and it happens, from this mode of reasoning in this place, that there subsists already a multitude of constituted magnitudes, from the fact of these affections following each of these places respectively, on the supposition of the foregoing we may ask whether, therefore, is this owing to the same number as that which is in the heaven, and which we ought to receive because that each of these exists, or, besides this, is there another number? For Plato says, indeed, that there is a different number: he, however, also thinks both these, and the causes of these, to be numbers, but numbers that are, indeed, intelligible causes; whereas those are merely sensible, according to Plato. Respecting then, indeed, the Pythagoreans, let us leave off our present discussions; for it is sufficient thus far to have touched upon their system.

9. But they who put forward ideas as causes, in their early investi- 990b gations, indeed, to acquire the causes of these entities, in the first place have adduced other things equal in number to these; as if one, desiring to have reckoned certain things, when these were less numerous, would consider this impossible, but, by creating a greater number, should succeed in counting them; for almost equal, or not less numerous, are the forms than those things respecting which, in investigating their causes, they have advanced from these to those: for, according to each individual thing, there is a certain homonymous form, and, in addition to the substances, also, of other things, there is the unity involved in the notion of plurality, both in the case of these and of things that are eternal.

Moreover, in the ways in which it is demonstrated that there are forms, according to none of these doth the subsistence of forms become apparent; for, indeed, from some there is no necessity, in the sequence of the reasoning, that a syllogism arise: but from other things, also,—not of such as we should expect to find forms,—of these are there forms generated. For according to the rational principles deducible from the sciences will there be forms of all things, of as many as there are sciences; and in accordance with the argument for ideas founded on the notion of unity involved in plurality, will there also be forms or ideas of negations: and according to the ability to understand something of what has been destroyed of things liable to decay will there also be forms, for of these there is a certain phantasm.

But further, as regards the most accurate of the arguments for the ideal theory, some of them, indeed, frame ideas of things relative, of which they do not say that there is an essential genus, whereas others speak of there being a third man.

And, upon the whole, the theories respecting forms overturn the things which they who affirm the existence of forms would wish should have a subsistence in preference to the subsistence of the ideas; for it happens that the dyad is not the first, but that the number is, and that the relative is, before the essential: and all those consequences ensue, as many as certain, who have followed up the opinions respecting forms—have set in contrariety to first principles. Further, also, according to the supposition in virtue of which we speak of the existence of the ideas, not only will there be forms of substances, but of many other things also; for, also, there is the one conception not only respecting substances, but also in the case of other substances; and there are sciences not only of substance, but of different things also, and innumerable other things of this sort occur: but according to necessity, and the opinions respecting forms, it follows, on the supposition that forms are things capable of participation, that there should be ideas of substances only; for not according to accident are they participated in, but things must participate in this respect in each idea, so far forth as each idea is not predicated about the subject. Now, I mean, for example, that if anything participates in the twofold itself, this also is a participant in what is eternal, but according to accident, for it is accidental for the twofold to be eternal. Therefore, the forms will be substance.

For the same things, both here and there, signify substance; or what will be the meaning of the assertion of the existence of a something that is independent of sensibles, drawn from the argument founded on unity, involved in the notion of plurality; and if there be the same form of the ideas, and of things that are participants of them, there will be something in common? For, by no means, in the case of perishable dyads—and, indeed, most dyads, but such as are eternal—is the dyad said to be rather one and the same, than in the case of this and one of some particular thing. But if there be not the same form there would be an homonymy; and it will be just as if one should call both Callias and a piece of wood a man, discerning no community whatever between them.

991a

But most of all would one feel perplexed as to what at all the forms contribute, either to those things that are eternal amongst sensibles, or to things that are being produced and being corrupted. For neither are they to them a cause of any motion or change whatever. But, truly, neither are they of any assistance towards the science of other things (for neither are those the substance of these, for in such a case they would be in these), nor do they contribute towards the existence of other things, inasmuch as they are not inherent in things that are their participants, at least; for so, indeed, they would perhaps be supposed as causes, just as if the white were mixed with the white it might be called the cause of a white body. But, indeed, this theory is very easily overthrown, which Anaxagoras, indeed, first, and Eudoxus subsequently, and certain others, advanced; for it would be easy to collect together, also, many impossibilities in reference to such an opinion: but, truly, neither do other things subsist from forms in accordance with any mode of existence of those that are wont to be mentioned.

But the assertion that these forms are exemplars, and that the rest of entities participate in them, is to speak vain words, and to utter poetic metaphors. For in what respect, may I ask, does that which operates look towards the ideas as a model? For it is possible that anything whatever that is similar both should exist and be produced, and yet that it be not made like in reference to that to which it is similar. Wherefore, also, on the supposition of the existence and nonexistence of Socrates, just such another one as Socrates is would be produced. And, in like manner, is it evident that this would follow, even though Socrates were eternal; and, besides, there will be many exemplars of the same thing; wherefore, also, the forms—for instance, of man, such as animal and biped, and at the same time, also, ideal man—will have a subsistence. Further, not only of things sensible are forms the exemplars, but also of forms themselves; as, for example, the genus as a genus will be an exemplar of species; wherefore, an exemplar and an image will be the same thing.

Further, it would seem impossible for the substance to be 991b separate from that of which it is the substance; therefore, in what way can the ideas, when they are substances of things, exist separately from them?

But in the Phaedo an assertion is made to this effect,—that the forms are causes of existence and of production. On the supposition, however, of the existence of forms, nevertheless, those things that are participants will not be produced, if there be not in existence that which is likely to be the origin of motion; and many other things are produced, such as a house and a ring, of which we do not say that there are forms. Wherefore, it is evident that it is possible, also, for other things both to exist and be produced from such causes, likewise, on account of which, also, arise those entities mentioned just now.

Moreover, if forms are numbers, how will they be causes? Whether is it because entities are different numbers,—as, for instance, this particular man is this particular number, indeed, and Socrates another, and Callias another, different from both,—in what respect are those, therefore, the causes of these? For neither will it make any difference whether those may be eternal, and these not so. But if it is because the things here are proportions or ratios of numbers,—as, for instance, a symphony,— it is obvious that there will be a certain one thing, at least, amongst those of which there are ratios or proportions. Now, if this is one thing—say matter—it is palpable that the actual numbers, also, will be certain proportions of one thing with another; but I say, for example, if Callias is a proportion in numbers of fire, and earth, and water, and air, to certain other subjects will belong the same man likewise; and if the idea constitute a number, the ideal man, also,—whether the idea may be a certain number or not,—nevertheless, will be a ratio in numbers of certain things without being himself a number; nor will there be a certain particular number on account of these things.

Further, out of many numbers one number results; but from forms how is one form produced? And if forms are not produced from forms, but from the units that are in numbers—as, for instance, in the myriad—how is it with the subsistence of the monads? For if they are of the same species, many absurdities will ensue; but if they are not of the same species, neither will they be the same with one another, nor all the rest the same with all: for wherein will they differ, since they are impassive? For such statements as these are neither rational nor consonant with the understanding. And, moreover, it is necessary to establish a certain other description of number, regarding which arithmetic is conversant, and all such things as are termed media by some; and how, or from what principles, will these arise? Or why will they be media between the things here and these?

992a Further, the monads which are in each dyad are from some prior dyad, although such is impossible. Further, why is there an aggregated number, as one thing? And further, in addition to the things that have been stated, if the monads are different, they ought to declare their opinions in this same way as those do, even as many as affirm the elements to be fourfold or twofold; for also, each one of these mentions not what is common as an element—for example, body—but fire and earth, whether body is anything that is common or not. But now, an assertion is made just as if the one were in existence as homogeneous fire or water; but if this be the case, numbers will not be substances; it is, however, evident, that if unity itself be anything, and if this be a first principle, that unity is expressed in many ways, for that it should be otherwise is impossible.

But they who wish to refer substances to first principles set down lengths, indeed; as consisting from the long and the short, from something small and large, and a superficies as from what is broad and narrow, and a body from what is deep and low. In what way, however, will the superficies involve a line, or the solid a line and surface, for the wide and the narrow are a different genus from deep and low? As, therefore, neither number is inherent in these, because the much and the few are different from these, so it is manifest that neither will anything else of those superior natures be inherent in those that are inferior. But, truly, neither is the wide a genus of the deep; for body would be a certain surface in this case. Further, may I ask from what will points be compounded? This genus, indeed, then, did Plato also oppose, as being a geometric dogma; but he used to call it the first principle of a line: and this he often set down (I mean the existence of indivisible lines), although of necessity there must be some limit to these; wherefore, from whatever principle a line is, therefrom also is a point.

And upon the whole, seeing that wisdom investigates into the cause, in respect of things that are manifest, this consideration, indeed have we omitted; for we say nothing regarding the cause of the origin of the principle of change: but, thinking to mention the substance of these, we say that there are different substances; but in what manner those may be substances of these we ineffectually describe, for as to such being accomplished by participation— as also we have stated on a former occasion—there is no advantage gained in saying this. Neither, truly, are ideas such causes as we see to be a cause to the sciences, on account of which both every mind and every nature operate; nor that cause which we affirm to be one of the first principles do forms in anywise touch upon; but to men, in the present age, mathematics have become *the* philosophy; although they say that persons ought to cultivate these sciences for the sake of other sciences.

But, further, one may suppose the subject-substance to be as 992b matter that is more mathematical, and rather to be converted into a predicable, and to constitute a difference of substance and of matter,—as, for instance, the great and the small,—just as, also, the natural philosophers mention the rare and the dense, saying that there are these primary differences of the subject, for these are a certain excess and defect. And respecting motion, if, indeed, these will constitute motion, it is evident that the forms will be moved; but if they are not, whence has motion originated? For thereby the entire investigation about Nature has been abolished.

And what seems to be easy—namely, the demonstration that all things are one—does not turn out to be so; for, according to the interpretation, all things do not become one, but a certain thing itself is one, if anyone would grant that all things are so: and neither would he allow this, unless one would admit the existence of a universal as a genus; but this, in some cases, is impossible.

But neither have those things that are after the numbers any grounds in reason,—namely, both lengths, and surfaces, and solids; nor is it so in regard of the mode of how they are, or shall be, or whether they involve any capacity; for these cannot possibly be either forms (for numbers they are not), or media (for those are mathematical), or things that are corruptible: but these, again, appear as this certain other fourth genus different from those other three.

But, upon the whole, the investigation of the elements of entities, seeing that they are expressed multifariously, it is impossible for any persons to discover a solution of who have not divided them; and, especially, if they investigate in this manner from what sort of elements they are compounded. For action, or passion, or the wide, it is not, doubtless, possible to receive from some things of which these consist; but, if this were 993a the case, it would be possible to receive them as subsisting from substances only. Wherefore, either to investigate or to think that you possess the elements of all entities is not true.

But how can anyone learn the elements of all things? For it is evident that it is not possible that he should be previously a person having prior knowledge thereof. For, as to one learning geometry, it is, indeed, possible to see beforehand other things; but of such things as the science consists of, and concerning which he is about to receive instruction, he can have no prior knowledge, so, also, is it in the case of other things. Wherefore, if there is a certain science of all things, as some affirm, nothing could this person know beforehand. Every system of learning, however, subsists, or is attainable, by means of previous knowledge, either of all things, or of certain particular things: and either by demonstration is this accomplished, or by definitions; for those things whereof the definition consists it is requisite to understand beforehand, and that they be known. In like manner is it the case with knowledge by induction. But, truly, if also it happens that there is in our possession a congenital knowledge of things, it is astonishing how we, in possession of the most excellent of the sciences, are unconscious of such a treasure.

Further, how will anyone know from what particulars all things consist, and how will this be manifest? For this also involves perplexity; for one would feel a doubt, just as also concerning some syllable: for certain affirm that *SMA* is composed of *S* and *M* and *A,* but others say that it possesses a different sound from its components, and none of those that are known.

Moreover, those things of which there is perception by sense, how could anyone know if he were not furnished with the capacity of perceiving by sense? Although one ought, if these are the elements of all things whereof they consist just as the compound sounds arise from their own proper elements.

That, therefore, all seem to seek the causes mentioned in our Physics, and, besides these, that we have no other to adduce, is likewise from the foregoing statements evident. But the early philosophers, I admit, have treated of these causes,—obscurely, however; and, indeed, in a certain manner, all such four causes have been enumerated by speculators of an age prior to ours: and, in a certain manner, by no means has this been the case; for the earliest system of philosophy concerning all things was like unto one articulating with a stammer, inasmuch as it was new as regards first principles, and a thing the first in its kind. For Empedocles says that a bone exists from form by the principle of composition; but this is the essence and the substance of that thing. But, truly, if this be admitted, in like manner, also, is it necessary that of both flesh, and everything else of the other things, there should subsist this principle of concretion, or that it should not subsist as a principle of anything at all; for on account of this are both flesh and bone, and each of the other things, in existence, and not on account of the matter, which he says is fire, and earth, and water, and air. But, also, with any other, indeed, who would make these assertions, he would of necessity concur; but he has not expressed himself with clearness respecting them. The case regarding such points, therefore, has been made evident on a former occasion; but as many doubts as anyone might indulge in respecting these same, we will a second time enumerate; for perhaps we shall thereby acquire a facility for having our difficulties resolved in reference to subsequent questions of doubt.

BOOK II[1]

1. SPECULATION respecting truth is partly difficult and partly easy. And a proof is the following, that, in the pursuit of truth, neither is any one philosopher, in a way worthy of the dignity 993b of the subject, able to attain this; nor can all investigators fail in reaching it, but that each says something to the point concerning Nature: and individually that, indeed, they add nothing or but little, to this speculation respecting truth, but from all these collected together that there ensues something of magnitude. Wherefore, if, indeed, it so seems to be the case, as we happen to say in the proverb, "Who will miss the door?" in this way, truly, would the speculation of truth be easy.

But for philosophers to have a certain whole and not to be able to have each some portion, indicates the difficulty of it: and perhaps, also, from the fact that the difficulty arises in two ways, the cause of this may not be so much in things themselves as in us; for as the eyes of bats are to the light that follows the dawn of day, so also is the mind of our soul to those things which, above all, are naturally the most splendid.

But not only is it just to return thanks to those whose opinions one may have fellowship with, but also to those, moreover, who have enunciated their sentiments more superficially; for even these, likewise, contribute something, for they have previously exercised our speculative habit. For if there had not been a Timotheus, we would not have had much melody; and unless there had been a Phrynis, there would not have been such a person as Timotheus. But, in the same manner, also, it is in the case of those who have declared their sentiments concerning truth; for, indeed, from some of them we have inherited certain opinions: but others have been the causes of these becoming opinions of theirs.

But it is correct, also, that philosophy should be styled a science, speculative of truth. For of speculative science the end is truth, but of practical science, a work; for even though they may examine how a thing is, practical men do not investigate into the cause of that thing in itself, but in relation to something else, and as connected with the present time: but we do not know the truth without the knowledge of cause. But, especially, is each thing that amongst other things according to which, also, there subsists in other things that which is synonymous,—as, for example, fire is a thing most hot; for also in the rest of entities is this a cause of their heat. Wherefore, also, most true is that which is a cause to posterior natures of their being true. Wherefore, is it necessary that the first principles of things, always existing, should always be most true; for not sometimes are they true, neither is anything the cause of being to those, but those are the causes of being in other things. Wherefore, as each thing is disposed in regard of existence, so, also, is it in regard of truth.

994a 2. But, truly, that there is, as least, some first principle, and that the causes of entities are not infinite, either in a progress in a straight forward direction, or according to form, is evident. For neither, as of matter, is it possible that this particular entity proceed from this to infinity; for instance, flesh, indeed, from earth, and earth from air, and air from fire, and this without ever coming to a standstill. Nor can there an infinite progression take place with the origin of the principle of motion; as, for instance, that man should have been moved by the air, and this by the sun, and the sun by discord; and of this that there should be no end. Nor, in like manner, can this infinite progression take place with the final cause,—that walking, for instance, should be gone through for the sake of health, and this for the sake of enjoyment, and this enjoyment for the sake of something else; and, similarly, that one thing invariably should subsist on account of another. And, in like manner, is it the case with the formal cause. For of media, to which externally there is something last and first, it is necessary that what is first should be a cause of those things which are subsequent to it. For if we must declare what is the cause of three things, we will assert that it is the first of the three; for, doubtless, it is not the last, at least, for that is not, at any rate, at the extremity of anything as a cause: but, truly, neither is it the middle, for this is the cause of one thing only. But it makes no difference whether one or many media be assumed, nor whether they are things infinite or finite; but in this way all the portions of things infinite, and of the Infinite in general, are similarly media up to the extremity; so that if there is nothing that is the first, there is, in short, no cause.

But neither, truly, is it possible, as regards a progession downwards, to proceed on to infinity, in case that which is in a progression upwards involves a first principle; as, for example, that from fire, indeed, water should be produced, but from this earth, and so invariably that a certain different genus be produced. For, in a twofold manner, is one thing produced from another,—not as this particular thing is said to take place after that; for example, the Olympic games from the Isthmaean,— either as a man is produced from a boy undergoing a change, or air from water.

As, indeed, then, we say that a man is produced from a boy as a thing that has been from that which is in a process of formation, or that which has been finished from that which is in a process of formation, or that which has been finished from that 994b which is being finished, or tends towards perfection, for always is there a certain medium; as production is a medium between existence and nonexistence, so also is the thing that is being produced between entity and nonentity: and a person receiving instruction is one becoming scientifically learned. And this is the meaning of what is affirmed,—that from a person learning is produced one that is scientifically learned; and just as water is generated from air on account of the air having undergone corruption. Wherefore, in the former instance, the things adduced, indeed, do not revert into one another, nor is a child produced from a man; for that which is being produced does not arise from the act of generation, but is subsequent to generation: for so, also, the day is generated from the dawn, because it is posterior to this; wherefore, neither is the dawn generated from the day: but the other instances revert into each other.

In both these cases, however, it is impossible to pursue the progress on to infinity; for, in the one case, of those that are media there must needs be an end, and, in the other case, the things adduced revert into one another, for the destruction of one is the generation of the other. But at the same time, also, it is impossible, that what is first, seeing that it is eternal, should be subject to corruption; for since generation is not infinite in an ascending progression, that nature must needs not be eternal from which anything has been produced as from that which is primary, and has been subject to corruption; but this is impossible.

Further, the final cause is an end; but a thing of this sort is that which does not subsist on account of another, but other things on account of that. Wherefore, if that which is last be a thing of this sort, there will not be a progression to infinity; but if there is not such thing—I mean that which is last—the final cause will have no existence. But they who introduce this infinite progression forget that they destroy the nature of the good. Although no one would undertake entering on any course of action not intending to go on to a termination of his undertaking; nor would there be design in such things: for one who is possessed of mind always does a thing for some purpose or other (for this is a termination for it), for the end proposed is a termination. But, indeed, neither can the formal cause admit of being referred to another definition more copious in reason. For the prior definition is invariably more the definition of a thing; but the subsequent is not so. But to that of which there is no first, neither has that which is next in order any existence.

Further, they destroy scientific knowledge who make assertions in this way; for it is not even possible to understand anything before we come to individual things; and scientific knowledge has no existence in this case: for things infinite, in this manner, how is it possible to apprehend? For the infinite here is not a thing similar to infinity in the case of a line, which, as regards its divisions, indeed, does not come to a standstill, but is indivisible; nor is it possible for one to apprehend these divisions, except he imposes some limit to their divisibility. Wherefore, he will not reckon the divisions or sections who goes through the infinite in detail. But also, as regards the matter,—so far as it is such, in what is being moved,—it is necessary to understand it thus far; and for nothing that is infinite is there any possibility of existence: but, if this is not the case, not infinite, at any rate, is that by which we may know the infinite. But, doubtless, if the species of causes were infinite in number, neither, in such a case, would the perception of our knowledge be possible; for then we think we know when we may make known the causes: but the infinite according to addition, it is not in finite duration possible to exhaust.

3. But lectures on philosophic subjects fall our according to our habits; for as we have been accustomed, so we deem it right a thing should be expressed; and whatever things are besides 995a these do not appear similar: but, from the fact of our not being habituated thereto, they seem more unknown and strange, for the habitual is more known. And how great force the habitual possesses, the laws make manifest, in which fabulous and puerile things have greater force from usage than the reality of our knowledge concerning them.

But some persons, indeed, so not admit those making assertions, unless one speaks with mathematical precision; but others do not approve of what is said, unless they express themselves by means of an exemplar; and others think it right to adduce a poet as a witness. And some require all things to be expressed with accuracy; whereas accuracy is troublesome to others, either on account of their not being able to carry on a train of reasoning, or on account of their considering such as mere quibbling about verbal niceties,—for the precise involves some such thing. Wherefore, as in the case of contracts, so also in that of philosophic discourse, precision seems to be a thing to some persons that is illiberal.

Wherefore, it is necessary that one should have been instructed what way we must admit each and all points of inquiry, as it would be absurd at the same time to seek for scientific knowledge and the mode of attaining such knowledge: but it is not easy to acquire either of these. Now, mathematical accuracy of language is not to be required in all things, but in those things that do not involve any connection with matter. Wherefore, such is not the natural mode of discovering truth; for perhaps the whole of Nature involves matter: therefore, first must we investigate what Nature is. For in this way, also, will it be evident about what only natural science is conversant, and whether it is the province of one science, or of many, to speculate into causes and first principles.

BOOK III

1. FOR the advancement of the science under investigation it is necessary for us, first, to take a review of those points respecting which one ought to doubt in the first instance; but these are whatsoever subjects some speculators have entertained opinions of after a different mode, and whatever beyond these may happen to have been overlooked. For it will contribute towards one's object, who wishes to acquire a facility in the gaining of knowledge, to doubt judiciously, for a subsequent acquisition in the way of knowledge is the solution of previous doubts; but when one is ignorant of the bond of a thing, it is not possible for such to loose it. But the perplexity of the intellect makes manifest this assertion respecting the matter in hand; for so far forth as the dianoetic faculty doubts, so far does it undergo something similar to persons loaded with chains; for it is possible, in both cases, to advance further. Wherefore, it is necessary, in the first instance, to speculate into all the difficulties involved in the present subject, both on account of those things, and also from the fact, that they who carry on an investigation, without doubting first, are similar to persons ignorant where they ought to walk; and, in addition to these things, neither can such know whether he has discovered the object of his speculation or not; for the end is not manifest to this speculator; but to one who has previously doubted, in a 995b judicious way, it is manifest. But, further, there is a necessity

that a person should be better qualified for forming a judgment who has heard all the reasons, as it were, of adversaries and opposing disputants.

Now, the first source of perplexity is concerning those things which we have expressed doubts of in our Preface; namely, whether to speculate into causes be the province of one or many sciences; and whether it be the province of this science to discover merely the primary principles of substance, or else to speculate concerning the first principles from which all derive their demonstrations; as, for instance, whether it is possible to affirm and deny one and the same thing, at the same time, or not, and concerning the other things of such a kind? And, if it is the province of this science to be conversant about substance, whether one may be about all, or whether there be many such in existence; and, if many, whether all are akin to each other, or it may be proper to style some of them sciences of "wisdom," and others of them, something else?

And this very thing is amongst the necessary points of investigation, whether it should be affirmed that sensible substances exist only, or whether others also subsist in addition to these; and whether there is a genius singly, or a number of genera of substances, according to the opinion of those who introduce both forms and mathematical entities as things intermediate between these and sensibles? Concerning these, therefore,—as we have said,—an examination must be made; and also concerning substances, whether the speculation extend only to them, or to the essential accidents of these substances? But, in addition to these points, we might inquire in regard to sameness and diversity, and similarity and dissimilarity, and identity and contrariety, and concerning priority and subsequence, and all the rest of such things, concerning as many as the Dialecticians endeavor to examine, instituting their inquiries from matters merely of opinion,—we might, I say, investigate whose province it is to speculate into all of these. Further, may one investigate whatsoever things are essential accidents in these very things, both not only what each of them is, but also whether, in truth, one be contrary to one?

And whether genera are first principles and elements, or those things into which, as being inherent, each thing is divided, and if the genera are so, whether they are such things as are predicted last or the first concerning individuals, as, for example, whether animal or man be a first principle, and be so rather than a singular? But most especially must we investigate and examine, with pains, as to whether besides matter there is any absolute cause or not, and whether this is separate or not, and whether it be one, or such causes may be many in number? And whether there is anything beside entirety (but I mean by entirety when anything has been predicated of matter), or nothing, or whether this is the case with some things, indeed, but not so with others, and what sort of entities such are? Moreover, whether first principles are limited in number or in 996a species, both those that subsist in formal causes and those that are in the subject? And whether of things corruptible and incorruptible the principles be the same or different? And whether all are incorruptible, or whether of corruptible things there are corruptible principles? Moreover, also, the most difficult of all, and involving the greatest perplexity, is the inquiry, whether unity and entity, as the Pythagoreans and Plato used to affirm, be not anything else but the substance of entities; or this be not the case, but that there be some other subject, as Empedocles says harmony is, and a certain other philosopher, fire, and another, water or air? And whether first principles are universal or are as the singulars of things? And whether they subsist in capacity or in energy? Further, whether they subsist otherwise than according to motion? For also these speculations would furnish much perplexity. But, in addition to these points, there remains the inquiry, whether numbers and dimensions, and figures and points, be certain substances or not? And, if they are substances, whether they are capable of being separated from sensibles or be inherent in them? For, concerning all of these questions, not only is it difficult successfully to attain unto the truth, but neither is a judicious doubting easy for the reasoning faculties.

2. In the first place, indeed, therefore, let us institute an inquiry concerning the first assertions which we have made; namely, whether to speculate concerning all kinds of causes be the province of one or many sciences? For how would it be the province of a single science to take cognizance of existing first principles when they are not contrary to each other? But, further, in the case of many of the entities all do not exist in all of them. For in what way is it possible for the principle of motion to be found in things incapable of motion; or that the nature of the good should, if everything which may be essentially good, and by reason of its own nature, is an end, and so a cause, inasmuch as on account of that other things are both produced and exist? But the end and the final cause are an end of any action. And all things in the act of doing are attended with motion; therefore, in things incapable of motion it would not be possible that this should exist as the first principle, or that there be therein any essential good. Wherefore, also, in mathematics nothing is demonstrated through this cause; nor is there any demonstration for the reason that a thing is better or worse: but neither does any mathematician make mention at all of any such thing whatsoever. Therefore, for this reason, certain of the Sophists, as, for example, Aristippus, regarded these with disdain; for in the other arts, even the mechanical ones themselves, as in those of carpentry and shoe-making, he said that wherefore a thing is better or worse could be declared in every respect, but that the mathematical sciences make no account concerning 996b things good and evil. But, truly, if there are, at least, many sciences of causes, and different sciences of a different first principle, which of these must be said to be the one under investigation; or whom of those that are in possession of them shall we pronounce scientifically informed, particularly in the matter under inquiry—for in the same subject is it possible that all the modes of causes exist; as, for example, of a house, the origin of the principle of motion is from art and the builder, and the final cause is the work, but the matter is earth and stones, and the form is the definition?

From the distinctions, therefore, laid down by us originally, as to which of the sciences we ought to denominate wisdom, is involved a reason for further styling each thus. For as far as a science is most qualified for the preeminence and for superiority over the rest, and so far as it is just that, as servants, the rest of the sciences should not contradict, so far such is a science of the end and of the good, for the rest of things are on account of this; but as far as wisdom has been defined a science of first causes, and of that which is especially capable of being scientifically known, so far such would be a science of substance. For seeing that persons may acquire the same knowledge by many methods, we say that he rather understands a thing who makes known by its being what that thing is than by its not-being; and of these themselves one in preference to another, and particularly he who knows what a thing is, and not he who knows the quantity or the quality of a thing, or what it is by nature fitted in for the way of action or of passion. Further, in the case of other things, the understanding each of those subjects concerning which there are demonstrations, we think then to have an existence when we may understand what a thing is; for instance, what the squaring of a right-lined figure is: that it is the finding of a mean proportional. In like manner is it in the case of the rest. But with regard to generations, and actions, and every kind of change, we are in a way of understanding each when we understand the first principle of motion; and this is different and in opposition to the end. Wherefore, it would appear to belong to the department of a different science to investigate each of these causes.

But, truly, also, with regard to demonstrative first principles, whether they belong to one science or more is a question open to doubt. But I term demonstrative even those common opinions from which all derive their demonstrations; for instance, that everything must needs be either an affirmation or negation, and that it is impossible for the same thing to be and not to be at the same time, and whatsoever other such propositions there are. It is, I say, a question open to doubt, whether there be one science of these and of substance or a different one; and if not one, whether it is necessary to denominate as such the science under investigation? Therefore it would not then appear reasonable, indeed, that it should be the province of one science; for why, in preference, should the perception concerning these peculiarly belong to geometry rather than to any other science whatsoever? If, therefore, in like manner, truly it belongs to any whatsoever, but it does not admit of belonging to all the sciences, as neither is it the peculiarity of the rest, so neither is it the province of that science which makes known the substances to investigate 997a concerning these. But, at the same time, also, in what way will it be the science of these? For what each of these happens to be we also now know; the rest of the arts, therefore, employ them as things known. But if there be a demonstrative science concerning them, it will be necessary that there be a certain subject-genus, and that some of these, indeed, should be passive properties and others axioms: for concerning all things it is impossible that there should be a demonstration; for demonstration must needs be composed of certain principles, and be conversant respecting some thing, and the demonstration of some things. Wherefore, it happens that there is one particular genus of all things that are being demonstrated, for all the demonstrative sciences employ axioms. But, truly, if there be a science of substance different from the one concerning these, which of them is by nature fitted to be more sovereign and prior, for especially and universally the principles of all things are the axioms? And if this is not the part of the philosopher, whose else will it be to speculate into the truth and falsehood regarding these?

And, upon the whole, whether of all substances is there one science or more? If, indeed, therefore, there is not one science of such, what sort of substance must we consider as the subject matter of this science of ontology? But that there should be one science of all substances is not reasonable; for there would be one demonstrative science concerning all things that are essential accidents, if every demonstrative science, in respect of a certain subject, speculates into essential accidents from general opinions. Respecting, then, the same genus it is the province of the same science to investigate the essential accidents from these same general opinions: for an examination respecting the wherefore belongs to one science, and to one respecting those elements whereof a thing consists, whether both investigations belong to the same or a different science? Wherefore, the like will take place in regard of accidents, whether these will investigate them or one of those? But, further, might we examine whether the speculation is confined only to substances, or is also concerning the accidents in these? But I say, for example, if a solid be a certain substance, and lines, and surfaces, whether it be the province of the same science to take cognizance of these things, and of the accidents of each genus about which the mathematical sciences demonstrate, or if it be the province of a different one? For if, indeed, of the same, there would be a certain demonstrative science, and that the science of substance; but of the essence or formal cause there does not appear to be a demonstration: but, if of a different science, what will be the science that speculates about the accidents of substance? For this would be altogether difficult to render an account of. Further, also, whether must we say that there are sensible substances only, or, also, besides these, others? And whether do the genera of these substances happen to subsist singly, or are they more 997b numerous, as, for instance, they who speak both of forms and media between forms, and things sensible, concerning which, they say, are conversant the mathematical sciences?

As to the assertion, then, indeed, that we have made, namely, that forms are causes, and substances absolutely subsisting, it has been declared in the earliest of our disquisitions concerning these: but as these inquiries in many ways are clogged with difficulties, it would be no less absurd the assertion that there are, indeed, certain natures besides those which are in the heavens, and that these are the same with things sensible, except that the former are, indeed, eternal, and the latter, corruptible. For they speak of the existence of ideal man, and ideal horse, and ideal health, but say nothing else in regard of these; acting, in a way, similar to those who affirm the existence of the gods, no doubt, but in the shape of men; for neither did these latter constitute aught save eternal men, nor do the former make species anything else but eternal sensibles.

But, further, if in addition, also, to forms and sensibles any will set down things intermediate, he will be involved in many doubts. For it is evident that, in like manner, there will be lines, and each of the other genera, besides also them that are sensible. Wherefore, since astrology is one of these, there will also be a certain heaven besides the sensible heaven, and a certain other sun and moon; and so with the rest, in like manner, of the bodies that are situated in the heavens. Although, how need one place confidence in such statements as these? For neither is it reasonable that this ideal heaven should be incapable of motion; but, also, that it should be capable of motion is altogether impossible. In like manner, also, is it the case concerning the objects whereof optical science treats, and that of harmonics in mathematics; for, also, it is impossible that these should have a subsistence different from sensibles through the same causes: for if things sensible and senses have an intermediate subsistence, it is manifest, also, that there will be animals which will be media between them and things corruptible. But one would doubt, also, concerning what sort of entities it is necessary for these sciences to investigate. For if geodesy will differ from geometry in this only, that one is conversant about things which we perceive by the senses, but the other, about things that are not cognizant by sense, it is manifest that besides the medicinal science, and besides each of the rest, there will be a certain science intermediate between the healing art itself and this particular art of medicine. Although, indeed, how is this possible? For, also, would there be, in such a case, certain salubrious qualities in addition to those that are sensible, and to the salubrious itself: but, at the same time, neither is this true that geodesy is conversant about sensible magnitudes and those that are corruptible; for it would fall into decay when they were in process of being destroyed. But, truly, neither will astronomy be conversant about sensible magnitude nor about yon heaven. For neither are the lines that fall under the cognizance of the senses the same as the geometrician describes them; for nought of the things that are perceived by the senses is 998a in this way strictly straight or round, for the circle touches the rule not in a point, but as Protagoras was accustomed to say in his refutation of the geometricians. Neither are the motions and the evolutions of the heaven similar to those about which astrology has formed its systems; nor have the symbols the same nature with the stars.

But there are some persons who say that these reputed media between forms and sensibles are not, indeed, separable from sensibles, at least, but inherent in them: and to enumerate all the impossibilities attendant upon these statements would require a more copious discourse; but even it will be sufficient to speculate thus much on this point. For neither is it reasonable that this should be so in the case of these merely; but it is evident that it would be possible, also, for forms to subsist in sensibles: for both of these are results of the same process of reasoning. But, further, must there needs be two solids in the same place; and these mathematical entities must needs not be things incapable of motion, seeing that they, at least, subsist in sensibles that are being moved, and, in short, on what account will any one lay down their having a subsistence, indeed, and a subsistence in sensibles? For the same absurdities with the things that have been previously spoken will ensue; for there will be a certain heaven in addition to the heaven we see, except that it will not be separate, but in the same place, which is still more absurd.

3. Now, respecting these points much doubt therefore prevails; namely, how it is necessary by forming one's opinion thereupon to attain unto the truth: and, likewise, respecting first principles, whether it is requisite to consider the genera as elements and first principles, or, in preference, those things from which, as inherent, each first thing consists? For example, the elements and first principles of voice appear to be those things from which all voices are composed primarily, but not the voice in common; and we say that those things are elements of figures

the demonstrations of which are inherent in the demonstrations either of all or of the greater part of other things. But, further, both some in affirming that there are many elements of bodies, and others that there is one, of which they are composed, and from which they consist, assert these to be the first principles; as, for example, Empedocles asserts that fire and water, and the elements subsisting along with these, are those from which, as being inherent, entities derive their existence: but he does not speak of those as the genera of entities. And, in addition to these statements, we may subjoin the remark, that if anyone wishes to contemplate the nature of the rest of things—as, for example, a bed, of what parts it consists, and how those parts are put together—in that case he is acquainted with the nature of it. From these reasons, therefore, it would appear that first principles would not be the genera of entities. But so far forth as we obtain a knowledge of each thing by means of the definitions, and so far as first principles are the genera of definitions, it is necessary, also, that first principles be the genera of things capable of definition. And, likewise, if to acquire the science of the forms according to which entities are denominated is to acquire the science of entities themselves, in this case the genera of the forms are first principles. But those, also, who affirm that the elements of entities are unity or entity, or the great and the little, appear to employ these as genera. But neither, truly, in both cases is it possible, at least, to affirm, also, that they are first principles. For, indeed, of substance there is one reason or formal principle; different, however, will be the definition through the genera, and that which declares the entities whereof, as inherent, a thing consists. If, also, most especially, in addition to these things, the genera are first principles, whether is it necessary to regard the first of the genera to be principles, or the lowest that are predicated of individuals? For this, also, is involved in doubt. For if, indeed, it is requisite that universals are first principles in a more eminent degree, it is evident that the topmost genera will be first principles; for these are predicated of all things. Therefore, the first principles of entities will be as numerous as the first genera; so that unity and entity will be first principles and substances: for these especially are predicated of all entities. But it is not possible that there should be one genus of entities, or that unity or entity should be such; for it is necessary, indeed, that the differences of each genus both exist, and that each should be one: but it is impossible either for the species to be predicated about the proper differences of the genus, or for the genus to subsist, independent of the species itself. Wherefore, if unity or entity be a genus, neither will entity or unity constitute any difference. But, doubtless, unless there be genera there will not be first principles, since genera are first principles. Further, also, media that are comprehended along with the differences will be genera as far as to individuals; but now this appears to be the case with some, and not with others. And further, in addition to these things, we may add that the differences are rather first principles than the genera; but if these, also, are first principles, first principles become infinite, so to speak: and this is especially the case if one should constitute the first genus a first principle.

But truly, if, also, the one rather be that which is principal, 999a and if one be a thing that is indivisible, and everything that is indivisible is so, either according to quantity or according to species, and if that which is according to species have a prior subsistence, and the genera are more divisible into species, one would be predicated last, for man is not a genus of certain particular men. Further, of those things wherein the prior and subsequent are inherent, it is not possible that what is predicated of them would be anything different from these; for instance, if a dyad be the first of numbers there will not be any number different from the species of numbers: and, in like manner, rather will there be figures in addition to the species of figures. But if this is not the case in regard of these, hardly, at least, will there be genera of other things in addition to the species, for of these there seem especially to be genera. But in individuals there is not one thing that is prior, and another that is subsequent. Further, where one thing is better and another worse, that which is better always is prior; so that none of these could be a genus. From these statements, indeed, therefore, it appears that those things that are predicated of individuals are first principles, rather than the genera. But, again, how, on the other hand, it is necessary to regard these as first principles, it would not be easy to express. For it is requisite that there should be a first principle and a cause exclusive of the things of which there is a first principle, and that it should be capable of subsisting in a condition of separation therefrom; but, as to the existence of some such thing besides the singular, why should one make a supposition to this effect, except that it is predicated universally, and of all things? But if, indeed, this is done on this account, in such a case universals are to be set down as first principles in a more eminent degree, so that the first genera would be principles.

4. But a doubt closely connected with the foregoing is one which of all is both the most difficult and the most requisite to examine into, concerning which our treatise, at present, is immediately occupied. For if there is not anything besides singulars, and if singulars are infinite, how is it possible to be in possession of a science of things that are infinite? For, as far as there is something that is one and the same, and as far as there is something that is universal, so far do we attain a knowledge of all things. But, doubtless, if this be necessary, and if there must needs be something in addition to singulars, it would be requisite that there be genera in addition to singulars, whether they are the lowest or the highest; but that this is impossible we have ourselves just now expressed a doubt.

But, further, if most especially there is something besides the entire when anything has been predicated concerning matter, whether, if there be a certain form, must there needs be something universal in addition to some, and not in addition to other things, or is there nothing universal besides singulars? If, then, there is nothing universal besides singulars, there would not be anything that is cognizable by the mind; but all things would fall beneath the notice of the senses, and there would not

999b

be a scientific knowledge of anything, unless one would assert the exercise of the senses to be science. Further, would there be nothing eternal or immovable; for all things sensible are in a process of corruption, and are in motion. But, truly, if there is, at least, nothing that is eternal, neither is it a thing possible that there should be generation; for there must needs be something, namely, that which is being produced, and wherefrom it is produced: and of these the last must be ingenerable if both the progress of successive productions is to stop at all, and if generation from nonentity should be a thing that is impossible. But, moreover, on the supposition of such things being in existence as generation and motion, there must needs be a limit likewise, for neither is any motion infinite; but of every motion is there an end: but that cannot be produced which it is impossible could have been produced; but that which has been produced must needs exist when first it has been produced. But, further, if matter be an existence from the fact of its being ingenerable, still it is much more reasonable that substance should have a subsistence when that is generated so as to have a being; for if neither substance nor matter shall have an existence, neither will there be anything at all in existence: but, if this be impossible, there must needs be something in addition to the entire, namely, the form and species; yet, if, on the other hand, anyone will establish this dogma, a doubt presents itself, both in the case of what things one should make this assertion, and in the case of what one should not. For that this is not possible, in the case of all, is evident; for we would not posit existence of any particular house in addition to certain houses.

But, in addition to the foregoing points, we may subjoin the inquiry, whether will there be one substance of all things, for instance, of men? Now, this is absurd, for all things are not one of which the substance is one, but are many and different; this, however, also, is an unreasonable statement. And, at the same time, also, how would matter become each of these? And how is the entire both of these? But, further, respecting first principles we would also entertain this particular doubt. For if, indeed, they are one in species, nought will there be that is one in number; nor will actual unity or entity have any existence: and how would scientific knowledge be in existence, unless there was a certain one in all things?

But, truly, if they are one in number, each of the first principles also will be one; and not, as in the case of sensibles, one principle of one thing, and another of another; as, for instance, of this syllable when it is the same in species, the first principles, also, are the same in species, for these, likewise, are different in number: and if this be not the case, but if the first principles of entities are one in number, there will not be in existence anything else besides the elements; for to speak of one in number, or of the singular, makes no difference, for so we speak of the singular as one in number, and of the universal as that which is common to these. Just, therefore, does the case stand as if the elements of voice should be limited in number, all the letters necessarily must be in number as many as the elements, since neither two, nor more than two, of them would be the same.

But a doubt of no less difficulty has been overlooked, both by modern investigators and by our predecessors, namely, as to whether the first principles of things corruptible and of things incorruptible be the same or different? For, if indeed, they are the same, how is it the case that some things are incorruptible and others corruptible, and from what cause does this difference arise?

Those of the Hesiodic school, and all as many as are theologians, fixed their thoughts only upon the probable, as it appeared to themselves; but they have treated us with disdain. For, seeing that they make the first principles gods, and to have been produced from gods, whatsoever did not taste of the nectar and ambrosia they say are mortal; palpably speaking of these denominations as expressive of things that are known to themselves. Respecting, however, the actual adducing of these causes, they have spoken beyond our comprehension. For if, indeed, the immortals partake of these for the sake of pleasure, the nectar and ambrosia are, in no respect, the causes of their existence;

1000a

and if these are the causes of their existence, how would they be eternal when thus requiring sustenance? But, respecting those fabulous systems of philosophy, it is not worth one's while considering them with seriousness.

But from those who make assertions by demonstration, it is necessary to ascertain in our inquiries, why, forsooth, if entities are from the same source, some of them are in their nature eternal, and why others of these entities are subject to decay? But, inasmuch as they neither mention a cause of this, and as it is not reasonable that the case should be so, it is manifest that the first principles of these would not be the same, nor would there be the same causes of them. For, also, one whom any person would suppose to speak particularly consistent with himself, namely, Empedocles, has, likewise, experienced the same difficulty. For he, indeed, is for establishing discord—which is a first principle in his system—as a certain cause of corruption. Nevertheless, this would seem, however, also, to produce entities that are beyond the one; for from this are produced all the other works of creation except the deity. The following, at least, are the words of Empedocles:

From which are all things, as many as were, and are, and
    shall be after;
And trees therefrom have blossomed, and men and women,
And beasts and birds, and water-fed fishes,
And even the long-lived gods.

And the subsistence of all things independent of these is manifest; for, unless discord were inherent in things, all things would have 1000b been one, as he says: for when they would have come together, then last in the conglomeration would stand discord.

Wherefore, also, it happens to him, in his system, that the deity, who is supremely happy, should be less prudent than the rest of beings, for he does not know all the elements, for he is not in possession of discord; but the knowledge of the like is through the like.

For, indeed, says he, by earth we see earth, and by water,
water,
And ether divine by ether, and through fire the ruinous fire,
And by concord, concord, and by gloomy discord, discord.

But, to return to the point from whence our discourse digressed. This, at all events, is evident, that it happens, according to the theory of Empedocles, that discord is no more the cause of corruption than of existence; and, in like manner, that neither is harmony a cause of existence more than of corruption, for while collecting things into unity it is a cause of corruption to other things. And, at the same time, also, he mentions no cause of the actual transmutation, save that the thing is thus constituted by nature to take place. Mark his words:

But when mighty discord was nourished in the members,
And rose up to the honors of deified Time, who, holding
The sway over them alternately, had, in the end,
Surpassed the ample objects of God's adjuration.

As if, indeed, it were a thing necessary that a change should take place; but he does not bring to light any necessary cause. But, nevertheless, thus much, at least, he only asserts consistently, for he does not constitute some entities corruptible and others incorruptible, but all corruptible, except the elements. But the source of perplexity now mentioned it this: why, if entities spring from the same source, some of them are incorruptible and some of them are not so? That, therefore, the first principles of things would not be the same, let this much suffice to have been spoken.

But, if the first principles of things be different, one matter of doubt, indeed, is, whether these also will be incorruptible or corruptible? For if, indeed, they are corruptible, it is manifest that it is requisite that these, also, should spring from certain entities; for all things perish into those from whence they derive their being. Wherefore, it happens that to principles there are other first principles that are prior; but this is impossible, both on the supposition of the progression being stationary, at some stage of its progress, and on the supposition of its going on to infinity. And, moreover, how will things perishable subsist if the first principles will be destroyed? But if these principles are imperishable, why, indeed, from these that are things imperishable will arise those that are perishable, but from the others those that are imperishable? For this is not reasonable, but either is impossible, or requires for its establishment much rational support. And, further, neither has anyone attempted to enumerate different ones; but speculators assign the same first principles of all things—the first subject of doubt, however, they 1001a entertain slightly, regarding it as something trifling.

But, also, the most difficult point of all to examine into, and the most necessary for the discovery of truth, is, whether entity and unity are substances of entities, and whether each of them not being anything else, this is unity and that is entity; or whether it is necessary to investigate what, at length, unity and entity are, as if another nature were the subject to these? For some, truly, in that way, and some in this, suppose their nature to be disposed. For Plato, indeed, and the Pythagoreans do not regard entity as anything different from unity, but that this is their nature that it should be the same thing for the substance to be one, and to be a certain entity. But amongst natural philosophers, Empedocles, for instance, as if conducting the inquiry to that which is more known, says that unity is entity. For he would seem to affirm that this is harmony—at least, this is a cause in his system of unity being found in all things. But others say that fire, and some that air, is this unity and entity from whence that entities both arise and are produced. So, in like manner, is it the case, also, with those who lay down the existence of more elements than these; for it is, likewise, necessary for these to reckon unity and entity such things as whatever, at least, they affirm first principles to be. But it happens, unless one will set down the existence of unity and entity as a certain substance, that not any of the rest of the universals will have any subsistence, for these are universal preeminently above all. But, if unity itself be not some particular thing, nor entity itself, much less will there be any of the other things that will have a subsistence, except those denominated singulars. But, further, on the supposition of unity not being a substance, it is evident that neither would number have a subsistence, as a certain nature that has been separated from entities, for number constitutes the monad; but the monad is the same as some certain unit. But, truly, if, at least, actual unity and actual entity be a certain particular thing, it is necessary that the substance of that thing be entity and unity; for it is not any different thing that is universally predicated about them, but these very same things.

But, doubtless, if actual entity and actual unity, at least, shall have any existence, much doubt will arise how there will subsist anything different from these. Now, I mean how there will be more entities in existence than one. For anything different from entity has no existence. Wherefore, according to the theory of Parmenides, it must needs happen that all entities are one, 1001b and that this one constitutes entity. But in both cases there is a difficulty; for even on the supposition whether unity, doubtless, be not substance, or whether any actual unity have a subsistence, it is impossible for number to be substance: but if, indeed, then, it has not a subsistence, it hath been previously stated why; but if it has the same doubt presents itself respecting entity also: for from what will there be another one besides the one itself, for must not that necessarily be not one, for all entities are either one or many, each of which is one? Further, if unity itself be indivisible, according, indeed, to the axiom of Zeno, nothing would there be having a subsistence. For that which neither when added nor subtracted makes anything greater or less, he affirms this not to belong to the category of entities, because entity is manifestly magnitude; and if it is magnitude it is corporeal, for this, in every way, is entity. But the addition of such things, in one way, will make what is greater, and, in another, will not make anything so at all. As a surface and a line make that which is greater; but a point and a monad, by no means, have this effect. But since this philosopher speculates clumsily, and it happens that there is something that is indivisible, wherefore, even in this way, also, hath one for him a certain reply as follows,—an addition of this sort will not make a thing greater, but will make it more; yet how, forsooth, from one, or more than one, of this kind will arise magnitude, for this is even like saying, that a line is made up of points? But, doubtless, if anyone makes a supposition in this way, so that, as some say, from actual unity, and a something else that is not one, is composed number, not the less should it form a subject for investigation, why, and how, what is produced will one time be number, and another time, magnitude, if what is not one be inequality and the same nature. For neither is it manifest how from one and this nature, nor how from a certain number and this nature, magnitudes would arise.

5. But a doubt connected with these is, whether numbers and bodies, and surfaces and points, are certain substances or not? For if they are not, it eludes our comprehension what being is, and what the substances of entities are. For passive properties, and motions, and relations, and dispositions, and ratios, do not appear to signify a substance of anything; for all these are predicated respecting a certain subject, and no one of them can be said to be this or that particular thing. But things which would seem particularly to signify substance, namely, water, and earth, and fire, from which compounded bodies consist, the heats and colds of these and such like qualities are affections, not substances; but 1002a all the while the body, which undergoes these passive conditions, alone sustains them as a certain entity, and as being a certain substance. But, truly, both body is less substance than a superficies, and this latter than a line, and this than the monad and the point, for by these is body defined. And these, indeed, seem capable of existence without body; but the existence of body, without these, seems impossible.

Wherefore, the majority of speculators and our predecessors considered substance and entity to be body, and the other things to be passive properties of this; so that, also, the first principles—those of bodies—are the first principles of entities. Subsequent investigators, however, and they, too, persons that appeared endowed with more wisdom than those, supposed such to be numbers. As, therefore, we have said, unless these are substance, there is, upon the whole, no substance in existence, nor no entity, for the accidents, at least, in these it would not, truly, be worthy to call entities.

But if, doubtless, this is acknowledged, that dimensions and points are substance, rather than bodies themselves, yet we do not perceive to what sort of bodies these would belong (for that they be inherent in things that fall under cognizance of the senses, this is impossible); in this case, then, there would not be any substance in existence. Further, however, it appears that all these entities are divisions of body, one indeed, into breadth, and another into depth, and a third into length. But, in addition to these things, in like manner, there is in the solid every kind of figure whatsoever; so that, if neither mercury is in the stone, nor the half of a cube in the cube, in such a way as has been defined neither, in this case, would surface exist in body: for if this would be the case with anything whatsoever, it would be with that which would separate the half. Now, there is the same mode of reasoning in the case of a line, and a point, and a monad; wherefore, if body especially be substance, and if these are substance rather than this, and these have no existence, nor do certain substances exist, there eludes our comprehension what entity is, and what is the substance of entities. For, in addition to the statements that have been made, those irrational consequences relating to generation and corruption, also, take place. For, indeed, substance—when not previously existing it comes into existence now, or when it which formerly had an existence afterwards ceases to exist—the substance, I say, appears to undergo these affections, namely, production and corruption; but points, and lines, and surfaces, cannot possibly arise or be destroyed, though sometimes these have a subsistence, and sometimes they have not. For when bodies mutually touch or 1002b intersect each other, at the same time that they touch they become one, and at the same time that they intersect they become two. So that points, lines, and surfaces, when bodies are compounded together, have no subsistence, but then have been reduced to corruption: but when bodies are divided, these rise into existence, though previously they had no existence. For a point, truly, that is indivisible is not capable of being divided into two; and, if they are produced and destroyed, they are produced from something. But, in a similar way, is it the case respecting the present time, which is contained in duration, for neither does this admit of being generated and destroyed, but, nevertheless, invariably seems to be a thing that is different, not that it is, however, any particular substance. In like manner, also, it is evident that it is the case both respecting points, and lines, and surfaces, for the reasoning is the same; for all these, in like manner, are either bounds or divisions.

6. But, upon the whole, would one feel perplexity why also it is necessary to investigate into certain other entities besides sensibles and media, for example, such as we posit as forms? For if it is on this account, because mathematical entities, indeed, differ from those that are here in a certain other respect, yet, in regard of there being many of them of the same species, there is no difference in this. Wherefore, the first principles of these will not be limited in number, as neither of all the lines which are here are the first principles limited in number, but in species, unless one takes the principle of this particular syllable, or of this particular voice, and the first principles of these will be limited in number. In like manner, also, is it the case with things that are intermediate; for there, likewise, things of the same species are infinite. Wherefore, unless, in addition to sensibles and mathematical entities, there are certain others, such as some call the forms, there will not be a substance one in number and species; nor will there be certain first principles of entities so many in number, but in species. If, then, this is necessary, the subsistence of forms, on this account, is necessary also. For even although they who make such assertions do not propound their theories with distinctness, yet it is this which they aim at; and they must needs affirm this, that each of the forms is a certain substance, and that not one of them subsists according to accident. But, doubtless, if we posit

the existence of the forms and of the first principles as one in number, but not in species, we have declared the impossibilities which must need come to pass.

Contiguous, also, to this inquiry is the question whether elements subsist in potentiality, or in some other manner? For if, indeed, in some other manner, there will be something else that is prior to first principles; for potentiality is prior to that cause: but it is not necessary that everything that is potential should be disposed in that way. But if elements are existent in potentiality, it is admissible that none of the entities should have a subsistence; for it is possible for that to exist which not as yet has any existence: for, indeed, that which has no existence is being produced, but nothing of things that are impotential is produced.

And these doubts, then, is it necessary to moot respecting first principles; and there remains, also, the inquiry whether universals exist, or, as we say, singulars? For if, indeed, universals exist, they will not be substances; for nought of those things that are general signify this particular thing, but a thing of such a sort; but the substance is this particular thing. But if it will be possible to exhibit this particular thing, and that which thereof may in common be predicated, in such a case many animals will Socrates himself be, and man and animal if each signify this certain particular thing, and that which is one. If, indeed, therefore, first principles are universal, these consequences take place; but if they are not universal, but are as singulars, they will not be objects of scientific knowledge; for the sciences are conversant about all things that are universal. Wherefore, will there be different first principles prior to principles, namely, those that are predicated universally, in case there is likely to be a science of them.

BOOK IV

1. THERE is a certain science which makes, as the object of its speculation, entity, as far forth as it is entity, and the things which are essentially inherent in this. But this is the same with none of those which are called particular sciences; for none of the rest of the sciences examines universally concerning entity so far forth as it is entity: but, cutting away a certain portion of it, they investigate what is accidental in regard of this; as, for example, the mathematical sciences. But, whereas we are in search of first principles and the topmost causes, it is evident that they must needs be absolutely of a certain nature. If, therefore, they, also, who investigate the elements of entities were accustomed to investigate these first principles, it is necessary, likewise, that the elements of entity should not have a subsistence according to accident, but so far forth as they are entities. Wherefore, also, must we ascertain the first causes of entity, so far as it is entity.

2. Now, entity is spoken of in various senses, indeed, but in reference to one, and to one certain nature, and not equivocally; but, in like manner, also, as everything conducive to health is termed so in reference to health, partly, indeed, in its preserving that state, and partly in giving rise to it, and partly in being an indication of health, and partly in being receptive of it; and, in like manner, as the medicinal is styled so in reference to the art of medicine; for, indeed, a thing is called medicinal partly in reference to its possessing the medicinal power, partly in its being by nature 1003b

65

adapted for the possession of such, and partly in its being the work of the medicinal art: and we shall receive the predication of other things in a similar manner with these. Thus, however, is entity, also, spoken of in various ways indeed; but every entity in reference to one first cause: for some things, because they are substances, are styled end-ties; but others, because they are affections of substance; but others, because they are a way to substance, either as corruptions, or privations, or qualities, or things formative or generative, of substance, or of those which are spoken of in reference to substance, or the negations of any of these or of substance. Wherefore, also, the nonentity we pronounce to be nonentity.

As, then, there is one science of all things pertaining to health, in like manner, also, is this so in the case of other things. For it is the province of one science to speculate concerning not only those things spoken of according to one, but also those spoken of in reference to a single nature. For these, also, in a certain manner, are spoken of in accordance with one. It is evident, therefore, that it is the province of a single science to speculate concerning entities, so far forth as they are entities. But in every respect is the science of ontology strictly a science of that which is first or elemental, both on which the other things depend and through which they are denominated. If, then, this is substance, the philosopher or metaphysician must needs be in possession of the first principles and causes of substances. Now, of every genus there is both one sense of each and one science; as, for instance, grammatical science is one, and speculates into all vocal sounds. Wherefore, to speculate into, also, the number of the species of entity, and the species of the species, belongs to a science one in kind.

If, therefore, entity and unity are the same thing, and one nature, from the fact of their following each other as first principle and cause, yet they are not manifested by a single definition; there is, however, no difference, should we even make our suppositions in regard of them after a similar manner, nay, even rather is it for the advantage of the present inquiry. For it is the same thing, one man and the entity man and man; and not anything different does it make manifest, according to a repetition of the expression, to say man is, and man and one man: but it is evident that there is no separation of being either in the case of production or corruption. But in like manner, also, is it the case with unity. Wherefore, it is manifest that addition in these implies the same thing, and that nothing different is unity from entity. And, further, the substance of each thing is one not according to accident; and in like manner, also, is it the case with any entity whatsoever. Therefore, as numerous as are the species of unity, so numerous, also, are those of entity, into the nature of which it is the province of the same science in kind to investigate: now I speak, for instance, of sameness and similarity, and of the other things of this sort, and of those that are in opposition to these. And almost all contraries are reduced to this first principle. These points, however, have formed the subject-matter of our 1004a inquiries in our treatise styled, "A Selection of Contraries."

And so many portions of philosophy are there as there are, as least, substances. Wherefore, is it necessary that there should be a certain first philosophy, and one next in order belonging to these; for unity and entity are things straightway involving genera; wherefore, also, the sciences will follow upon these. For the philosopher or metaphysician is as one that is styled a mathematician, for his science also has parts; and there is a certain first and second science, and another next in order, in mathematics. But whereas it is the province of one science to investigate things that are in opposition, and since plurality is opposed to unity, it is also the province of one science to specu-late into negation and privation, on account of both kinds of inquiry being possible in the case of unity, of which there is the negation or the privation, either absolutely affirmed that such does not reside therein, or in a certain genus thereof. In this case, indeed, therefore, the difference is present in unity with the exception of that which is inherent in negation (for negation is the absence of that). And in privation, also, is there a certain sub-ject nature of which the privation is predicated. Now, plurality is opposed to unity; wherefore, also, the things that are in opposition to those that have been mentioned—namely, both diversity, and dissimilarity, and inequality, and as many other qualities as are denominated either according to the same, or according to plurality and unity—it is the province of the science of metaphysics that we have alluded to, to examine into; among the number of which, also, a certain one is contrariety; for contrariety is a certain difference, but difference is diversity.

Wherefore, since unity is spoken of in various ways, these, also, shall in many ways be spoken of; but, nevertheless, it is the province of one science to make known all such; for even though unity be spoken of in many ways, on that account it is not the province of a different science to investigate them: if, however, neither the definitions are capable of being reduced in accordance with one, nor in reference to one, then is it the province of a different science. But since all such are referred to what is first— as, for example, as many things as are styled one are spoken of in reference to the first one—in the same manner may the assertion be made, that this science is concerning sameness and diversity, and the rest of the contraries. Wherefore, in dividing how many modes each is expressed by, in this way must reference be made to what is first or original in each category, in order to ascertain how it is expressed in reference to that. For things will be denominated partly by reason of having those primaries, and partly that they are causes of them, and partly according to other such modes. Therefore, is it evident, as has been stated in the doubts, that it is the province of one science to institute an inquiry concerning these and concerning substance. But this was one of those inquiries that have been mentioned in the doubts.

1004b   And it is the part of the philosopher to be able to speculate about all the foregoing subjects of inquiry. For, if it be not the province of the philosopher, who shall there be that will be likely to examine whether he be the same person, Socrates, and Socrates sitting; or whether one be contrary to one, or what a contrary is, or in how many ways it is denominated? In like manner, also, is it in the case of the rest of such points for investigation.

Since, therefore, these of themselves are affections of unity, so far forth as it is unity, and of entity, so far forth as it is entity, but not so far forth as they are numbers, or lines, or fire, it is evident that it is the province of that science of ontology to make known both what these are, and the accidents that are inherent in them. And not in this respect do they err who examine concerning these, as not philosophizing, but because substance, about which they understand nothing, is a thing prior in existence. Since, as there are peculiar affections of number, as far as it is number (for instance, oddness, evenness, commensurability, equality, excess, defect), and as these both absolutely and relatively to one another are inherent in numbers, and since in a similar way there are other peculiar qualities, in what is solid and incapable of motion, and in what is being moved, both that which is without weight, and that which has weight, so, also, in entity, so far forth as it is entity, are there certain peculiar properties; and these are they about the truth of which it is the province of the philosopher or ontologist to inquire.

Now, a proof of this is the following: for dialecticians and sophists assume, indeed, the same figure as the philosopher (for sophistical is only apparent wisdom, and dialecticians dispute about all things); to all, however, is entity common. But they dispute concerning these, evidently, from the cause of these being proper subjects of inquiry for philosophy. For, indeed, sophistry and dialectics are employed about the same genus as philosophy is; but philosophy differs from the one in the mode of power, and from the other in the choice of life. And again, dialectic science is merely tentative of the knowledge of those things that philosophy has already actually reached; but sophistic science is only apparent, and not real. And the same is further proved from the fact that a different coordination of contraries is privation, and all things are referred to entity and nonentity, and to unity and plurality: as, for instance, rest in its nature partakes of unity, and motion of plurality. But that entities and substance are compounded of contraries almost all men acknowledge—all, at least, assert the first principles to be contraries: according to some, indeed, these principles being odd and even; and according to others, hot and cold; and according to others, finite and infinite; and others, harmony and discord. But all the rest of such are referred apparently to 1005a unity and plurality; for let this reduction be received by us as is done in the first book of our work "Concerning the Good." Now, there it appears that first principles, both altogether and as is acknowledged by others, fall under these genera.

From these statements, therefore, is it also evident that to investigate entity, so far forth as it is entity, is the province of one science. For all things are either contraries or composed from contraries: but the first principles, also, of contraries are unity and plurality; and these are belonging to the department of one science, whether the predication be made according to one or not, as, perhaps, the truth is. But, nevertheless, even though unity be spoken of in many ways, to the first will the rest be reduced, and the contraries in like manner. And for this reason, even though entity and unity be not universal and the same, in the case of all things, or separable, as, perhaps, they are not, yet some things, no doubt, are referred to unity, but others to that next in order; and for this reason it is not the business of the geometer to investigate into what the contrary is, or the perfect, or unity, or entity, or identity, or diversity, save only from hypothesis.

That, therefore, it is the province of one science to investigate entity, so far forth as it is entity, and the things therein existing, so far forth as they constitute entity, is evident; and that the same science is speculative not only of substances, but also of things that are inherent in substances, and of the particulars enumerated, both concerning priority and subsequence, and genus and species, and whole and part, and the rest of each, this is evident also.

3. But we must determine whether it is the province of one science, or a different one, to speculate concerning axioms, as they are called, in mathematics; and concerning substance? Doubtless, it is manifest that it is belonging to one, and that the

science of the philosopher, and the investigation of such inquirer is respecting these; for in all entities are they inherent, but not in any genus separate distinctly from the rest. And all investigators employ them, indeed, because they belong to entity, so far forth as it is entity; each genus, however, constitutes entity. And thus far do they employ them as is sufficient for their purpose, but that is as far as they comprise the genus about which they bring forward their demonstrations. Wherefore, since it is evident that they are inherent in all things, as far as they are entities (for this is held by these in common), the speculation of them belongs to the philosopher, whose business it is to make known the truth concerning entity, so far forth as it is entity, and concerning these. Therefore, no one of those who are partial inquirers attempts to say aught concerning these, whether they are true or not, neither, for instance, the geometer nor the arithmetician.

Some of the natural philosophers, however, in doing so, act reasonably; for they alone are accustomed to think that it is their province to examine concerning the whole of nature, and concerning entity. But since there is something of a higher order than the physical (for nature is merely one certain genus of entity), the investigation in regard of these should belong to the universal, and to that which is speculative of the first substance. 1005b Now, I admit there is a certain wisdom, namely, even the physical; but it is not the first. As many things, however, as certain of those who speak concerning the truth of axioms attempt to lay down, in what way they ought to be admitted, they do this from ignorance of analytics; for they ought to approach such a subject who are instructed therein beforehand: but whilst hearers they should not be investigators. That, therefore, it is the part of the philosopher, and of the inquirer concerning substance in its entirety, so far forth as it is such by nature, to examine, also, in regard of syllogistic principles, is evident.

But it is becoming that one especially furnishing information about each genus should be competent to speak of the very surest principles of the thing; and, therefore, the same holds true of a person that is engaged in the investigation of entities, so far forth as they are entities—I mean, that he should be able to adduce the most firm principles of all. Now, this is the philosopher; and the most firm first principle of all is that concerning which there can be no possibility of deception, for such must needs be that which is most known; for those points respecting which men do not impart knowledge are all exposed to deception in; and it must needs, likewise, be a thing independent of hypothesis. For a principle which one must be in posssession of who understands any entity whatsoever, this is not an hypothesis; but what one must make known, in the manifestation of anything whatsoever, he must also needs come forward furnished with this. That, therefore, indeed, such is the most firm first principle of all is evident. Now, what this principle is we shall after this declare. For the same thing to be present and not be present at the same time in the same subject, and according to the same, is impossible (and whatsoever things we have further defined, let these be so defined in respect of their logical difficulties). This, however, is the most firm of all first principles; for it involves the distinction spoken of above. For it is impossible to suppose that anything whatsoever is the same, and is not the same, as certain think that Heraclitus asserts; for it is not necessary, as far as concerns what one asserts to exist, to suppose that these also do exist. But if it is not admissible that contraries at the same time should subsist in the same subject (now the usual definitions have been additionally made by us to this proposition) and if an opinion contrary to an opinion be that of contradiction, it is evident that it is impossible for the same inquirer to suppose that at the same time the same thing should be and not be; for one laboring under deception in regard of this would entertain contrary opinions at the same time. Wherefore, all who employ demonstration reduce the matter to this last opinion; for by nature this, also, is the first principle of all the rest of the axioms.

4. Now, there are certain philosophers who, as we have intimated, themselves both affirm that it is possible that the same thing may and may not be, and that they really think so. This

principle, however, do many of the investigators of Nature 1006a
employ. But we just now have assumed it as a thing impossible, in
the case of an entity, that it should be and not be at the same
time; and by means of this have we demonstrated that this is the
most firm of all first principles. Now, some also demand a
demonstration of this, from ignorance; for it *is* ignorance the
not knowing what things one ought to seek a demonstration of,
and of what things he ought not. For, indeed, upon the whole, it
is impossible that there should be a demonstration of all things;
for one would go on in this case to infinity, so that there would
not be any demonstration at all in this way. If, however, there be
some things of which we should not seek a demonstration,
what they in preference require such a first principle to be
they have not the ability to affirm. But it is possible to demonstrate concerning this, by refutation, that it is impossible, if only
he would affirm anything who doubts; but if he makes no assertion, it would be ridiculous the seeking an argument against him
who had not a reason to put forward about anything, so far as he
had no such reason; for an adversary of this sort, as far now as he
is such, would be like unto a plant. Now, I say, demonstration by
refutation differs from demonstration simply or properly so
called, because he that employs demonstration would seem to
require what is the principle in the beginning; but, on the
supposition of the existence of another cause of such a kind, it
would be a refutation, and not a demonstration.

Now, a commencement of a discussion in regard of all such
points is, not the demanding the declaration that either a thing
exists or doth not exist (for this, one would imagine, perhaps,
was the asking the principle assumed originally), but the
demanding the signification, at least, of a thing, both as for
oneself and for another. For this also amounts to a necessity, if
he is to say anything at all; for if he does not, there would be no
possibility of a rational discussion with such a one, neither for
himself relatively to himself, nor to another. If any one, however,
would grant this, there will be a demonstration in existence; for
now will there actually be in existence something that has been

determined. But the cause is not the person demonstrating, but the person sustaining the argument; for, by overturning the discussion, he yet sustains the discussion. And further, he that acquiesces in this, hath acquiesced in the truth of something independent of demonstration; so that not everything would be so and not so.

In the first place, indeed, therefore, it is evident that this very assertion is true, because the name signifies the existence or the nonexistence of this particular thing; so that not everything would be so, and not so in this particular way. Further, if man 1006b signifies one thing, let this be a two-footed animal. Now, I say, that this signifies one thing; if this be man, whatever is a man, this, namely, the being a two-footed animal, is the being in man: but there is no difference should any one assert that more is thereby signified, provided only they have been reduced under proper definitions; for grant that upon each definition a different name may have been imposed. Now, I say, for example, if he would not assert that man signifies one, but many things, of one of which there is a single definition, namely, two-footed animal, yet, also, are there many others, but defined according to number; for its own proper denomination might be set down according to each of the definitions. But if its proper denomination should not be thus set down, but one would say that such signified an infinity of things, it is palpable that there would not be a definition of it at all; for the signifying not any one thing is the signifying nothing. And when the denominations are devoid of meaning, there is an end to mutual discussion, and, also, in reality, to discussion on the part of a man with himself. For it is not possible that a person should understand anything that is not capable of understanding one thing: but, if it were possible, one name would be imposed on this thing. Let it, doubtless, be granted, as has been stated in the commencement, that a name significant of something be significant of one thing also.

It is not, therefore, possible that being in man signifies the same particular thing as the not being in man, if man is significant not merely of what is predicated of one, but even one thing itself;

for this we do not require that the one should signify that which is predicated of one: since, if the case stands in this way, at least, the musical, and the white, and the man, would signify one thing; so that all things would be one, for they would be synonymous; and it will not be possible that the same thing be and not be, save by equivocation; just as if we would call any one a man whom others would call a not-man. The subject of doubt, however, is not this, if it is possible that the same thing at the same time should be and not be the man nominally, but really. But if the name man, and the name not-man, do not signify anything different, it is evident that the not being man will not differ from the being man. Wherefore, the being man will be the not being man, for they will be one thing; for this signifies that they are one—as a tunic and a cloak—if there is one definition of each. And if they shall be one, the being man and the not being man signify one thing: but it has been demonstrated that they signify a different thing.

There is a necessity, therefore, of this consequence, if there be a particle of truth in the assertion, that man in signification is equipollent with being a two-footed animal; for this was what the expression man was assumed to signify. Now, if there exists a necessity that this be the case, it is not possible for this very thing not to be a two-footed animal then, for this doth the phrase "the being a necessity," signify, namely, the impossiblity of its not being man. Accordingly, it is not possible to be true to say at the same time that the same thing is both a man and is not a man. But there prevails the same mode of reasoning in the case of the not being man also; for the being of a man and the not being of a man signify a different thing, if, truly, both the being white and 1007a the being man are different; for much more is there opposition in this case to justify the difference of signification. But if, also, one would say that the white signifies one and the same thing with the being man, again will we make the same assertion, as has been declared on a former occasion, namely, that all things will be one, and not merely things in opposition. But, if this be not possible, that which has been declared will happen, if the question asked be answered.

If, however, when a simple question is put, one subjoin negations also, the question actually put is not replied to: for nothing hinders the same thing being both man and white, and other things ten thousand in multitude; but, nevertheless, if the question be asked, if it is true to affirm man to be this, or not to be so, the reply should be, that it signifies one thing, and no addition should be made that it is both white and large. For, also, it is impossible to go through accidents when, at least, they are infinite; either, therefore, let one go through all or none. In like manner, therefore, if, also, ten thousand times over they are the same thing, namely, man and not man, the reply to the question, if man is, should not be that at the same time also not man is, unless the reply likewise states, in addition, the rest of whatsoever things are accidents, as many as are so, and as many as are not; if this, however, be not done by the person asked the question, there is nothing under discussion at all.

But, in general, they who make this assertion overturn substance and essence, or the formal cause and very nature of a thing; for they must themselves needs affirm all things to be accidents, and that the essence of man or animal, whatsoever it be, has no existence. For if there will exist the essential nature of anything whatsoever, such as is that which is to be man this will not be to be not man, or not to be man, although these are negations of this; for it was one thing which it signified, and this was the substance of a certain thing. But the signification of the substance of a thing is, that not anything else is the being of that thing: but if the being whatsoever man is will be found in this, being either whatsoever is not man or whatsoever not is man, is a thing impossible; for it will be a something different. Wherefore, it will be necessary for them to say that a formal and substantial definition of this kind, and one invariably suited unto the subject, will be one of a nonentity: but all things, as we have supposed, are according to accident; for in this lies the distinction between substance and accident, for the white is an accident in man, because he is white, but not anything whatsoever that is white.

But, if all things are spoken of according to accident, there will be no primary universal, if an accident always signifies a predication about a certain subject. There is a necessity, then, of 1007a going on in a progression to infinity. But this is impossible (for more than two of such are not connected together), for accident is not a thing that is accidental to that which is an accident, unless that both are accidental in the same subject. Now, I say this, for example, in the instance of the white being musical, and the latter being white, because both are accidents in man; but not on this account is Socrates musical, because it happens that both are accidents in a certain other subject. Since accidents, therefore, are spoken of some in this way and some in that, as many as are so expressed, as the white in Socrates, it is not possible should be infinite in an ascending series of productions in the case of man; as, for example, that in Socrates the white there should be some other different accident, for any one thing is not produced from all: nor, truly, in the white will be found any different accident; as, for instance, the musical: for, also, in no wise rather is this an accident in that, than that in this. And, at the same time, the distinction has been made that some things are accidents after this manner, but others, as the musical in Socrates. But as to as many things as are accidental in this way, such are accidents not in such a way as an accident in what is accidental; but this is the case with whatsoever is accidental in that other way. Wherefore, all things will not be spoken of according to accident; something, then, will there be significant, also, as of substance; and if this be so, it has been demonstrated that it is impossible that at the same time contradictions should be predicated of the same subject.

Further, if all contradictions are true at the same time concerning the same thing, it is manifest that all things will be one. For the same thing will it be, both a trireme, and a wall, and a man, if it is possible to affirm or deny anything of everything, as there is a necessity for those to do who assert the opinion of Protagoras. For if, also, to anyone a man seems not to be a trireme, it is evident that he will not be a trireme: wherefore, also, he is, if the contradiction be true. And, doubtless, comes to pass a saying of Anaxagoras: "At the same time subsist together all things," so that, in reality, nothing is one. The indefinite, therefore, they seem to speak of, and, thinking that they mention entity, they talk about nonentity; for an entity in capacity, and not in actuality, constitutes the indefinite. But, doubtless, must we say to the authors of this hypothesis, that of everything either an affirmation or a negation must be predicated; for it would be absurd if in each thing there will be inherent the negation of itself, but that the negation of what is different, and which is not inherent therein, will have no existence. Now, I say, for example, if it is true to assert of a man that he is not a man, it is manifest also that he is not a trireme; if, indeed, therefore, there is truth in the affirmation, there is a necessity that also there be truth in the negation: but if there is not truth in the affirmation, the negation, at least, of a trireme will more appertain to him than the negation of himself. If, therefore, that also be true, there will also be truth in the negation of the trireme; and if in the negation of this, in the affirmation also. And these consequences happen to those who make such a statement, even to the effect that it is not necessary to employ either affirmation or negation. For, if it is true that the same individual is man and not man, it is evident that such a one will be neither man nor not man; for of those two qualities there are two negations. But if that is one which is composed of both, this one would also be in opposition.

Further, indeed, respecting all things it is so; and a thing will be white and not white, and entity and nonentity, and it will be so respecting the rest of the assertions and negations in a similar manner; or this will not be the case, but only so regarding some, and not regarding others. And if, doubtless, it were not so respecting all, these would be indisputable; but if it be true concerning all, again, no doubt, in the case of whatsoever there is an assertion there will also be a negation; and in the case of whatsoever there is a negation there will likewise be an assertion;

1008a

or in the case of whatsoever there is an assertion there will also be a negation; or of whatsoever, indeed, there is an assertion there is also a negation: but of whatsoever things there is a negation, of all such there will not be an assertion. And if this be so, there would be something indubitably a nonentity, and this will be a firm opinion; and if to be a nonentity be something both firm and known, more firm would be the opposite assertion. And if, in like manner, also, it is necessary that in the case of whatsoever things one employs a negation he should employ an affirmation also, it would be true, undoubtedly, by dividing, to say either that a thing, for instance, is white, and again that it is not white, or that this would not be true. And if, indeed, it is not true, by dividing, to say so, he does not affirm these things, and there is nothing in existence; but how can one speak of nonentities, or understand anything respecting them, or thus move forward in the paths of knowledge? And all things would be one, as it has been said heretofore, and both man, and god, and trireme, and the contradictions of them, will be the same. But if, in like manner, this be so in the case of each thing, in no wise will one thing differ from another; for if there will be a difference, this will be true, and a peculiarity of this. In like manner, also, if it is possible that he who makes the division should speak the truth, there happens that which has been declared. And to this reason we may subjoin the following: that all would speak the truth, and all would speak falsely, and one would acknowledge himself to be speaking what is false. At the same time, however, it is evident that the investigation with such a person is concerning nothing; for he affirms nothing. For neither in this manner nor in that is the assertion made with such a one, but in this manner and not in this manner. And again, at least, with respect to these points he makes a negation of both, because the assertion is made that they are neither so in this manner nor not in this manner, but both in this manner and not in this manner; for, if this were not the case, there would now be in existence something that has been defined. Further, if when an assertion be true the negation be false, and if when the latter itself be true the affirmation be false, it would not be possible at the same time to assert and deny the same thing with truth. But, perhaps, persons will say that this is what has been laid down from the commencement.

Further, does one who supposes that in a manner a thing either is so and so, or that it is not so, labor under a misapprehension? But he who thinks that it is both, does he speak truth, or can he verify his assertion? For if he affirms truth, what is the assertion, save that such is the nature of entities? And if he does not affirm the truth, but rather he speaks truth who makes a supposition in that way, entities, in such a case, would, in a certain manner, be now disposed thus; and would this be true and not so at the same time, and yet, in reality, not true? But if, in like manner, all both speak falsehood and speak truth, it is not possible for such either to utter or to declare anything, for at the same time he says the same things and not the same things. But if he makes no supposition, but in the same way thinks and does not think, in what way will he be disposed differently from plants?

Whence, also, it is especially manifest that no one either of the rest of the skeptics, or of those making this statement, is so affected. For why, may I ask, does he walk towards Megara, but not remain still, thinking that he is actually walking? Nor straightway, at dawn, does he proceed to a well or a precipice? If he may chance to meet with such, he, however, appears cautious, as not considering the falling into it to be not good and to be good in the same sense. It is evident, accordingly, that the one he considers preferable but the other as not preferable. And, if this be the case, both the one he must needs consider a man and the other not a man; and the one thing sweet, and the other not sweet. For not as of equal importance doth he investigate and regard all things, inasmuch as he thinks it better to drink water and to visit a certain person, and then seeks, in point of fact, for those very things. Although he ought to seek for all things with equal zest, if, in like manner, it were the same thing—I mean to say, both man and not man. But, as has been declared, there is no one who does not appear cautious in regard of the one set of things and not so in regard of the other. Wherefore, as it appears all men suppose that the case is absolutely so, if not concerning all things, at least, concerning what is better and worse. Now, if they do so not from scientific knowledge, but from opinion, much more must attention be paid to truth; just as also the health of one that is diseased must be looked after more than that of a person that is sound: for he that indulges in theory or surmise, compared with one possessed of scientific knowledge, is not healthfully disposed towards truth.

Further, although as much as possible all things should especially be so and not so, yet, at any rate, the more and the less are inherent in the nature of entities; for one would not say that two and three were similarly even, nor does a person in the same manner assert an untruth who thinks four five, as he who thinks it a thousand. If, therefore, he be not deceived, in the same manner, it is evident that the other is less deceived in this way, so that he affirms what is more true. If, therefore, that which is more true be more immediate to the truth, there would be something true, at 1009a least, to which what is more contiguous will be more true. And even if nothing should be true. And even if nothing should be true, yet now, at any rate, is there something that is more firm and more true than another; and so in this way would we be liberated from that intemperate theory alluded to, and one which forbids the definition of anything mentally.

5. Now, from the same opinion originates also the theory of Protagoras; and in like manner is there a necessity that both of them should be or not be capable of verification. For if all things that seem so are true, and if all things that are apparent are true, then must all things, at the same time, be true and false. For many entertain contrary opinions to one another; and those who do not happen to think the same with themselves they regard as victims to delusion; so that the same thing must needs be and not be. And, if this be the case, it is necessary that all things that seem so should be true; for opposite sentiments do they hold with one

another who speak falsehood and who speak truth. If, then, things be so, all will speak truth: that from the same opinion, then, both of these theories originate is evident.

There does not, however, exist the same method of conducting our controversy as regards all such philosophers, for some of them require persuasion, and some compulsion. For as many indeed, as have formed opinions in this way from doubt, the ignorance of these is remediable, for the refutation is directed towards not the theory, but the understanding; and as many as speak for argument's sake, refutation is a cure also of these, both of that discourse which consists in voice, and of that which consists in names. But unto those persons who labor under doubt in this way has the opinion itself originated from sensibles; the opinion, I mean, that contradictions and things contrary subsist together, inasmuch as they see contraries arising from the same thing. If, therefore, it is not possible that nonentity should come into existence, in a similar way, according to them, must the thing have preexisted, namely, as both contraries at once; as also Anaxagoras says and Democritus, that everything was mingled in everything; for, also, this latter philosopher maintained that vacuity and fullness are similarly resident in any part whatsoever, although the one of these is entity and the other nonentity.

Respecting, indeed, therefore, those who form their opinions from these data we will say that in a certain manner they speak correctly, and that in a certain sense they are involved in ignorance. For entity is spoken of in a twofold point of view; so that it is in a way admissible that something should arise from that which has no being, and that it is in a way not admissible that it should be so; and that the same thing at the same time should be an entity and a nonentity, but not according to the same entity; for in capacity, no doubt, is it admissible at the same time for the same thing to be contraries, but in actuality not so. And, further, shall we deem them to suppose the existence of a certain other substance of entities in which is inherent neither motion, nor corruption, nor generation at all.

And, in like manner, also, has the truth respecting the 1009b things apparent reached some speculators from sensibles. For they do not consider it fitting that the true should be decided by plurality or fewness; but the same thing seems sweet to some on tasting it, and to others bitter. Wherefore, if all persons were sick, or all beside themselves, but two or three were sound in health, or in possession of their mind, it would happen that these latter would appear to be ill and laboring under an aberration of intellect, but that the rest would not seem so. Further, to many of the rest of the animal creation do contraries appear to be the same thing as well as to us; and to each very person with himself things do not always, according to sense, appear to be the same: which description of these, therefore, is true or false is obscure; for nothing the more is this true than that, but both in like manner are affected as regards truth. Wherefore, Democritus says, at least, that, positively, either nothing is true, or that, if it be so, that to us it is wrapped in obscurity.

But, upon the whole, on account of their supposing prudence, no doubt, to be sense, and that this sense constitutes an alteration, these persons affirm that the apparent, according to sense, is necessarily true; for from these skeptics both Empedocles and Democritus, and each of the other philosophers, so to speak, have become entangled in opinions of this sort. For Empedocles, also, asserts that those changing their habit change their prudence; witness his words:

For for the present counsel varies in men.

And in other passages he says, that

As far as diverse men become, so far
Is present, also, in them always diverse thought.

And Parmenides evinces the same mode of thinking; for instance, in the words:

For as each has a tempering of graceful limbs,
So present in man is mind. For the same thing
With whatever thinks is the nature of limbs in men,
Both every and all, for more than this is mind.

And the apothegm of Anaxagoras, also, is remembered amongst certain of his associates; namely, that entities are such to them as they may have supposed them. Now, they say that even Homer seems to have been in possession of this opinion, because he made Hector, after he was deranged from the wound, to lie in a delirious state; as if even those of unsound mind were capable of exercising thought, indeed, but not the same thoughts as with those of sound mind. It is evident, therefore, if both be exertions of prudence, that also entities subsist in this way, and not in this way, at the same time.

Wherefore, also, most difficult is that which ensues from this theory; for if they who particularly perceived as true that which it is admissible should be true (but these are they who especially seek after it and love it); if these persons hold such opinions, and manifest such tenets respecting truth, how is it not becoming those to despair who attempt to philosophize? For the pursuit of things eluding their grasp would constitute the investigation 1010a of truth. But a cause of this opinion of theirs is the following: that from time to time they have examined into the truth, concerning entities, no doubt, but the entities they have supposed to be sensibles merely. Now, in these is inherent much of the nature of the indefinite and that of entity, which subsists in such a manner as we have declared. Wherefore, they speak naturally; but they do not speak things that are true. For so is it more in harmony for them to speak after this manner than as Epicharmus in his reply to Xenophanes.

But, moreover, seeing the whole of this visible nature in motion, but respecting what is being changed seeing nothing verified,—regarding, at least, what is being changed altogether and everywhere,—they considered that verification was not a thing that is possible: for from this hypothesis blossomed that most extreme opinion of those philosophers mentioned just now; namely, that of those speculators who professed to adopt the philosophy of Heraclitus, and such as Cratylus held, who at last was of opinion that one ought to speak of nothing, but moved merely his finger; and who rebuked Heraclitus for saying that it is not possible to enter the same river twice: for he himself was of opinion that you could not do so once.

In reply, however, to this theory we will also say, that there is some foundation in reason for their supposing with these, that that which undergoes a change, when it does change, may not be considered as existing. This, however, is a circumstance attended with doubtfulness, for the rejecting substance retains something of that which is rejected; and of that which is being produced must there now necessarily exist something: and if, in short, it is undergoing corruption, there will subsist a certain entity; and if it is being produced, there must needs be that from which it is produced, and by which it is generated, and that this process goes not on in a progression to infinity. Omitting, however, these arguments, let us make those assertions following; namely, that not the same thing is the alteration according to quantity and according to quality; grant, indeed, that, as far as quantity goes, it does not abide the same; but it is according to form that we know all things. But, further, it is worth while reproving those who think thus, because, although knowing the number of sensibles themselves, and that in the case of the fewer number of sensibles this state of flux and mutation was to be found, they have yet manifested similar sentiments respecting the whole heaven. For the place about us, of what is sensible, continues alone to subsist in a condition of corruption and generation; but this in no wise, so to say, is part of the universe: wherefore, more justly would it be, on account of the greater number of witnesses, to have acquitted these, than on account of these, the fewer, to have condemned those. And, further, is it evident that in reply, also, to these we may use the same arguments with those that have been originally laid down by us; for that there is some nature immovable has been demonstrated to their satisfaction, and has gained their assent. It happens however, to those, at least, who say that a thing is and is not at the same time, to affirm all things to be in a state of rest, rather than of motion; for, on this hypothesis, there exists nothing into which anything is changed, for all things are inherent in all.

1010b   Regarding, however, the truth that not everything that is apparent is true, in the first place, indeed, it might be replied, that sense, to be sure, is not deceitful in what falls within its own peculiar province, but that imagination is not the same with sense. It is worthy of consideration and wonder, in the next place, if they really are in doubt of this, whether magnitudes are so great, and colors such as they appear to those at a distance, or such as they appear to those that are near; and whether they are such as they appear to persons in health, or such as they appear to persons in sickness? And, in regard of weight, whether things more weighty are such as appear so to the weak, or such as seem so to the strong? And lastly, in respect of truth, whether things are true such as appear so to the sleeping, or such as seem so to those who are awake? For that they do not, in reality, think so, at least, is evident; for one, if even he supposes when asleep by night that he were in Athens, when he is in Libya, goes when he awakes, to the Odeion.

And, further, respecting the future, as also Plato says, doubtless, not similarly decisive is the opinion of the physician and that of the ignorant quack; for example, as to the likelihood that one will be sound, or that one will not be so: and, further, in the case of the senses themselves, not similarly decisive is the testimony of sense in respect of what is foreign, and in respect of what is its peculiar province, or of that which is near and of that which is remote from itself. But respecting color it is sight and not taste that judges; and respecting juices it is taste but not sight, each of which never at the same time affirms about the same thing that simultaneously a thing is so and not so disposed. But neither in a different period have the senses doubted about the passion, at least, to which they are subject, but about that in which the passion is an accident. Now, I say, for example, that the same wine, either from being changed, or from the bodily organ being changed, might so appear at one time to be sweet, and at another time not sweet; but the sweet then, at least, when it is sweet is not such, for it never has undergone a change; but always verification thereof is possible, and of necessity is it that such will be a thing that is sweet. All these theories, however, overturn this conclusion, since, also, if there is not a substance of anything neither is there anything necessarily subsisting; for it is not admissible for the necessary to be at one time disposed one way, and at another time another: wherefore, if there is anything of necessity, it will not be disposed both so and not so.

If, also, upon the whole, what is sensible exists merely, nothing would there be subsisting, inasmuch as animated beings would have no existence; for sense would have no existence. Perhaps, then, on the supposition of the nonexistence of sense, the truth would be, that neither sensibles nor sensations exist (for of the percipient is sense an affection); but that it is impossible that the subjects themselves which produce sense have not any existence, even though sense exist not. For, doubtless, sense itself is not of itself; but there is something else, also, different from, and independent of, sense, which must needs be prior to sense; for the moving cause is prior in nature to that which is being moved: and if these assertions are made one with another, 1011a not a whit the less is the same theory true.

6. But there are some who doubt and are skeptics both amongst those who are persuaded of the reality of these opinions and those who merely affirm these theories, for they ask, who is it that judgeth him that is in good health, and him that, upon the whole, is capable of forming his decision correctly about each particular? Now, doubts of such a sort as this are similar to one's doubting whether we now sleep or are awake. For all such doubts are tantamount to the same; for these persons demand that there should be a reason of all things: for they seek for a first principle, and expect to obtain this by demonstration, whereas, at least, that they are not persuaded of the validity of

their position they make manifest in their acts. But, as we have said, this is the characteristic property of these philosophers, for they seek for a reason of things of which there is no reason; for the principle of demonstration is not demonstration. These therefore, indeed, would be easily persuaded of this, for it is not difficult to apprehend.

They, however, who seek in reason compulsion merely, seek an impossibility; for what is contrary they deem it right to speak, immediately uttering contrary things. But if all things are not relatives, but some are also themselves by themselves, that is, absolute, in such a case everything apparent would not be true, for the apparent is apparent to someone: therefore he that says that all things apparent are true, makes all entities relatives. Wherefore, also, must the precaution be adopted by those who seek for compulsion in reason, and at the same time, also, think right to subjoin a reason that not the apparent is true, but that the apparent is true to whomsoever it appears so, and when it appears, and how far, and in what matter.

But if they subjoin a reason, to be sure, but do not in this way subjoin it, it will happen speedily unto them that they should speak things that are contrary. For it is possible for the same thing to appear honey, as far as the sight goes, and not to appear so to the taste; and, as we have two eyes, not the same will a thing appear to each organ of vision if they be dissimilar. Whereas, in reply to those, at least, who, on account of the causes originally enumerated, affirm the apparent to be true, and for this reason contend that all things in like manner are false and true; in reply to these, I say, it may be affirmed that neither the same things appear the same to all men, nor to the same person do the same things invariably appear the same, but frequently things contrary at the same time; for the touch, in the alteration of the fingers, says that there are two objects, but the organ of sight one; but neither to the same sense, at least, do the same things seem the same, and according to the same, and in like manner, also, in

1011b the same moment of time: wherefore, this would be true. But, perhaps, for this cause it is necessary to say to those who speak not on account of doubt, but for talk's sake, that this is not absolutely true, but that it is true relatively to this person.

And, as doubtless it has been formerly affirmed, it is necessary, also, to make all things relative, both in reference to opinion and sense; so that nothing either has been produced or will arise except on the supposition of some person previously exercising thought. But if anything has been generated or will arise, it is evident that all things would not be according to opinion. Further, if one things exists, it exists in relation to one, or in relation to a definite thing; and if the same thing is both half and equal, such things exist in relation to these; yet the equal is not in reference to the double. Now, in relation to opinion, if man and the subject of the opinion be the same, man will not be the thinking subject, but the subject of opinion. But if each thing will be in relation to the thinking subject, the thinking subject will subsist in relation to things infinite in species. That, indeed, therefore, most indisputable of all is the opinion, that assertions in opposition are not at the same time true; and what happens in the way of consequence unto those who say that they are true, and why they say so, let thus much suffice to have been spoken.

But since it is impossible that contradiction should be true of the same subject at the same time, it is evident that neither can contraries possibly subsist at the same time in the same subject. For, indeed, of contraries one or other is not the less privation. But privation of substance is negation from some definite genus. If, therefore, it is impossible at the same time to affirm and deny with truth, it is impossible that also contraries should be inherent in the same subject at the same time; but either both must be inherent partially, or the one partially and the other simply or absolutely.

7. But, truly, neither is it possible that there is any mean between a contradiction; but there is a necessity either of asserting or denying any one thing whatsoever of one. Now, in the first place,

this is evident to those who define what truth and falsehood are. For, indeed, the assertion that entity does not exist, and that nonentity does, is a falsehood, but that entity exists, and that nonentity does not exist, is truth. Wherefore, the person who affirms that this medium is in existence or is not will speak truth or utter falsehood. But neither is entity nor nonentity said not to exist or to exist.

Further, either will there be a mean between contradiction, as that of a darkish color between black and white, or it will be as that which is neutral between man and horse. If, therefore, this subsist in this way, there would be no change (for a change takes place from something that is not good into that which is good, or from this latter into what is not good); but now it is always apparent as taking place, for there is not a change existing but one into opposites and media. If, however, there is a mean, so also would there be a certain production into a thing that is white, not from that which is not white; but this is not perceived as being the case.

1012a   Further, everything intelligible and mental the understanding either affirms or denies; and this is manifest from definition when truth is spoken or falsehood; when, indeed, in this way it is composed, as an assertion or negation, truth is spoken; but when in that way, falsehood. Further, must there be in all contradictions a mean, save where the assertion is made only for argument or talk's sake, so that also one will neither utter truth nor not utter truth. And, besides entity and nonentity, there will be something in subsistence: wherefore, besides generation and corruption, some change will there be. Moreover, in whatsoever genera negation introduces the contrary, in these also will be found this medium as, for example, in numbers a number neither odd nor not odd: such, however, is impossible, and from the definition is this evident. Further, would we go on in a progression to infinity, and not only will there be sesquialterate entities, but even more than this. For, again, it will be possible to deny this in regard of the assertion and negation of the medium of the former contradiction; and this will be something, for there will be a certain other substance of this. Moreover, as to the question if a thing is white when one says that it is not, nothing has he denied than that it is; but that a thing is not, amounts to a negation.

But from the same source as other paradoxes has this opinion reached unto certain speculators; for when they are unable to solve arguments open to dispute, giving in to reason, they consent to the truth of whatever is brought out by syllogism. Some, therefore, make assertions from some such cause as this, but others on account of requiring in their investigations the reason of all things.

The principle, however, in respect of all these is to be derived from definition. But definition arises from their necessarily signifying something; for the sentence of which the name is a sign becomes the definition of a thing. And the theory of Heraclitus, affirming all things to be and not to be, appeared to make all things true; but that of Anaxagoras was, that there is a certain medium between contradiction; so that all things are false, for when they are mingled, neither is the mixture good nor not good: wherefore, there is nothing that one can affirm as true.

8. Now, these distinctions having been laid down, it is evident that the predications made in one way only, and also those that are made about all, it is impossible should be as certain affirm they are; some, indeed, saying that nothing is true (for nothing, they say, hinders all things from being in such a way as that the diagonal of a square is commensurable with its side); but others affirming that all things are true. For almost all these assertions are the same with those of Heraclitus; for this philosopher, in affirming that all things are true and all things false, affirms also separately 1012b each of these theories. Wherefore, if those are impossible, it is impossible, likewise, that these should be so.

But, further, are those palpably contradictions which, likewise, it is not possible should at the same time be true. Nor, doubtless, is it possible that all should be false, although, at least, it would the rather seem to be admissible from what has been stated. But, in reply to all such theories, must the question be asked (as also has been declared in the discussions above), not if there is something or if there is not, but if something has a signification. Wherefore, from the definition is the discussion to be drawn, by assuming what falsehood or truth signifies. But if the true and the false be nothing else than to assert what is true or deny what is false, it is impossible that all things be false; for it is necessary that either portion of the contradiction be true. Further, if it be necessary either to assert or deny everything, it is impossible for both to be false; for either part of the contradiction is false.

Truly, also, doth the common saying happen unto all such theories, that they overthrow or stultify themselves. For the person that says that all things are true renders the statement contrary to this true also: wherefore, he makes his own affirmation not true; for the contrary says that it is not true; but he that says that all things are false, even himself falsifies his own position. If, however, they make an exception, the one making an exception in the case of the contrary that it is not alone true, and the other in the case of his own assertion that it is not false, in no wise the less does it happen unto these skeptics that they require the truth and falsehood of an infinite number of assertions; for he who says that a true theory is true agrees with the affirmation that it is true; but this will go on in a progression infinity.

It is evident, however, that neither they who lay down that all things are at rest speak the truth, nor they who say that all things are in motion. For if, indeed, all things are at rest, the same things will always be true and false. Now, this appears to be a thing undergoing a change. For he who speaks once himself was not, and again will not be. If all things, however, are in motion, there will be nothing that is true; all things, in that case, are false. But it has been demonstrated that this is impossible. Further, must entity needs undergo a change; for from something into something is the change made. But, doubtless, neither are all things at rest or in motion at any particular time; but nothing subsists in such a condition of rest or motion eternally: for there is something which always moves the things that are in motion, and the first imparter of motion is itself immovable.

BOOK V

1. THAT is called a principle from whence anything has had motion imparted to it in the first instance; for example, the principle of length and of a way: from hence, indeed, is the actual principle, but from the contrary a different one; but, 1013a again, that is called a first principle from whence each thing would spring in the most beautiful manner: as, for instance, even in the case of discipline the beginning must be made sometimes not from what is first, and the principle of a thing, but from whence one may learn with the greatest facility. And, again, that is a principle from whence is produced the first of a thing that is inherent; as, for example, a keel of a vessel and a foundation of a house: and some suppose the heart of animals to be a thing of this sort; but others the brain, and others whatever else of this kind they may happen with. And, again, that is a principle from whence the first of a thing not inherent is produced, and whence motion and change have first been naturally fitted to commence; as, for example, the child from the father and the mother, and the battle from abuse. And that is a first principle according to the free impulse of which things in motion are moved, and things undergoing a change, are changed, as in cities dominions and dynasties, and kingdoms and tyrannies are styled principles. And both the arts, and especially those of them that are architectonic, are called principles. Further, whence a thing is known first, this is called a principle of that thing; as, for example, the hypotheses

are principles of demonstration. In as many ways, also, as first principles are styled are causes in like manner denominated; for all causes are first principles.

Common to all first principles is the being the original from whence a thing either is, or is produced, or is known. But of these principles some, indeed, are inherent, and others are extrinsic. Wherefore, Nature constitutes both a first principle, and an element is so likewise, and understanding, and free-will, and substance, and the final cause; for, in the case of many things, the principle of knowledge and of motion is the good and the fair.

2. In one way that is called cause from which, as inherent, anything is produced; as, for example, the brass of a statue, and the silver of a cup, and the genera of these; but, in another way, the form and exemplar are regarded as causes: and this is the reason of the formal cause and the genera of these; as, for instance, in the diapason the cause is the ratio of two to one; and, in general, number and the parts, those that are in the ratio, belong to this order of cause. But, further, that constitutes a cause from whence is the first principle of change or of rest; for instance, the designing cause and the father of a child; and, generally speaking, the forming of that which is being formed, and that capable of effecting a change of that which is undergoing a change. Further, a cause is as the end; this, however, is the final cause, as, for instance, health of walking. For why does one walk? We say, that he may have good health; and, saying so, we think that we have assigned the cause. And as many operations, doubtless, as take place between any other source of motion and the end are regarded as causes; for example, of health, tenuity, or purging, or 1013b medicines, or instruments, for all these are on account of the end; but they differ from one another in respect of being, some as instruments, and others as things done. Causes, indeed, therefore, are enumerated almost somehow after this manner.

And seeing that causes are thus multifariously denominated, it happens that many of them are causes of the same thing, not according to accident; for instance, of the statue both the statuary art and the brass, not according to anything that is different, but so far forth as it is a statue; this, however, does not take place in the same manner, but the brass is as matter, and the art as the origin of motion, or the efficient cause. And some things are reciprocally causes of one another; as, for example, labor of a good habit of body, and this latter, again, of labor: yet not in the same manner, but the one is as the end, and the other as the principle of motion. Further, the same thing sometimes is the cause of things that are contrary; for that which when present is the cause of this particular thing, this when absent we sometimes denominate the cause of the contrary: for example, the absence of the pilot is the cause of the capsizing of the boat, the presence of whom is the cause of its preservation. Both, however, as well the presence as the absence of the pilot, are as efficient causes, that is, causes imparting motion.

Now, all the causes just enumerated fall under four modes the most evident. For, indeed, the elements of syllables, and the matter of things constructed by art, and the fire and earth, and all such bodies, and the parts of a whole, and the hypotheses of the conclusion, are causes, as that whereof other things are produced. But of these some are as the subject; as, for instance, the parts: but others, as the formal cause; for example, both the whole, and the composition, and the form. But the seed, and the physician, and the deliberator, and, in short, the maker, all are the causes of the principle of change or of stability. But the rest, as the end and the good, are causes of other things; for the final cause aims at being the best, and an end to the other things: let there be, however, no actual difference in saying a thing is good or appears good.

These causes, indeed, therefore, are so many in species, but the modes of causes are, doubtless, many in number; these, however, become less numerous by being reduced under heads. For causes are called so in many ways; and of those things of the same species, antecedently and subsequently, one thing is the cause of another; as, for example, of health the physician and the artisan, and of the diapason the double and number, and always those things that comprise anything whatsoever of singulars. But, moreover, cause is denominated as the accident and the genera of these; as, for instance, of a statue, in one sense, Polyclitus is the cause, and, in another, the statuary, because it is accidental with the statuary to be Polyclitus: and the things embracing the accidental are causes; for instance, man is a cause of a statue, or also, in general, animal, because Polyclitus is a man, and man is an animal. But also of the accidents one is more remote, and another more contiguous than others; for example, just as if the white and the musical should be termed a cause of the statue, but not merely Polyclitus, or man. But besides all things, both those that are denominated appropriately or strictly, and those according to accident, some causes are denominated as things endued with a capacity, but others as things energizing; as the cause of the house being built is the builder, or the builder considered as in the act of building. In like manner with what has been stated will be mentioned, also, the causes in the case of which there are causes; as, for example, of this statue, as far forth as it is a statue, or, in general, of an image, or of this brass, so far forth as it is brass, or, in short, matter; and in the case of the accidents it is so in like manner. Further, also, these and those shall be predicated as connected together; as, for example, not Polyclitus nor a statuary, but Polyclitus a statuary. But, however, all these at least, are six in number, yet are expressed in a twofold manner. For either as a singular are they denominated, or as the genus thereof, or as the accident, or as genus of the accident, or as these connected together or simply expressed; further, all of them as energizing, or according to capacity. But thus far is there a difference, that causes energizing and singulars, and those of which they are the causes, subsist at the same time and at the same time cease to be; as, for example, the person healing with that person that is being restored to health, and this person the builder with that which is being built. Not invariably, however, is this the case with regard to causes in capacity; for not at the same time sink into decay the house and the builder.

1014a

3. An element is called that from which, as an inherent first principle and indivisible in species, something is compounded into a different species; as, for instance, the elements of voice are those things of which the voice is composed, and into which it is ultimately divided: those elements, however, no longer are divided into other voices different from them in species; but, even though they be divided, the parts would be of the same species; as, for example, the portion of water is water, but a portion of the syllable is not a syllable. In like manner, also, do the old philosophers, who enumerate the elements of bodies, say that they are those entities into which bodies are ultimately divided; but those no longer are divisible into others different in species; and whether such may be one or many, these they yet call elements. Similarly, also, are denominated the elements both of diagrams and, in general, those of demonstrations; for the primary demonstrations, and those that are inherent in many more demonstrations, themselves 1014b are styled elements of demonstrations; but of such kind are the first syllogisms, which are composed of three terms by means of the one middle.

And, by a transference of the meaning, they hence call an element that which being one and small may be useful for many purposes; wherefore, also, what is small, and simple, and indivisible, is styled an element. Hence it has come to pass that those things which are most especially universal are elements, because each of them is one and simple, and is inherent in many things, or in all, or in as many as possible; and to some speculators it seems that the one and the point are first principles. Since, therefore, those things called genera are universal and indivisible (for there is one definition of them), certain persons call the genera elements; and that, too, in preference to difference, for the genus is more universal. For in whatsoever the difference resides, the genus also follows; but in what the genus resides does not, in every way, constitute the difference. Common, however, to all is the characteristic that the being of the element of each body is the first inherent quality in each.

4. Nature is called, in one way, the production of things that are by Nature; as, for instance, if one putting forth his voice should articulate the letter *U*: and in another, as that from which, as being inherent, that which is being naturally produced is primarily formed. Moreover, Nature is the origin of the earliest motion in each of the things in itself subsisting by Nature, so far as it is this very thing. Now, those things are said to be produced by Nature as many as involve growth through another body, by means of contact and growth along with, or growth beside, just as embryos. But the being connascent differs from contact; for in the latter there must needs be nothing else besides the touch: but in things that are connate there is some one thing that is the same in both, which, instead of involving contact, causes them to be connascent, and causes them to be one according to what is continuous and involving quantity, but not according to quality. Moreover, is that styled Nature from which, as its primary matter, there either is or arises anything of the things that subsist by Nature, being without regular motion, and unchangeable from the power which belongs to itself; for instance, of a statue, or of brazen vessels, the brass is called the nature, and of wooden vessels the wood: but in like manner is it in the case of the rest. For each thing is from these, the primary matter remaining in a state of conservation; for in this way, also, do they affirm the elements of those things that are by Nature to constitute Nature; some saying that this is fire, but others, earth, and others, air, and others, water: but others asserting some other such thing and others, some of these, but others, all of them.

In another way, however, Nature is styled the substance of things that exist by Nature; for instance, those who affirm that Nature is the earliest synthesis, as Empedocles says that

1015a   Nature is there of no one of entities,
         But merely mixture and of things mixed,
         A change, and thus by men is Nature styled.

Wherefore, as many things, also, as by Nature exist or are produced, that being in existence already from which it is natural that they should arise, or should have their being, not as yet do we say that such is in possession of Nature, unless they have the species and the form. By Nature, then, subsists that which is composed from both of these, as, for instance, animals and their parts. Nature, however, constitutes the primary matter, and this in a twofold sense,—either the primary in reference to a thing itself, or, upon the whole, the first; for example, of brazen works the first in reference to these is the brass; and water, perhaps, in general, if the primary matter of all things that are capable of being liquified be water. And Nature constitutes both species and substance; and this is the end of production. But now, metaphorically speaking and generally, every substance is called Nature for this reason, because Nature, also, is a certain substance.

Doubtless, from the things that have been stated, the earliest nature, and that termed so with precision, is the substance,— I mean of those things possessing the principle of motion in themselves, so far forth as themselves are such. For matter, in respect of its being susceptible of this, is styled Nature; and generations and the act of production are termed so in consequence of their motions being from this. And the first principle of motion, in those things that by Nature subsist, is Nature, inherent as a first principle in a manner either potentially or actually.

5. Necessary is defined that without which, as a cooperating cause, it is not admissible for a thing to exist; as, for instance, respiration and nourishment are necessary conditions for an animal: for without these it is impossible that an animal can exist. And that is necessary without which it is not possible for what is good either to subsist, or to arise, or to cast aside any evil, or that any evil should be exterminated; for instance, the drinking a certain medicine is a necessary precaution against sickness, and the sailing to Aegina, against the loss of one's property. Further, the compulsory and compulsion are styled necessary;

but this is that which constitutes an obstruction, and is capable of offering an hindrance to impulse and free-will. For what is compulsory is styled necessary: wherefore, also, is it a thing that is sad; as also Evenus has it:

For everything necessary is a thing doleful.

And force, or compulsion, involves a certain necessity, as also Sophocles says:

But force compels me to do these things.

And necessity seems to be a something that is inevitable (correctly so), for it is contrary to the motion that results according to freewill, and according to the power of reasoning. Further, that which does not admit of being otherwise than it is, we say is in this way disposed as a necessary thing. And, according to this acceptation of the word, what is necessary, and all the other things that are so, are also, in a manner, styled necessary; for the violent, or compulsory, is called necessary, either in regard of 1015b action or passion, at such times as when a person cannot make any move according to impulse, on account of some constraining cause; so that this is a necessary impulse on account of which the thing could not be otherwise. And in the case of the cooperating causes of the principle of vitality, and the good, it is so in like manner; for when it is not admissible, on the one hand, to obtain, indeed, the good, and on the other, to live and to exist without certain things, these things then are necessary, and this cause constitutes a certain necessity.

Further, does demonstration belong to those things that are necessary, because it is not possible that the things that are being demonstrated should be otherwise, if the thing be absolutely demonstrated; but causes of this are things primary, which it is impossible should subsist otherwise than they do; put of which is formed the syllogism. Of some things, truly, is there a different cause from themselves of their being necessary, but of others there is no such cause; but on account of these are other things that are from necessity. Wherefore, what is primary and what is absolute, or simple, are strictly necessary; for it is not possible that this can be disposed in many ways: therefore, neither can it subsist in different ways at different times; for on such a supposition would it now be disposed in many ways. If, therefore, there are certain things that are eternal and immovable, there is in them nothing compulsory or contrary to Nature.

6. One is called that which subsists as such according to accident in one way, and in another, that which subsists essentially. A thing is called one according to accident; for instance, Coriscus and what is musical, and the musical Coriscus; for it is one and the same thing to say, Coriscus and what is musical, as to say, Coriscus the musician; also, to say the musical and the just is one with saying the just musician Coriscus. For all these are called one according to accident; the just, indeed, and the musical, because they are accidents in one substance; but what is musical and Coriscus, because either is an accident in the other. Likewise, also, in a certain sense, the musical Coriscus is one with Coriscus, because either of the parts of those that are in this sentence is an accident in the other; as, for example, what is musical in Coriscus and the musical Coriscus in just Coriscus, because one portion of either is an accident in the same one. For there is no difference whether what is musical is an accident in Coriscus, or Coriscus the just in the musical Coriscus. In like manner, however, will one be denominated according to accident, though it should be predicated of the genus, or of some universal names; as, for instance, if man were said to be the same with a musical man: for that it should be so either because the musical is an accident in the man being one substance, or because both are accidents in any one of those which are singulars, as in Coriscus; nevertheless, both are not inherent in the same manner, but the one, perhaps, as genus and in the substance, and the other, as a habit or passion of the substance. Therefore, as many things as are expressed according to accident are styled one after this manner.

But of things denominated one essentially, some are styled
so on account of their being continuous; as, for instance, a
bundle held together by a string and a piece of wood by glue;
and a line, even though it be curved, yet, if it be continuous, is
called one; as also each of the parts of the body: for instance, a
leg and an arm. Now, of these very things those are more one
which by nature are continuous than those that are continuous
by art. But that is called continuous of which the motion is one
essentially, and also which it is not possible should be otherwise.
And motion is one when it is indivisible, and indivisible according
to time; those things, however, are essentially continuous as
many as are not one by contact; for if you were to place sticks
touching one another, you would not say that these are one,
either one piece of wood, or one body, or anything else that is
continuous. And, indeed, in general, things that are continuous
are called one, even though they may have a curve, and still
rather things that have not a curve; thus the leg and thigh are
more one than the leg and foot together, because it is possible
that the motion of the leg and foot be not one. And the straight
line is one rather than the curved line. But the curved, and that
which has an angle, we call both one and not one, because it is
admissible that both the motion of the whole should not be at
the same time, and yet that at the same time should be the
motion of a part; but part and the whole of a straight line are
always at the same time in motion together, and no such portion
as involves magnitude partly remains at rest and partly is in
motion, as of a line that is curved.

Further, in another way a thing is called one in respect of the
subject being in species indifferent or destitute of a difference.
But things that are indifferent are those of which the form,
according to sense, is indivisible, and the subject is either the
first or the last in respect of the end. For both wine is called one
and water one, so far forth as either is indivisible according to
the form; and all fluids are styled one, as oil, wine, and things
that are soluble, because the ultimate subject of all these is the
same; for all these are, in reality, water and air. But those things

are styled one, also, of which the genus is one, differing by opposite differences. And all these care called one because one genus is the subject of the differences; for instance, horse, man, dog, is a certain one because all of them are animals; and, doubtless, they are one in some similar manner as the matter is one. These things, however, sometimes in this way are styled one, and sometimes the superior genus is regarded one, which is denominated the same, if those higher up than these be the ultimate species of the genus; as, for example, the isosceles, to be sure, and the equilateral, are one and the same figure because both are triangles; but they are not the same triangles.

Further, are those things styled one the definition of whatsoever of which, denominating the essence of them, is indivisible, as far as regards another definition signifying the being of the thing, for every actual definition is essentially indivisible. For so, also, both that which has undergone increase and diminution is one because the definition is one, as in the case of surfaces possessing length and breadth the definition of the species is 1016b one. In general, however, are those things one of which the perception is indivisible; I mean, that which perceives what the essence or formal principle is, and which cannot be separated either in time, or place, or definition; these most especially, I say, are one; and of these as many as are substances.

For, universally, whatever things do not involve division, so far forth as they have it not, so far are they styled one; for example, if man, as far as he is a man, has not a division, he is one man; and if an animal, as far as it is an animal, is indivisible, animal is one: but if magnitude, as far as magnitude is concerned, is indivisible, magnitude is one. The most things, no doubt, then, are styled one because some one different thing they either effect, or suffer, or possess, or because of their being relative to some one thing; but those things primarily denominated one are those of which the substance is one: one, however, either in continuity, or species, or definition; for also we reckon as plural, or many, either those things that are not continuous, or those of which the form is not one, or of which the definition is not one.

But, further, is it the case that we say sometimes that anything whatsoever is one, provided only it involves quantity and continuity; and we sometimes say that it is not one, if it be not a certain whole, that is, if it does not possess one form; for instance, we would not say that in like manner a shoe is one, when looking at the portions of that shoe any way whatsoever put together, although there may be continuity involved therein: but if it be in such a position of its parts as to be in reality a shoe, and to have a certain form, it would already then be one. Wherefore, also, of lines the circular is particularly one because it is entire and perfect.

Of the one, however, the very essence consists in this, that it is the principle of a certain number; for the first measure is the principle of each genus thereof; for that whereby, as primary, we make a thing known, this is the first measure of each genus: therefore, the first principle of that which may be known constitutes, in regard of each genus, the one. But the one is not the same in all the genera; for here it is diesis and there a vowel, or a mute; but of gravity there is a different one, and of motion another. Everywhere, however, is unity indivisible, either in form or in quantity. That, indeed, therefore, which is indivisible according to quantity, and so far forth as it is a quantity (I mean, what is in every direction indivisible, and is without position), this is called an unit or monad; but that which is in every direction indivisible, and involves a position, is a point; and that which is divisible in one direction is a line, and that capable of a twofold division, a surface; but that which in every way and in three directions is divisible according to quantity is a body. And, conversely, that which is divisible in a twofold respect is a surface, and that in a single direction, a line, and that divisible everywhere in three directions is a body, but that divisible nowhere according to quantity, a point and a monad; the one, without position, a monad, and the other, with position, a point.

And, moreover, some things are one according to number, but others according to species, and others according to genus, and others according to analogy. Those things are one in number of which the matter is one, but in species of which the definition is one, but in genus of which there is the same figure of predication; but according to analogy are things one as many as are disposed as one thing in relation to another. The subsequent, however, invariably follows the things that are prior; as, for instance, whatsoever things are one in number are also one in species, but whatsoever things are one in species are not all one in number; but all things are one in genus, whatsoever are likewise so in species; but whatsoever are one in genus are not all one in species, but are so in analogy; and whatsoever 1017a things are one analogically are not all so in genus.

It is manifest, however, also, that plurality will be spoken of in an opposite manner to the one, partly from the fact of its being not continuous, and partly from having its matter divisible according to species either as the first matter or the ultimate matter, but partly from possessing many of those reasons or definitions which declare the essence of a thing, or its very nature.

7. Entity is denominated partly as that which subsists according to accident, and partly that which subsists essentially; an entity subsists according to accident as when we say that a just man is musical, and that the man is musical, and that the musician is a man; speaking in a similar manner as when we say that the musical man builds because it is an accident to the builder to be a musician, or for the musician to be a builder: for the affirming that this particular thing is that signifies that this thing is an accident in that. So, also, in the case of the instances that have been mentioned; when we say that the man is a musician, and that the musician is a man, or that one who is white is the musician, or that the latter is white, we say this because both of these are accidents in the same subject; but we say that because they are accidents in entity: but that the musician is a man we say because the being a musician is an accident to this person. So, also, is it said that what is white is a man because that is a man to which the being white is an accident. Things, indeed, therefore, said to subsist according to accident are expressed in this way, either because both are inherent in the same entity, or because

they are inherent in that entity, or because they are the same with that in which the accidents are inherent, and of which the thing itself is predicated.

Entities, also, are said to subsist essentially whatsoever signify the figures of predication; for as often as they are predicated, so often do they signify essence. Since, therefore, of the things that are predicated some signify what a thing is, or quiddity, and others quality, and others quantity, and others relation, and others action or passion, and some the place where, and others the time when, to each of these the being or essence signifies the same thing. For there is no difference in the expression, the man is in a healthy state, from this, namely, the man is healthy, or, the man is walking or is cutting, from the expression, man walks or cuts. And in like manner, also, is it in the case of the rest.

Further, the words "to be" and "it is" signify that a thing is true, but the words "not to be," that it is not true, but false; in like manner is it the case both in respect to affirmation and negation; as, for example, he who says that Socrates is musical says so because this is true; or he who says that Socrates is not white says so because it is true; he, however, who says that the diameter is not incommensurable says so because this is false. Further, "to be" and "being" signify that which is expressed partly as potentially, and partly as actually, of those things that have been enumerated. For we say, also, that seeing is both seeing in potentiality expressly, and in actuality; and similarly we say that he is endued with scientific knowledge who both has the ability to employ scientific knowledge and does actually employ it, and that a thing is in a condition of rest both in which rest is at present inherent, and which involves the capability of remaining in a state of quiescence. But in like manner, also, is it in the case of substances; for we speak of the existence of Mercury in the stone, and the half of the line; and we call that corn which not yet has reached a state of maturity. When, however, a thing is potential, and when it is not as yet potential, must be defined elsewhere.

1017b

8. As regards substance, both simple bodies, as, for instance, earth, and fire, and water, and such like, are called substances; and, in general, bodies are styled so; and animals consisting of these, and those beings that are of the nature of demons, and the parts of these. Now, all these are denominated substances because they are not predicated of a subject, whereas other things are predicated of these. But in another way is that styled substance whatever may be the cause of being, and may be inherent in such as are not predicated of a subject; for example, soul in an animal. Further, as many parts as are inherent in such things that both define and signify "the what" a certain thing is, on the removal of which the whole is taken away,— as, for example, if superficies be taken away body also is destroyed, as some say; and superficies is destroyed by taking away a line; and, in general, number seems to some to be a thing of this kind: for that if it is removed away nothing can subsist, and that it defines all things,—such parts we may consider substances. Further, the essence of which the formal cause is the definition, this, also, is styled the substance of each thing.

Now, substance happens in two ways to be styled substance, both as the ultimate subject which no longer is predicated of anything else, and as that which may be this certain particular thing, and may be separable; but such is the form and the species of each thing.

9. But the same are styled partly according to accident, as the white and the musical are the same because they are accidents in the same subject, and man and musician are the same because either is an accident in the other; I mean, that man is musical because the musical is an accident in man: and this is the same with either, and either of these the same with this; for also with the man that is musical both man and musical are styled the same, and that is regarded the same with those. Wherefore, also, all these are not predicated universally; for it is not true to say that every man is the same thing with what is musical: for universals are absolute existences, but accidents are not absolute

1018a existences, but are simply predicated of singulars. For it seems the same thing to be Socrates and Socrates the musical, for the expression Socrates is not affirmed of all; wherefore, not every Socrates is predicated as every man is. And some things in this way are called the same. Some things, however, are called the same essentially in the same way as unity also; for those things likewise of which the matter is one either in species, or in number, or in genus, are called the same, and those of which the substance is one are called the same. Wherefore, it is evident that sameness is a certain unity of the being of either many things, or when one employs anything as many, as when one affirms the same thing to be the same with itself, for he employs that thing as two.

But diverse are those things called of which either the species are numerous, or the matter, or the definition of the substance; and, in general, is the diverse denominated in a manner opposite to the same. And those things are styled different whatsoever are diverse; being, however, in some respect the same, not merely in number, but either in species, or genus, or analogy. Further, things are considered different of which the genus is diverse, and the things that are contrary, and whatsoever involve diversity in the substance. Similar are those things styled both which everywhere undergo the same affection and undergo more of the same affections than of the diverse, and of which the quality is one, and in as many of the contraries as a change is possible, that which possesses more of these, or the more important amongst these, is similar to that thing. Things that are dissimilar, however, are denominated in an opposite way to those that are similar.

10. Things that are opposite are called contradictions, and contraries, and relations, and privation, and habit, and those things from which ultimate things arise, and those into which they are resolved: as, for instance, the generations and corruptions of bodies, and whatsoever things it is not admissible at the same time should be present in that which is receptive of both, these

are said to be opposite either themselves or those whereof they are compounded. For black and white at the same time are not inherent in the same subject. Wherefore, those colors of which they are compounded are opposite to these. Those things are called contraries, both those which cannot be present in the same subject at the same time, of things that differ in genus; and those things are called contraries which involve the greatest amount of difference, of those that are in the same genus, and things that widely differ in the same recipient, and which widely differ of those under the same capacity, and those of which there is the greatest difference, either simply, or according to genus, or according to species. And other things are styled contraries; some as having such things in possession, and others as being recipients of such, and some in being effective, or in being capable of undergoing passive conditions, or in being agents, or being passive, or being rejections, or affinities, or habits, or privations, of these and of things of this sort. Since unity and entity, however, are spoken of in many ways, there is a necessity of the other things also following as many as are expressed according to these. Wherefore, also, will there be a distribution of the same, and the diverse, and the contrary; so that there must needs be something diverse in each category.

And diverse in species are those things called as many as 1018b being of the same genus are not subalternate, and as many as being in the same genus involve a difference, and as many as in the substance are related in the way of contrariety. And contraries are diverse in the species of one another, either all or those which are denominated primarily, and are those of whatever in the ultimate species of the genus the definitions are diverse; as, for instance, man and horse, which are individuals in the genus, but the definitions of them are diverse. And those are contraries as many as being in the same substance involve a difference. Those things, however, are in species the same which are expressed in an opposite way to these.

11. Prior and subsequent are things called. Some, as in the case of a certain thing existing as first, and as a first principle, in each genus; for prior is that which is nearer a certain first principle, defined either simply and by nature, or relatively, or according to place, or by certain things: as, for instance, some things are prior in place from the fact of being nearer either by nature to a certain definite place as to the mean or the extreme, or by some ordinary relation in this way; and that which is more remote from this definite locality is subsequent. Other things prior and subsequent, however, are so in accordance with time; for some things, indeed, are considered prior as they are more remote from the present moment: for instance, in the case of things that have taken place in time past; for the Trojan annals are prior to the Medean because they are further removed from the present time; and other things are prior in regard of being nearer the present time, as in the case of things to come: for the Nemean games are prior to the Pythian because it is an event nearer the present, using the present as a first principle and a thing that is first. Some things, also, according to motion are prior and subsequent; for that which is more immediate to the first moving power is prior: as, for example, a boy is prior to a man; and this, also, is a certain first principle simply considered. Some things, also, are prior according to potentiality; for that which is supereminent in potentiality is prior, and that which is more potential is prior: but that nature is of such kind as according to the free-will of which another must needs follow which is also posterior. Wherefore, in the event of that one not imparting motion, the consequence will be that no motion should ensue in the other; and, in the event of that one imparting motion, that motion should ensue in the other; but free-will constitutes a first principle. Also, things according to order are styled prior and subsequent; but these are such as according to some one relation defined are distant proportionally: as, for example, in a dance the person standing second is prior to one that stands third, and the paranete to the nete in a musical instrument; for in the former is the person who presides, and in the latter the medium is a first principle.

These things, indeed, therefore, are styled prior in this way; but in another way is a thing prior in knowledge as if it were even absolutely prior. Of these things, however, that are otherwise, some are according to reason, and some according to sense; for, certainly, according to reason things that are universal are prior; but according to sense the singulars are prior. And according to the reason, also, the accident is prior to the whole, as the musical is before a man that is musical; for the entire reason will not be without the part, athough it is not possible to be musical when there is not a certain one that is musically gifted. Further, the passive conditions of things that are prior are called prior; as, for instance, straightness is prior to smoothness: for the one is an essential affection of a line, and the other of a superficies.

Some things, therefore, are called prior and subsequent in this way; but others are termed so according to nature and substance, as many as it is admissible can be in subsistence without others, but others cannot subsist without them; which opinion Plato adopted. But since "the being" is in many ways denominated, in the first place the subject is prior through which the substance is prior; in the next place the things according to potentiality and actuality are otherwise; for according to potentiality are some things prior, and others according to actuality, subsequent; as, for instance, according to potentiality is the half prior to the whole and the part to the whole, and the matter to the substance; but according to actuality is this a thing that is subsequent: for when dissolution has taken place things will subsist according to actuality. In a certain manner, it is true, all things that are styled prior and subsequent are expressed according to these; for some according to generation it is admissible may subsist without others, as the whole without the parts: but some according to corruption, as the part is prior to the whole. But it is in like manner with the rest. 1019a

12. Potentiality is called the first principle of motion or change in another thing, or so far forth as it is another thing; as the building art is a potentiality that does not reside in the thing that

is built: but the art of healing, when it constitutes a potentiality, would reside in the person who is being healed but not so far forth as he is a person that is being healed. Therefore, in general, the first principle of change or of motion is said to be potentiality in another thing, so far forth as it is another, and potentiality is styled such from another thing, or so far forth as it is another; for according to this sense of potentiality is what is passive in any degree passive. Sometimes, then, if it may be possible also that anything whatsoever undergoes passion, we say that thing involves the potentiality of being passive; but sometimes we say that this is not the case as regards every passion, but if it be passive in reference to what is better. Further, is potentiality the capacity of accomplishing this particular thing well, or doing so according to free-will; for sometimes persons who merely have been walking or speaking, but yet who have not done so well, or not as they would choose, we would not say possessed the power or potentiality of speaking or walking: but also, in like manner, is it in the case of passion. Further, as many habits as according to which things are entirely devoid of passion, or unchangeable, or not capable of being easily altered into a worse state, such are styled potentialities. For things are broken, indeed, and rubbed together, and bent, and are, in general, subject to decay, not from the having capacity, but from the not having capacity or potentiality, and from deficiency in some point: other things, however, are impassive by such as scarcely, and in a small degree, become affected on account of potentiality, and the possession of potentiality, and the being in a certain manner disposed.

Now, seeing that potentiality is denominated in so many ways, in the first place will also the potential be styled as that which possesses a first principle of motion or of change (for even what is stationary is something potential in another thing, or so far forth as it is another), and in the second place, if anything else of this should possess a capacity of this sort, and in the third place, if it involve such a capacity of bringing about a change in anything whatsoever, whether into what is worse or into what is

1019b

better. For, also, that which is in a state of decay seems to be a thing capable of falling into decay, otherwise it would not be corrupted if such were impossible; but already has it a certain disposition of parts, and a cause and first principle of such a passive condition. Sometimes, however, from the fact of possession, and sometimes from the fact of privation, does it seem to be a thing of this sort. And if privation in a manner constitute a habit, all things by the fact of the possession of something would be potentialities; but the entity would be also expressed equivocally. Wherefore, is a thing potential in respect of having a certain habit and first principle, and in respect of involving the privation of this, if it is admissible that it should involve privation. And in the fourth place is a thing potential from the non-possession of a potentiality—or a first principle of this in another, or so far forth as it is another—which is subject to corruption. But, moreover, are all those things potential either in the mere accident of their being generated or not being generated, or in respect of their being generated in an excellent manner. For, also, in things that are inanimate is there such a capacity inherent; as, for instance, in musical instruments: for one lyre, they say, can send forth sound, but that another does not possess this capacity, if it be not fair sounding.

Impotentiality, however, is a privation of potentiality, and a certain removal of a first principle of such a sort, as has been mentioned, either entirely so, or from being by nature adapted to have such, or already to have such when it has been naturally fitted thereto also; for we would not say that in like manner was it impotential or impossible for a man and an eunuch to beget a child. But, moreover, according to both sorts of potentiality is there impotentiality opposed, both to that merely which is capable of motion, and to that capable of motion in an excellent manner. And things are styled impotential, some in accordance with this kind of impotentiality, and others in another way; as, for instance, both the possible and the impossible. That, indeed, is a thing impossible the contrary of which is necessarily true; as the commensurability of the diameter is a thing that is impossible because such a position in mathematics is false; and the contrary of this is not only true, but also must necessarily be so, namely, the incommensurability of the diameter. Its being commensurable, accordingly, is not merely false, but must be false. The contrary, however, to this is the possible, when it is not necessary that the contrary should be false; as, for example, the possibility of a man's sitting: for not necessarily is his being in a posture not of sitting a thing that is false. The possible in one way, therefore, as has been stated, signifies that which is not necessarily false, but in another it signifies the being true, and in another that which it is admissible may be true. Now, this is what in geometry is figuratively styled potentiality. These, indeed, therefore, are things possible—not so according to potentiality.

1020a But all the things that are expressed according to potentiality are enumerated with reference to one original potentiality or capacity; and this is a principle of change in another, so far forth as it is another. For the rest are styled potential, partly in some other of them possessing such potentiality, and partly in its non-possession thereof, and partly in its being thus disposed. In like manner, also, is it the case with things that are impotential. Wherefore, the precise definition of the first potentiality would be a principle capable of bringing about a change in another thing, or so far forth as it is another.

13. Quantity is denominated that which is divisible into things that are inherent, of which either or each thing is adapted by nature to be a certain one thing, and a certain particular thing of this sort. Multitude, then, indeed, is a certain quantity if it may be numerable, but magnitude if it may be measurable; and multitude is styled that which is divisible in capacity into what is not continuous, but magnitude into that which is continuous. Now, of magnitude that which is continuous in one direction is length, and that in two directions breadth, and that in three, depth. But of these finite multitude is number, and length is a line, and breadth a superficies, and depth a body.

Moreover, some things are said to be certain quantities in themselves, or to be essential quantities; but others, quantities according to accident: as a line, to wit, is a certain essential quantity, whereas what is musical is a quantity according to accident. Now, of quantities that are so essentially, some are a certain quantity according to substance; as, for instance, a line (for in the definition expressive of what anything is, a certain quantity is inherent); but other quantities are passions and habits of such a substance: as, for example, much and little, and long and short, and broad and narrow, and high and low, and heavy and light, and the rest of such properties. Likewise, both the great and the little, and the greater and less, expressed both in reference to themselves and in relation to one another, are the essential passions of quantity. These names, indeed, are also transferred to other things. Of quantities, however, that are expressed according to accident, some are so expressed as has been declared, because what is musical is quantity, and what is white is so in respect of there being a certain quantity in that subject wherein they are inherent; and other things are quantities as motion and duration: for these, also, are termed certain quantities, and things continuous in respect of those things being divisible of which these are passive states. Now, I mean not that which is in a state of motion, but that which has had motion imparted to it; for from the fact of that being quantity, motion is likewise quantity, and duration, from the fact of this latter being quantity, is regarded as quantity itself also.

14. Quality is styled in one way the difference of substance; as, man is a certain quality of animal because he is a biped, and horse is a certain quality of animal because he is a quadruped, and a circle is a certain quality of figure because it is without angles: so that the difference constitutes the quality according to the substance. Now, in this one way is quality styled the difference of substance, but in another, as things incapable of motion and mathematical entities, just as numbers are certain qualities; 1020b

for example, those that are compound, and not only those which subsist in respect of one, but those of which surface and solid are an imitation (now these are plane, square, or cube numbers), and, in general, whatever besides quantity inheres in substance, for the being assumed once is the substance of each thing; as, for example, the substance of the six is not twice three, or thrice two, but the being taken once, for once six is six. Moreover, as many things as are passive conditions of substances in a state of motion are called qualities, as heat and cold, and whiteness and blackness, and gravity and lightness, and whatever such-like properties there are according to which the bodies of those things that are undergoing a change are said to be altered. Further, are things qualities so far as they subsist according to virtue and vice, and, in general, to what is bad and good.

So that almost in two ways may quality be expressed; and in one of these which would be the most strict or appropriate; for first, indeed, as quality, is the difference of substance. And a certain part of this, also, is the quality contained in numbers; for this is a certain difference of substances, yet either not of things that are being moved or not so far forth as they are being moved. These, however, are passive conditions of things that are in motion, so far forth as they are being moved and are differences of motions. And virtue and vice are a certain portion of such passions; for they make manifest the differences of motion and of energy in accordance with which those things that are in motion are agents and are passive in an excellent or a worthless manner: for that which in this way possesses the power of motion, or of energizing in this way, is good, and that which is moved and energizes in that way, and in a contrary manner, is worthless. And most especially do what is good and bad signify quality in the case of animated natures, and amongst these particularly does this apply to the case of those that possess free-will.

15. With respect to relatives, they are denominated, some of them, as a twofold to a half, and a threefold to a third, and, in general, a multiple to a submultiple, and excess to that which is

exceeded; and others of them, as the calorific to that which is heated, and the divisible to the divided, and, in general, the active to the passive; and others of them, as the measurable to the measure, and the object of scientific knowledge to science, and the sensible to sense.

Now, regarding these relatives, the first of them are expressed according to number, either simply or by definition, in respect of them or in respect of one; as, for example, the twofold in respect of one is a definite number, and the multiple is according to number in respect of one, but such as is not defined; as, for example, this or this particular number; but the sesqualiter, in relation to the subsesqualiter, is according to number in relation to a definite number. Superpartient, in relation to 1021a superpartient, is according to the indefinite in the same manner as the multiple is in relation to one. But that which exceeds, in relation to that which is exceeded, is, in short, indefinite according to number; for number is commensurable: but the excess and what is exceeded are denominated according to a non-commensurable number; for that which exceeds is such in relation to that which is exceeded, and something further than this: but this is indefinite; for whatsoever chances to be the result is either equal or not equal. These things, therefore, which are relatives, are all denominated according to number, and are passive properties of numbers: and, further, the equal, and similar, and same, according to another manner, are termed thus; for all these are expressed according to the one. For the same, indeed, are those things of which the substance is one; but similar are those things of which the quality is one; and equal are those of which the quantity is one. And the one is the first principle and measure of number; so that all these are denominated relations according to number, indeed, yet not in the same manner.

Things active and passive, however, subsist according to an active and passive potentiality, and according to energies that belong to potentialities; as that capable of promoting heat to that which is heated, because of its being endued with potentiality:

and again, the making warm in relation to that which is made warm; and one who severs in relation to that which is severed—as things energizing—are relatives. But of those things that are relatives according to number, these are not energies, save only in the manner it has been mentioned elsewhere; but energies according to motion do not subsist in numbers. And of those things that are relatives according to potentiality, some are already styled so according to periods of duration; as, for example, that which forms in relation to that which has been formed, and that which is likely to form in relation to that which is likely to be formed. For so, also, is a father called a father of a son; for there is something that partly has been active and partly passive. Further, are some things considered relations according to the privation of potentiality; for instance, just as the impossible, and as many things as are expressed in this way as, for example, the invisible.

Things, therefore, denominated relatives according to number and potentiality are all of them so called because each derives that which it is from reference to another, but not because something else is denominated with reference to it; and the measurable, and that which may be scientifically known, and that which is an object of the intellect, on account of something else being denominated in respect of them, are styled relatives. For, also, being an object of the intellect, signifies that the intellect is exercised about this; the intellect, however, does not subsist in relation to that about which the intellect is conversant, for the same thing, doubtless, would be said twice. In like manner, also, the power of sight is that of something, and not of him to 1021b whom the sight belongs. This, however, is a true statement, but it is in relation to color, or something else of this kind; yet in that way the same thing would be expressed twice: I mean that sight is the sight of him of whom it is the sight.

Things, indeed, therefore, called relatives essentially are denominated partly in this way, and partly if their genera are of this kind; as, for instance, the art of healing belongs to those things that are relative, because the science which is the genus of it seems to belong to those that are relatives. We may subjoin, as such, those things according to which, whatever they may be, things that possess them are spoken of as relatives, for example, equality is a relation because of the equal being relative, and similarity is a relation because of the similar being relative. Some things, however, are called relatives according to accident, as man is a relative because it is accidental to him his being twofold; and this belongs to those things that are relatives; or the white is a relative if it is accidental to the same thing to be twofold and white.

16. Perfect is denominated that beyond which it is not possible to assume anything or any one single portion; as, for instance, the time of each thing is perfect beyond which it is not possible to assume any period of duration which is a portion of this time: and that which according to virtue, and to what belongs to the excellent, doth not involve excess with respect to any genus; as, for instance, a perfect or finished physician, and a perfect or finished musician, are such when they are in no wise deficient as far as regards the species of the excellence that is proper to their professions, so, also, transferring our remarks to the case of evil things, we say a perfect or finished sycophant, and a finished thief, since we also denominate these characters good, as a good thief, and a good sycophant. And virtue is a certain perfection; for each thing is then perfect, and every substance is then perfect, when, in accordance with the species of its proper excellence or virtue, no portion of the natural magnitude is deficient. Further, in whatever things resides an admirable end, these are styled perfect; for in respect of involving an end are they perfect. Wherefore, since the end is something belonging to extremes, and transferring, also, our remarks to the case of things that are worthless, we say that a thing is perfectly lost and perfectly corrupted when nought of the corruption and of what is bad is deficient, but when it has arrived at the ultimate limit of these. Wherefore, also, death, metaphorically, is called the termination, because both are extremes. The end, however, together with the final cause, is a thing that is ultimate.

The things indeed, therefore, denominated essentially perfect are styled in thus much number of ways, partly in their being no wise deficient according to subsisting in an excellent manner, nor involving excess in each genus, nor there being anything extrinsic belonging to them; and the other things now are termed essentially perfect in respect either of the doing some 1022a such thing, or the having it in possession, or of the adaptation of itself to this, or in accordance, at least, with some other mode of expression in relation to things that are primarily called perfect.

17. A termination is called the last of each thing, and beyond which, as first, it is not possible to assume anything, and within which, as first, are comprised all things, and that, likewise, which may be a form of magnitude, or of that which is in possession of magnitude, and which is the end of everything. Now, a thing of this kind is that towards which motion and the mode of an action tend, and not from which they originate. Sometimes, however, a termination is both of these; both that from which motion and action originate, and towards which they tend; also, that for the sake of which other things operate, and the substance of each thing, and the essence or the formal cause of each: for this is a termination of knowledge, and if of knowledge, also of the thing done. Wherefore, it is evident that even as often as the first principle is predicated so often also is the termination, and still more multifariously; for the first principle, to be sure, is a certain termination: not every termination, however, is a first principle.

18. "The according to which" is denominated in many ways. In one way, indeed, as the species and the substance of each thing; as, for instance, that in accordance with which a man is good, itself is good; and, in another way, as that in which first a thing has been fitted by nature to rise into being, as color in a super-ficies. Therefore, what has, indeed, in the first instance been mentioned as "the according to which" constitutes form; but that mentioned secondarily, as such, is as the matter of each thing,

and the first subject in everything. And, in general, "the according to which" will have a subsistence as often as the cause; for according to what a man has come is an expression of the same import as on account of what he has come; and the inquiry according to what false reasoning, or correct reasoning, may be drawn is the same as an inquiry into what is the cause of the syllogism, or the paralogism, in such cases. Moreover, "the according to which" is denominated that which subsists according to a position, according to which one stands, or according to which one walks; for all these signify position and locality.

Wherefore, "that according to itself," or the essential, is necessarily expressed in many ways. For in one way is "that according to itself," or the essential, the very nature of each thing, or the formal cause; as, for example, Callias essentially is the very nature also of Callias; and, secondly, it signifies whatsoever things are inherent in the "what anything is"; as Callias essentially is an animal; for in the definition of Callias is to be found animal, for Callias is a certain description of animal: and, thirdly, may we denominate "that according to itself," or the essential, as a thing that has primarily been a recipient in itself, or a certain part of things that belong to itself; as, for instance, superficies is essentially white, and man essentially is an animal, for the soul is a certain portion of the man in which vitality is primarily inherent. Fourthly, does it signify that of which there is not any one other cause; for of man there are many causes, such as animal, biped; but, nevertheless, man is man essentially. Fifthly, we consider "that according to itself," or the essential, as many things as are inherent in some one particular thing alone, and as far forth as it is alone. Wherefore, whatever has a separate has also an essential subsistence.

19. Disposition is styled an arrangement of that which has parts 1022b either according to place or to potentiality, or according to species; for it is necessary that there be a certain position, as also the name disposition makes manifest.

20. Now habit is denominated, in one way, as a certain energy of the possessor and the possessed, just as it were a certain action or motion; for when the one accomplishes, and the other is accomplished, the act of accomplishing is a mean between them, so also between one having in possession a garment, and the garment had in possession, habit is a mean. Therefore, indeed, is it evident that it is not admissible that this should involve another habit; for the thing would go on to infinity if it be the case that one habit should involve the habit of that which is possessed. And in another way is habit styled a disposition according to which that which is disposed is disposed well or ill; and this either according to itself, that is, essentially, or in relation to another: as, for example, health is a certain habit, for it is a disposition of this sort. Further, is a thing called habit in a case where it may be a portion of such a disposition. Wherefore, also, is the virtue or excellency of the parts a certain habit.

21. Passion is denominated in one way, quality according to which a thing admits of alteration; as white and black, and sweet and bitter, and gravity and lightness, and whatsoever other such things there are: and in another way now are energies and alterations called passions of these; still more than these are noxious alterations and motions, passions, and particularly those motions that along with being noxious or injurious are painful likewise. Further, the crushing burdens of misfortunes, and of things that are fraught with suffering, are called passions.

22. Privation is denominated, in one way, in case a thing does not involve any of the things that by nature are adapted for being possessed, even though itself may not by nature be adapted for the possession of such; as, for example, a plant in this sense is said to be deprived of eyes. And in another way is that termed privation if a thing be by nature fit for possession of a thing, either itself or the genus, and yet may not have possession of that thing; as in one sense is a blind man deprived of sight, and a mole in another: the latter, indeed, according to the genus, and

the former according to itself, or essentially. Further, is that privation if a thing be by nature adapted to possess a quality; and when it is so adapted by nature to possess it, yet possesses it not, for blindness is a certain privation; but for an animal to be blind is not in accordance with every age, but with that only in which it is fitted by nature to have sight, and yet may not have it at all. And in like manner may privation be found in "the what," and according to "what," and for "what," and so far forth as it may be adapted by nature for the possession of such, and yet may not possess them.

Further, the violent removal of each thing is styled a privation. And as often, also, as are expressed negations from *A*, so often, likewise, are expressed privations; for the unequal is denominated thus from the fact of the non-possession of equality when by nature it is fitted for it, but the invisible, both from being entirely without color and in consequence of having it defectively; and an animal is called "apous," or without feet, both from its being without feet entirely, and in consequence of having them attended with some defect. Further, do we call a thing privation when that thing has anything small; as, for instance, any fruit 1023a with a small kernel: and this amounts to the being, in a manner, disposed defectively. And, again, we say privation exists where a thing cannot be effected with facility, or in a proper manner; as, for example, that which cannot be severed is so not only in respect of the incapacity of being severed, but also in respect of the incapacity of being severed easily or properly. Moreover, privation is found in the non-possession of a thing in every way; for a person blind is not called such from being one-eyed, but from being deprived of the power of vision in both eyes. Wherefore, not every man is good or evil, or just or unjust; but also there are shades of character intermediate between these.

23. Possession is denominated in many ways; in one way as the action of a thing according to the nature of what thing, or according to the impulse of it. Wherefore, both a fever is said to possess a man, and tyrants are said to possess states, and those

that are clothed a garment. And in another way we term possession as that in whatever anything is inherent, as being receptive; as, for instance, the brass possesses the form of a statue, and the body possesses disease. And in another way we term possession as a thing that embraces the things that are comprised; for wherein anything is comprised, by this it is said to be possessed: as, for instance, we say that the vessel possesses moisture, and the city inhabitants, and the ship sailors; and so, also, the whole possesses the parts. And, further, that which hinders, in accordance with its own force, anything from motion or action is said to possess this very thing; as, for example, both the pillars possess the superincumbent weights, and just as the poets make Atlas to possess the heaven, so that it should otherwise fall upon the earth; as, also, certain of the physiologists affirm. And in this way, likewise, is the connecting said to possess the things which it connects, as if they would otherwise have severally been separated according to their own proper force. And the being in anything is expressed in a similar manner with, and as a consequence upon, possession.

24. "The being from anything" is said in one way to be that from which a thing is as from matter; and this in a twofold respect, either according to the first genus, or according to the last species: as, for instance, all liquids, in a way, are from water, and the statue is from brass. And in another way we consider "the being from anything" as that which springs from the first moving cause; thus from what doth the battle arise? From invective, because such is a first principle of the battle. In another sense, however, is this defined as that from what is composite (I mean from matter and form), as the parts from the whole, and the verse from the *Iliad,* and the stones from the house; for form is an end to be sure, but that which possesses an end is finished. And in some respects it is as the species from a part; for instance, man is from biped, and a syllable from a letter: for these are from those otherwise than the statue from the brass, for from the

1023b

matter cognizant to the senses is the composite substance; but also form consists from the matter of the form. Some things are styled in this way as "that from anything," and others, if they subsist according to any part of these modes: as from the father and mother the child, and from earth the plants, because they spring from some part of them.

And, lastly, is this styled as that which subsists after anything in time, as night is said to be from day, and a storm from a calm, because the one follows after the other. But of these some are so called in respect of possessing the power of mutual change, as also those particulars just now enumerated; but others only in respect of their being successive in time: as from the equinox is made a voyage, because it is made after the equinox, and the Thargelia are from the Dionysia, because they are celebrated after the Dionysia.

25. A part is said to be in one way that into which any quantity whatsoever may be divisible; for always that which is subtracted from quantity, so far forth as it is quantity, is called a portion of that thing; thus, of three is the two in a manner called a part: and in another way that which measures it is called the part of things of this sort merely. Wherefore, two, in one way, is a part of three, as is stated, and in another is not so. Moreover, those things into which the species of animal may be divided without quantity, these also are called parts of this species. Wherefore, they say that species are parts of the genus. We further call those things parts into whatsoever anything is divided, or those things whereof the whole is made up, or the species, or that which involves the species, even as the brass is a part of the brazen sphere, or of the brazen cube (but this is the matter wherein the form resides), and an angle also is a part. Moreover, those things that are contained in the definition which manifests each thing, these also are parts of the whole. Wherefore, the genus is called a part also of the species, and in other respects the species is regarded a part of the genus.

26. A whole is styled, first, that from which is absent no part of those things whereof the whole by nature is said to consist; and secondly, that which contains the things contained, so that they form one certain thing. And this is the case in a twofold way; for it is so either in such a manner that each may be one, or that one thing may arise from these. For the universal, indeed, and that which is predicated in general as being a certain whole, are universal in such a way as that the predication of each contains many things, and that all are one as each predicated thing is; for example, man, horse, god, is individually one thing, because all are animals. And the continuous and the finite may we regard as a whole when there may be produced one thing from many things that are inherent, especially when this is the case in potentiality, but if not in energy.

Now, of these very things rather are those wholes which subsist by nature than such as are made by art; as also we say, in regard of the one, that entirety is a certain unity. Further, seeing that quantity 1024a has a first principle, and a mean, and an extreme, of whatsoever quantities position does not cause a difference "all" is predicated; but of whatsoever it does, a "whole" is predicated; and as many things as admit of both, both "whole" and "all" are predicated. There are those things, however, whose nature abides the same in the act of transposition; but not so with the form, as wax and a garment: for both whole and all are they styled, for they possess both. But water, and whatsoever things are moist, and number, are called "all," no doubt; yet number is not styled a whole, and water a whole, unless metaphorically. All those, however, are predicated thus of which the entire is predicated; as in the case of the one, in the case of these I say all things are predicated; as in the case of things divided we say all this is number, and all these monads.

27. But the mutilated is styled, amongst quantities, not every indiscriminate quantity, but it must needs be itself divisible and a whole. For two things are not mutilated when either one is being

subtracted (for both the mutilation and what remains nowhere are equal), nor, in general, is any number mutilated, for also must its substance needs remain: thus, if a goblet be mutilated, still must the goblet exist; but a number is no longer the same when a part is taken away. And, in addition to these, if also things may be of dissimilar parts, neither can all these be considered mutilated; for number is that which also contains dissimilar parts: as, for example, a dyad, a triad. But, in short, none of those things of which the position does not make a difference is mutilated, as water or fire; but such must needs be mutilated which have a substantial position. Further, things continuous must needs be mutilated; for harmony consisting from things of dissimilar parts, indeed, also possesses position; but it does not become mutilated.

And, in addition to these, neither are those things mutilated, whatsoever are wholes, by the privation of any part whatsoever indifferently. For it is not necessary that either the principal parts of the substance, or those that are taken away anywhere whatsoever, should make what remains mutilated; as, for instance, if a goblet be bored it is not mutilated, but if its handle, or if any of its extremities, be, it is mutilated: and a man is not mutilated if he have flesh or spleen, but if he have an extremity taken away, and not every such indifferently; but should it be that which does not possess the power of reproduction when entirely taken away. Wherefore, bald persons are not mutilated.

28. Genus is styled so partly when there may be a continuous generation of things that possess the same species; as, for instance, there is said to be a genus of men, because as long as the generation of them may be continuous there would exist such. And it is that also from which things derive their being as the first disposing cause towards existence; for so are the Ellenes styled the genus, and the Ionians: the former as springing from Hellen, and the latter from Ion, as the first generator. And rather are those things a genus that are from the generator than from

the matter. For they are said to be the genus, also, that are from the female, as those from Pyrrha. Further, are they termed as the 1024b surface is called the genus of superficial figures, and the solid of such as are solid; for, as regards each of the figures, the one is such a surface, but the other is such a solid, and this is the subject in the differences, which, of course, is the genus. Further, do we regard genus as that which first is inherent in definitions, which is predicated in the case of the essence of a thing the differences of which are called qualities. The genus, therefore, indeed, is denominated in thus many ways; partly according to the continuous generation of the same species, and partly according to the original moving power of the same species, and partly as matter; for that to which the difference and the quality belong; this constitutes the subject which we style matter.

And things are called diverse in genus of which the first subject is diverse, and in the case of which one is not resolved into another, nor both into the same (as the form and the matter are something different in the genus), and whatsoever things are denominated according to a different form of the predication of entity; for some entities signify quiddity, and some a certain quality of a thing, and some have a signification in accordance with our former division; for neither are these resolvable either into one another or into any one thing.

29. The false is denominated in one way as a false thing; and, in regard of this, partly in the fact of its not being composed, or in the impossibility of its being in a state of composition; as the expression of the diameter being commensurable, or of your being in a sitting posture; for of these the former is, indeed, always, but the latter sometimes false: for thus are these not in being. For things are false as many as are in being, no doubt, but yet are fitted by nature, to appear either not such as they are, or what they are not; as, for example, a rough painting and dreams; for these, truly, are something, but not those things of which they cause an imagination or impression. Things, indeed, therefore, are thus termed false either in respect of themselves

not being, or in respect of the impression that is conveyed from them being that of a nonentity; and a false discourse is a discourse about nonentities, so far forth as it is false.

Wherefore, every false definition, or discourse, is employed about something that is different from that of which it would be a true discourse; as the discourse about a circle is a false one when transferred to a triangle. Now, the discourse, or definition of everything is partly as one—namely, that explanatory of the essence; and it is partly as many, since, somehow, a thing itself, and this thing, viewed as passive, may be regarded the same as Socrates and Socrates the musical. And a false discourse is a discourse simply about nothing.

Wherefore, Antisthenes entertained a silly opinion when he thought that nothing could be predicated, unless one, in regard of one thing, by a proper definition or discourse; the result of which statements was, that there can be no contradiction in existence, and almost no way of making a false assertion. It is possible, however, to express each thing not only in a discourse proper to itself, but also in that which belongs to a different thing—falsely, no doubt, and altogether so: notwithstanding, then, is it possible to express the same, in a manner, also with truth; as, for instance, eight are twofold, from the definition of the dyad. Some things, indeed, therefore, are denominated in this way false.

But a false man is called one who is ready and disposed to 1025a admit false assertions of such a sort, not on account of anything that is different, but on account of their being false, and who, in the case of others, is the cause of the adoption of such false assertions; as also we say that those things are false as many as create a false impression.

Wherefore, the reasoning in the Hippias of Plato is sophistical, so far as it endeavors to establish that the same man is false and true. For one that is capable of deceiving he receives as false, and this person is one that is knowing and prudent; further, a man who is voluntarily worthless he pronounced a better man. Now, this falsehood he gathers by induction; for one that is lame voluntarily is superior to one that is so involuntarily, considering the voluntary lameness as an imitation of lameness. Since, if were he lame voluntarily he would, perhaps, be a worse individual, as this also would be the case as regards moral deportment.

30. An accident, however, is denominated as that which is inherent in something, and which it is true to affirm is so, yet not either necessarily, or for the most part; as, for example, if anyone in digging a furrow for a plant should discover a treasure. This, then, would be an accident to the person engaged in digging the trench, namely, the discovery of the treasure; for neither does the one necessarily follow from the other, nor after it; nor, should one be occupied in planting, does he, for the most part, find a treasure. And the case is the same should anyone who is musical be white: since, however, this takes place neither of necessity nor as for the most part, we pronounce this an accident. Wherefore, since there is something which has a subsistence, and a subsistence in something, and some of these both in a certain place and at a certain time, whatsoever would be so, indeed, but would involve no allusion as to why it was this particular thing, either now or here, such will be an accident: nor, doubtless, is there any definite cause of what is accidental; but the cause of this is the casual or ordinary, and this is the indefinite. Thus, it has been accidental to a certain individual, his arriving at Aegina, if he has not left home for this purpose that he should go thither, but has been driven there by a storm or captured by pirates. The accidental, doubtless, has been generated, and will have a subsistence, not, however, so far forth as itself is concerned, but as far as something else is; for the storm was the cause of his going to the port he was not sailing for, and this was Aegina. And in another way is a thing called an accident; for example, in the way whatsoever things are inherent in each thing essentially, and yet are not contained in the substance of that thing, as in a triangle to have angles equal to two right angles. And accidents of this sort it is admissible should be eternal, yet this is not the case with any of those others. The reason, however, of this may be found elsewhere.

BOOK VI

1. THE first principles and causes of entities are under inves- 1025b
tigation; and it is evident that the investigation regards the
causes and first principles of entities, so far forth as they are
entities. For there is a certain cause of health, and of a good
habit of body, and of mathematical entities; likewise are there
first principles, and elements, and causes; and in general, also,
every science which is an intellectual one, or in any degree
even partaking of the faculty of thought, is conversant about
causes and first principles, which are either more accurate or
more simple, as the case may be. All of these, however, being
descriptive of one particular subject, and a particular genus,
are engaged about this; but not concerning being or entity
simply considered, nor so far forth as it is entity: nor do they
make any account of the substance of a thing, but from this
one particular subject, partly from sense making this manifest,
and partly assuming an hypothesis as to substance or quiddity;
they, accordingly, demonstrate the things that are essentially
inherent in the genus about which they subsist, either more
necessarily or more feebly. Wherefore, it is evident that there
is not a demonstration of substance, nor of "the what" a thing
is, that is, of quiddity, by means of an induction of such a
kind; but there is some other mode of manifestation. In like
manner, also, these sciences say nothing as to whether the
genus about which they are engaged is or is not, an account of

its belonging to the same faculty of thought or understanding, and of its making manifest the nature of a thing, and whether it is this particular thing.

But since, also, physical science happens to be conversant about a certain genus of entity (for about such a sort of substance is it conversant in which is contained in itself the first principle of motion and of rest), it is evident that it is neither practical, nor productive, that is, effective; for the first principle of things that are productive resides in the producer or efficient cause, whether that principle be mind, or art, or a certain capacity, but the first principle of things that are practical is free-will in the agent; for the same thing is an object of action and of free-will. Wherefore, if every dianoetic faculty be either practical, or productive, or speculative, the physical dianoetic energy would be some speculative science; but speculative about such an entity as it is possible should have motion imparted to it, and about such a substance as, existing according to reason, for the most part has not a separable subsistence merely. It is requisite, however, as regards the essence or formal cause, and the definition how things are so, that this should not escape our notice, as without this knowledge, at least, the present investigation would be the accomplishing of nothing. But of things that are defined, and to which the inquiry what they are belongs, some subsist in such a manner as the flat-nose, and some as the hollow. And these differ, since flat-nose is conceived along with matter, for, in truth, a flat-nose is a hollow-nose; but hollowness or concavity is without sensible matter. If, therefore, all physical or natural things are predicated in the same way as flat-nose—as, for instance, nose, eye, face, flesh, bone, in short, animal, leaf, root, bark; in short, plant (for the definition of none of these subsists without motion, but such invariably involves matter)—it is plain how it is necessary in physical inquiries to investigate the nature of a thing, and to define it, and why, also, it is the part of the natural philosopher to institute an inquiry concerning a certain soul, namely, such a soul as is not unconnected with matter; that therefore the physical dianoetic energy is speculative is evident

1026a

from these statements. But also the mathematical dianoetic energy is speculative also; whether it is conversant, however, about entities that are immovable, and capable of a separate subsistence is a point that at present is obscure: but that certain mathematical systems investigate certain entities, so far as they are immovable, and so far as they have a separable subsistence, is clear.

Now, if there is something that is eternal and immovable, and that involves a separate subsistence, it is evident that it is the province of the speculative, that is, of the ontological, science to investigate such. It is not, certainly, the province of physical science, at any rate (for physical science is conversant about certain movable natures), nor of the mathematical, but of a science prior to both of these, that is, the science of metaphysics. For physical science, I admit, is conversant about things that are inseparable, to be sure, but not immovable; and of mathematical science some are conversant about entities that are immovable, it is true, yet, perhaps, not separable, but subsisting as in matter. But Metaphysics, or the First Philosophy, is conversant about entities which both have a separate subsistence and are immovable; and it is necessary that causes should be eternal, all without exception, but particularly these: for these are the causes of the things that are manifest or phenomenal amongst those that are divine.

Wherefore, according to this view of things, there would be three speculative philosophies; namely, the mathematical, the physical, the theological. For it is not obscure that if what is divine exists anywhere, it resides in such nature as this; and it is requisite that that should be the most honorable science which is conversant about a genus of things which is most entitled to our respect. The speculative sciences, accordingly, are more eligible than the rest of the sciences; and of such as are speculative, this science of metaphysics, now under investigation, is more eligible than all the others.

For one would feel a doubt as to whether at all the first philosophy, or ontology, is universal, or conversant about a certain genus and one nature. For neither is there the same method of conducting our inquiries in the mathematical sciences; but geometry, in fact, and astronomy, are conversant about a certain peculiar nature: yet, in reply to this, I would say that pure mathematics universally is common to all the branches of that science, and thus that the first philosophy universally is common to all the sciences. If, then, there is not some different substance besides those that consist by nature, the physical would be the first science; but if there is a certain immovable substance, this will be prior, and the subject of the first philosophy, and in this way will subsist universally, because it is the first of the sciences; and it would be the province of this science of metaphysics, or ontology, to institute an inquiry respecting entity, so far forth as it is entity, and respecting quiddity, or the nature of a thing, and respecting those things that universally are inherent in it, so far forth as it is entity.

2. Since, however, entity, simply so called, is denominated in many ways, of which one was that which subsists according to accident, and another that which is as a thing that is true, and the nonbeing of which is as a thing that is false, and besides these, since these are figures of predication; as, for example, quiddity, and quality, and quantity, and the place where, and the time when, and whatever else there is that is significant in this way: further, besides all these, is there that which subsists in potentiality, and that which subsists in energy: since, however, I say entity is denominated in many ways; in the first instance, as far as regards that subsisting according to accident, must we declare that respecting this there exists no speculation.

1026b

And a proof of this statement is the following; for in no science is there any attention paid to this, neither in practical, nor productive, nor speculative science. For neither does one who builds a house make at the same time as many things as are accidental to the house when it is built, for these are infinite; there is no hindrance, for example, but that the house, when it has been constructed should prove to some persons agreeable, but to others injurious, and to others serviceable, and, as I may say, different from all entities, of none of which the building art is productive. And, in the same manner, neither does the geometrician speculate into things which in this way are accidental to figures, nor whether there is any difference between a wooden triangle and a triangle having angles equal to two right angles.

And this coincidence takes place rationally; for the accidental subsists as it were in name merely. Wherefore, after a certain mode, Plato judiciously arranged nonentity about the art of the Sophist. For the arguments of the Sophists are employed about the accident, as I may say, most especially of all things; for they ask, for instance, whether a musician and a grammarian are a different person or the same; and whether the musical Coriscus and Coriscus are the same; and whether everything which may exist, yet not always, has been generated? Wherefore, whether in case a man is musical he has been made grammatical; and whether in case he is grammatical he has been made musical? And as many arguments, no doubt, as there are of this kind; for accident appears to be a something that hovers on the confines of nonentity. Now, this is evident also from such arguments as the foregoing; for of those things that subsist in a different way from accidents there is generation and corruption: but this is not the case with those things that subsist according to accident.

Nevertheless, however, must we further discuss concerning accident, as far as is possible, what is its nature, and on account of what cause it exists; for at the same time, perhaps, will it be evident on account of what reason also there is not a science of it. Since, therefore, there are in entities some things that are always disposed in a similar manner, and from necessity—a necessity that is not denominated according to what is violent, but that which we have spoken of in the case of its not being admissible for a thing to be otherwise than it is,—and since other things, though these are not of necessity, to be sure, nor always, yet are in existence for the most part, this is the first principle, and this the cause of the subsistence of accident.

For whatever may be neither always, nor for the most part, this we pronounce to be an accident, as, for instance, in the dog-days, that is, when the sun is in Canis, if there should prevail storm and cold, we say that this is accidental; we should not, however, speak in this manner should stifling heat and warmth be generated, because the latter invariably, or at least for the most part, is prevalent at such a season of the year, whereas the former is not. And that a man is white is an accident; for neither is he always so, nor for the most part: but that man is an animal is not according to accident. And for a builder to have been 1027a instrumental in producing good health is an accident, because a builder is not fitted by nature to accomplish this, but a physician is; but it would be an accident for the builder, his being a physician. And a cook, aiming at furnishing pleasure, would probably make something calculated to promote health, but not in accordance with, or by virtue of, the art of cooking. Wherefore, we say that this would be accidental, and that in a certain respect the cook makes something that is salubrious, but, simply considered, that he does not so.

For of some things are there other potentialities that sometimes are productive, but of others there is no definite art or potentiality; for of those things that are, or are generated according to accident, the cause also is according to accident. Wherefore, since all things are not from necessity and always either are entities or are in generation, but since most things have a subsistence for the most part, it is necessary that there be in existence something which subsists according to accident, and that it should be such as is a white musician, who exists neither always, nor for the most part. Since sometimes, however, such is produced, there will be a subsistence according to accident, and if not, all things will subsist from necessity. Wherefore, matter will be the contingent cause of what is accidental, differently from that which has a subsistence, for the most part.

We must, however, assume this as a beginning of the inquiry, whether there is nothing which subsists neither always, nor for the most part, or whether this is impossible? Accordingly, in addition to these things is there something which in one way or other has a casual subsistence, and a subsistence according to accident. Shall we, however, admit that that

which has a subsistence for the most part, and that which has a
perpetual subsistence, is not inherent in the nature of anything,
or are there certain entities that are eternal? Concerning these
points, indeed, we will afterwards examine.

That, however, there is not a science of the accidental is
manifest; for, certainly, every science is a science either of that
which subsists always, or of that which subsists as for the most
part. For, otherwise, how should one learn anything or instruct
another? For it is necessary that the object of the science be
defined, either by that subsisting always, or that having a subsistence for the most part, as that mead is useful, for the most part,
for one that is sick of fever. What, however, is beyond this it will
not be allowable to affirm; namely, as to the time when it may not
be useful: as, for instance, during new-moon, for either always,
or for the most part, is the mead serviceable during new-moon,
also; and what is different from these is accidental. What, in
truth, therefore, the accidental is, and from what cause it arises,
and that there is no science of it in existence, has been declared.

3. Now, that there are first principles, and causes that are generable and corruptible, without anything rising into existence and
falling into decay, is evident. For if this were not the case all
things would subsist from necessity, if of that which is being
produced and corrupted there must needs be a certain cause
which does not subsist according to accident. For whether will
this particular thing take place or not? If, at least, this be produced it will, but if not, by no means will it take place; but this
latter will take place if something else is accomplished.

And so it is manifest that when a store of time is subtracted
from finite duration you will invariably come to the present
moment. Wherefore, this person will die either by disease or 1027b
violence if he, at least, go forth out of the city, and this will take
place if he should be thirsty, and this will happen if something
else happens; and so will he come to that which now is, or to
something of those things that have been: as, for instance, if he
may have felt thirst; and this will happen if he eats things that are

137

pungent to the taste; and this, assuredly, is the case or is not: wherefore, he shall necessarily either die or shall not die. In like manner, also, if anyone pass over in his inquiry to the things that have been done, the reasoning is the same; for already does this subsist in something: but I speak of that which has been done. Accordingly, all things that are likely to be in future will subsist from necessity: as, for instance, the death of one that is living; for already has something been accomplished which shows a tendency toward dissolution; I mean, the existence of things that are contrary in the same body: but if the death of this person is to be brought about by disease or violence, not as yet has this taken place, but should this particular thing be effected.

It is evident, then, that this reduction advances towards a certain principle, and this principle no longer extends to anything else. Therefore, will this be the principle of what is casual, and there will be nothing as a cause of its generation. But into what sort of first principle, and what sort of cause such a reduction may be made, whether as into matter, or as into the final cause, or as into the power that imparts motion that is the efficient cause, is particularly worthy of consideration.

4. Therefore, indeed, respecting the entity which subsists according to accident, let the discussion be dismissed, for the subject has been determined with sufficient accuracy. Now, that which subsists as true is entity, and that which subsists as false is nonentity, since they are employed about composition and division, and entirety about a portion of contradiction; for that which is true involves an affirmation in the case of composition, and a negation in the case of division; but that which is false involves the contradiction of this division.

But how it is possible to understand what subsists at the same time, or has a separate subsistence, this is another question. Now, I mean, that things which subsist together, and that which subsists apart, are disposed in such a way as not to subsist in a consequent order, but so as to become one certain thing; for not in things themselves are the false and the true,—as that which is good is true, but that which is bad is false,—but in the understanding and the truth and falsehood concerning things that are simple, and concerning essence, are not in the understanding either. As many points, then, as it is requisite to examine into as regards entity subsisting in this way, and regarding nonentity, must be investigated on a subsequent occasion.

Since, however, composition and division are in the intellect but not in the things themselves, and that which is an entity after this manner is different from those things that are properly termed entities (for either the nature of a thing, or its being of a certain quality or quantity, or something else of the kind, doth the intellect conjoin or separate),—that which, as an entity, subsists as an accident, and that which is as it were what is true—the consideration of these must be omitted. For the 1028a cause of the one, is indefinite, but of the other a certain affection of the understanding; and both are conversant about the remaining genus of entity, and do not render manifest any nature that is of an higher order than entity. Wherefore, let these points be omitted, to be sure; but we must examine the causes and the first principles of entity itself, so far forth as it is entity. And it is evident, in what we have laid down concerning the multifarious predication of everything, that entity is denominated in many ways.

BOOK VII

1. ENTITY is denominated in many ways, as we have previously made the division in the case of those statements relating to its multifarious predications; for one signification of entity is "that what a thing is," or quiddity, and this certain particular thing; and another is quality or quantity, or each of the rest of the things that are so predicated. Now, seeing that entity is spoken of in thus many ways, it is evident that the first entity amongst these is quiddity, or "the what a thing is," which signifies substance. For when we say that this particular thing is of a certain quality, we term it either good or bad; but not as of three cubits, or that it is a man: when, however, we say what a thing is, we term it not white or warm, or of three cubits; but a man or a god. But the other entities are denominated so in regard of belonging to entity that is really such; some, to wit, as being quantities, and some qualities, and some passions, and others, some other things of the sort. Wherefore, one might feel perplexed as to whether walking, and health, and sitting, were each of them an entity or a nonentity. And, in like manner, also, is it the case with any whatsoever of the other things of this kind respecting which similar doubts are entertained; for none of them is adapted by nature either to subsist essentially or is capable of being separated from substance, but rather (if I may express myself so) this is to be said of any amongst the entities which is walking, and sitting, and being in sound health. And these rather than those appear to be entities, because they have some

definite subject, and this is substance, and these singular which appears in the category of this kind; for that which is good, or the sitting posture, is not expressed without this also. It is evident, therefore, that each of those also subsists on account of this. Wherefore, that which is primarily entity, and not any particular entity, but entity simply or absolutely, will constitute substance.

Therefore, that which is first is denominated in many ways; nevertheless, first of all is substance, both in reason, and knowledge, and time, and nature. For no one of the rest of the categories is capable of a separate subsistence, but this alone; and in definition is this first: for in the definition of everything there is a necessity that the definition of substance be inherent. And then we think we know each particular thing, especially, when we know what man is, or fire is, rather than when we know the quality, or the quantity, or the situation of a thing; since we then come to know each of these things when we know what the quantity of them is, or the quality.

1028b

And unquestionably, also, was that originally, and at the present time, and always, a subject of investigation, and invariably of doubt; namely, what entity is, that is, what substance is: for some say that this is one, but others, that it is more than one; and some maintain that things which are finite are this entity, but others, things that are infinite. Wherefore, also, especially, and primarily, and exclusively, as I may say, we must investigate concerning that which subsists as entity after this manner, as to what it is.

2. Now, substance seems to subsist, no doubt, in bodies most palpably. Wherefore, we say that both animals, and plants, and the parts of them, are substances; and we say the same of natural or physical bodies, as fire, and water, and earth, and everything of this sort; and as many as are either parts of these or are composed of these, either partly or entirely, as both the heaven and its parts, stars, and moon, and sun. Whether, however, these are the only substances, or whether there are others besides, or whether no one of these, but certain different ones, are substances, this must be examined into. But to some the boundaries of

bodies (as superficies, and line, and point, and monad) seem to be substance, and that, too, rather than body and solidity. Further, with the exception of things that are sensible, some are not of opinion that there is anything in existence of the kind, but others, that there are many such, and that especially those entities have a subsistence which are eternal; as Plato considered both forms and mathematical entities as two substances, and, as a third, the substance of sensible bodies. But Speusippus, starting from one, says that there are many substances and first principles of each substance; one of numbers, but another of magnitudes, then another of soul; and in this way extends therefore, the classes of substance. And some affirm that forms and numbers have the same nature, but that other things that are connected therewith, as lines and surfaces, belong to a second class of substances as far as to the substance of the heaven and to sensibles.

Accordingly, respecting these we must consider what it is that is said well or not well, and what substances exist, and whether there are certain ones besides sensibles, or are not, and how these subsist? Also, whether there is any separable substance, and why there is, and after what mode of subsistence; or whether there is no substance besides sensibles? This, I say, must form the subject of our investigation, having first delineated substance in a sketch of what it is.

3. Now, substance is denominated, if not multifariously, yet, at least, in four ways particularly; for both the essence of the formal cause, and the universal, and the genus, seem to be substance in each thing; and fourth of these is the subject. But the subject is that of which other things are predicated, while itself is no longer predicated of any other thing. Wherefore, concerning this point we must come to a determination in the first instance; for substance appears especially to be the primary subject. Now, in some such manner is matter denominated substance, but in another way form, and in a third, that which results from, or is a compound of, these; now, I mean by matter, brass, for instance, but by form the figure of the idea, and by what

1029a

which is composed of these the statue in its entirety. Wherefore, if form be prior to matter, and rather than it is entity or being, also for the same reason will be prior that which is a compound of both. Now therefore, by way of a rough delineation has it been declared what substance is at all; namely, that it is not that which is predicated of the subject, but is that of which other things are predicated. It must needs, however, be spoken of not in this manner solely, for such is not sufficient; for this account of it is obscure.

And, further, matter becomes substance: for if matter is not substance, what else is escapes our comprehension; for when other things are removed away, nothing appears remaining. For other things are the passive conditions of bodies, and are productions, and potentialities; but length, and breadth, and depth, are certain quantities, but not substances: for quantity is not substance but rather that wherein these very qualities are inherent primarily—*that* is substance. But, unquestionably, if we take away length, and depth, and breadth, we see nothing left except whatsoever is bounded by these. Wherefore, to persons conducting the inquiry in this way, matter must needs appear only as substance; and I call matter that which essentially is termed neither quiddity, nor quantity, nor anything else of those things whereby entity is defined. For there is something of which each of these is predicated from which "the being" is different, as well as from each of the categories; for the other things are predicated of substance, but this of matter. Wherefore, that which is ultimate essentially is neither quiddity, nor quantity, nor quality, nor any other such thing. Neither, therefore, are negations so; for these also will have a subsistence according to accident. In consequence of these things, no doubt, therefore, it happens with speculators that matter is regarded as substance.

This, however, is impossible; for both a capability of separation in its subsistence, and the subsisting as this particular thing, seem to inhere especially in substance. Wherefore, form, and that which is composed of both, would appear to be substance rather than matter. Indeed, then, as regards the substance which is composed of both (I mean composed of matter and form), the consideration of this must be omitted, for it is posterior and manifest; but somehow matter also is plain. But respecting the third substance must there be an inquiry made, for this is most perplexing. Now, certain substances of sensibles are acknowledged to exist; wherefore, in the case of these, let us, in the first place, 1029b institute an examination.

4. But since in the beginning of this book we have made a division in how many ways we define substance, and of these a certain one seems to be the essence of the very nature of a thing, we must make an inquiry respecting this, for advantageous is the transition to what is more known. For in this way is instruction imparted to all by means of advancing through those things that are less known to Nature to things that are more known; and this is something accomplished, as in practical things the having made from those things that are good to each, things that are good to each generally; so, from things that are more known to oneself, the having made things that are known to himself, to be known to Nature, as well as things that are known to individuals, and such as are first, and are often but little known, and often involve little or nothing of entity. Nevertheless, however, from things badly known, to be sure, yet known to oneself, must we endeavor to attain a knowledge of things generally known, making a transition, as has been stated, by the way of these very things.

And, in the first place, let us speak thereof some things logically, because the very nature of everything is that which is denominated as subsisting essentially or absolutely. For your essence does not consist in being in one that is musical, for not according to yourself are you musical; your essence, then, subsists according to yourself. For, truly, not everything that is essentially present to a thing is the very nature of that thing; for that is not the case with that which is so essentially present, as a white surface, since the being of a surface is not the same thing with the being of what is white. But, doubtless, neither is that which is composed of both, namely, the being of a white surface, the same as the essence of superficies. Should the question be asked why it is not, our reply is, because superficies is contained in the definition of white surface. In whatever definition, then, expressive of this, this will not be found inherent, this will be the reason of the essence or very nature of each thing. Wherefore, if the being of a white surface is the being of a smooth surface, the being white and smooth is one and the same thing.

But since, also, in accordance with the rest of the categories there are natures that are composite (for there is a certain subject to each as to quality and quantity, and the time when, and the place where, and motion), we must examine if there is a definition of the very nature or essence of each of them, and, also, whether the essence of a thing is inherent in these; as, for example, if in man the essence of white man is inherent. Now, let his name be garment, what then is the being of a garment? But, doubtless, neither does this belong to those things that are expressed absolutely; or, shall we say that a thing which is not essential is predicated in two ways, and that of this the one is from addition, but the other is not so? And in regard of this being added to another thing, it is denominated as that which is defined; for instance, if one defining the being white should assume the definition of white man, another thing is so denominated because something else is not added to it; for example, if a garment signifies a white man, but someone should define the garment as white, in this case a white man is, doubtless, something that is white, yet his essence or very nature does not consist in being white, but in being a garment. Is there, then, in short, in 1030a existence such a thing as the essence or very nature of entities or not? For whatsoever is the very nature of a thing is the essence of that thing. But when one thing is predicated of another, it is not this certain particular thing; as, for instance, a white man is not this certain particular thing, if the being this particular thing belong to substances only. Wherefore, the very nature of a thing appertains to those things the discourse respecting which is a definition. But not every discursus which signifies the same thing as the name is a definition (for, in this case, all discourses would be definitions), for the name will be the same with any discourse whatsoever. Wherefore, also, the term *Iliad* will be a definition; but if it may be one of some primary thing, a discourse is then a definition. And things of this kind are such as are spoken of not in respect of the predication of one thing of another.

The very nature of a thing will not, accordingly, be found in any of those things that are not the species of a genus, but in these only; for these seem to be predicated not according to participation and passion, nor as an accident: but, no doubt, there will be a discourse of each thing, and it will signify something of the other things, if it be a name; I mean, that this particular thing is inherent in this, or instead of the simple assertion is there one that is more accurate; but it will not be a definition, nor the essence or very nature of a thing.

Or also shall we say that definition, as well as the essence of a thing, is expressed in many ways? For also the inquiry what the nature of a thing is, in one way signifies substance, and the being this particular thing, but in another each of the categories, quantity, quality, and whatever things else there are of this sort. For as the inquiry what a thing is also belongs to all things, though not after a similar manner, but to one thing primarily, and to others in a consequent order, so also the nature of a thing inheres in the substance simply, but in other things in a sort of a way; for also as to the quality of a thing we could ask the question what it is: wherefore, likewise, quality belongs to those things to which the inquiry what they are appertains, but not simply considered; but just as in the case of nonentity certain speculators say that it is nonentity, logically speaking, not simply, but that is nonentity, so also is it with respect to quality. It is necessary, therefore, to examine also how one should speak of everything not, certainly, at any rate, more than how each thing subsists or is disposed.

Wherefore, now, also, since what is spoken is manifest, the very nature or essence of a thing will also, in like manner, be inherent primarily and simply in substance, and afterwards in other things; as in the inquiry what a thing is, the essence or very nature of that thing will not be inherent simply, but with the addition of quality or quantity will the essence be inherent. For it is requisite to speak of the existence of these entities either equivocally or with addition and ablation, as, also, that which is not the object of scientific knowledge is a thing that may be scientifically known; since this is correct, at least, neither to 1030b speak of these equivocally, nor in like manner, but just in such a way as that what is medicinal is predicated in reference to one and the same thing, without, however, being one and the same thing, and yet, indeed, is not equivocally predicated either; for no medicinal body is termed a work and an apparatus either equivocally or according to one, but in relation to one thing.

Therefore, in whatsoever way one chooses, indeed, to express these things makes no difference. This, however, is evident, that definition, primarily and absolutely considered, and that the essence or very nature of a thing, belong to substances. Notwithstanding, they belong to other things, also, in a similar manner, except not primarily. For there is no necessity, even though we should admit that a name has the same signification with a certain discourse, that a discourse about that which the name signifies should be a definition of this; but this will take place if the name may have the same signification with a discourse, at least a certain discourse. And this takes place if it be of one thing not by continuity, as the *Iliad,* or whatever things else are one by connection, but if it is as multifariously expressed as one thing is. Unity, however, is predicated in as many ways as entity; and entity signifies partly this particular thing, and partly quantity, and partly quality. Wherefore, also, of white man will there be a certain discourse and definition; and in another way will there be the same, both of that which is white and of substance.

5. This statement, however, involves a doubt—in case anyone denies definition to be a discourse subsisting from addition—of what the definition will be of those things that are not simple, but connected together; for from addition it is necessary to make them manifest. Now, I say, for instance, there is nose and hollowness, and flatness of nose—I mean, that which is called from

both of these in respect of this being inherent in that; and neither the hollowness nor the flatness of nose is, according to accident, at least, a passion of nose, but subsists eseentially; nor do they subsist as the white in Callias, or man, because Callias is white, to whom it is an accident to be man: but they subsist as the male in animal, and the equal in quantity, and in the same way as all those things that are said to be essentially inherent. But these are those in whatsoever is inherent either the definition or the name of which this is an affection, and which it is not possible to manifest separately, as it is possible to make manifest the white without man, not so, however, the female without animal. Wherefore, the very nature and definition of these are either of nothing, or, if there is a definition of these, it is in a manner otherwise from what we have declared.

And there is also another matter of doubt about these. For if, in truth, a flat-nose and a hollow-nose are the same, the same thing will be flat and the hollow; but if not, on account of its being impossible to use the word flat even without the thing of which it is an essential affection, and if flatness of nose will be a hollowness in the nose, the speaking of flat-nose either is a thing not possible, or the same thing will be said twice over; as thus, nose is hollow-nose; for the nose, that is, the flat-nose, will be a hollow-nose. Wherefore, the inherence in things of this sort of what is the essence or formal principle would be absurd; and if it were not absurd there would be a progression *ad infinitum*; for in a nose, a flat-nose, will there further be inherent something else that is essential. It is evident, therefore, that of substance only is there definition; for if it were also of the rest of the categories, it must needs be from addition, as in the definition of quality and unevenness; for it is not framed without number, nor is the definition of female framed without animal. Now, definitions formed from addition I call those in whatever the same things happen to be said twice, as in these.

And, if this be true, neither will there be definition of those things that are conjoined together as of an odd number: it escapes their notice, however, that not accurately are the definitions of the

1031a

settings expressed by them. But if there are definitions of these things also, doubtless in a different way do they subsist; or, as has been affirmed, definition must be spoken of as subsisting in many ways, and so with the essence, or the very nature of a thing, likewise. Wherefore, in one way there will not be a definition of any of these, nor will essence be inherent in any one of these, save in substances; and in another way they will be inherent. That, therefore, indeed, definition is a discursus or description of the very nature or essence of a thing, and that the essence or formal principle belongs either to substances only, or especially both primarily and simply, is manifest.

6. Let us now consider whether the essence or very nature of a thing, and each individual thing, are the same, or different? For this will be of advantage in reference to the inquiry concerning substance; for both each particular thing does not seem to be different from its own substance, and the essence, or very nature of each thing, is said to be the substance of that thing. Therefore in the case, no doubt, of things that are predicated according to accident, these would seem to be different, as that a white man is a thing different from the being of white man. For if they were the same, both the being of man, and the being of white man, would be the same; for man and white man, as they say, are the same thing. Wherefore, also, the being of a white man, and the being of man, would be the same. Or is there no necessity for whatever things that are according to accident to be the same, as those things that have an essential subsistence? For not, in like manner, do the extremes become the same. But, perhaps, at least, it would seem to happen that the extremes should become the same according to accident; as, for instance, the being of white, and the being of a musician; but this does not seem to be the case.

And as regards things that are predicated absolutely there always is a necessity that they be the same, as must take place if there are certain substances belonging to which there are not different substances, nor different antecedent natures, such as some affirm ideas to be. For if the actual good be a different

1031b thing from the being good, and animal from the being animal, and entity from the essence of entity, there will exist both different substances, and natures, and ideas, besides those mentioned; and those substances will be prior if there be in existence the essence of substance. And if they are, indeed, unconnected one with another, of such there will not be a scientific knowledge, and they will not be entities. Now, I mean by the phrase "unconnected," if neither in the actual good is inherent the being good, nor if the existence of good pertains to this; for the scientific knowledge of each thing subsists when we know the essence or very nature of each thing: and in the case of what is good, and of other things, the same takes place. Wherefore, if the being good be not good, neither will the being in entity constitute entity, nor that in unity be unity. In like manner, also, all or not one of the essences will have an existence. Wherefore, if neither it be so with the being in entity, neither will it be so with anything else. Further, in whatever is not inherent the being good is not good.

Accordingly, it is necessary that the good and the being of good—be one, also the fair and the being fair; in fact, whatsoever things are not predicated of another, but have an absolute subsistence, and are things which are primary. For, also, this is sufficient if it takes place, even though forms may have no existence; but rather, perhaps, if forms do subsist. But, at the same time, it is evident that also if ideas are such things as some say they are, the subject of them will not be substance; for it is necessary that these be substances, I admit: but it is not necessary that they be predicated of a subject, for in this they will be inherent by participation. And, doubtless, from these arguments it is evident that each particular itself, and the essence, not according to accident are one and the same thing, and that to have a scientific knowledge, at any rate, of anything is to know scientifically the very nature or essence of that thing. Wherefore, according to this exposition, it is requisite that both be a certain one thing.

But that a thing predicated according to accident, as the musical or white, should be the same as the very nature of a thing itself, on account of the twofold signification of that in

150

which it is an accident and the accident itself, this is not a true assertion; so that in a certain respect a thing itself is the same, and in a certain respect is not the same, with the very nature of that thing. For the being of man is not the same with that of a white man; but so far as the essence of man is passive to whiteness it is the same. Now, it would appear absurd, also, if any would impose the name on each thing of the essences; for there will be another essence besides also that: as besides the essence of horse there will be a different essence of horse. Although what hinders certain essences even from being now directly the same as the things of which they are the very natures, if the very nature of a thing be substance? But, truly, not only are they one, but also the definition of them is the same, as is also evident from the statements that have been 1032a made; for to be one and one are not according to accident. Further, if they be different they will go on in a progression *ad infinitum*; for the one will be the essence of being one, but the other the one itself. Wherefore, also, in the case of those will there be the same definition. That, therefore, in the case of the first existences, and of things predicated essentially, the being of each thing, and that very thing itself, are one and the same thing is evident.

As regards, however, the refutations of the sophists in reference to this position, it is palpable that they are decided by the same solution; for example, these sophists inquire whether Socrates and the being Socrates are the same? For there is no difference in the things either from which one would ask the question, or from which he should light upon an answer in his attempted solution of it. How, then, the essence or very nature is the same, and how it is not the same, with each particular thing, has been declared.

7. Now, of things that are being produced, some are produced by Nature, and others by Art, and others from Chance. All things, however, that are produced are produced by means of something, and from something, and become something. But I mean that

they become something according to each category; for they are generated either as quiddity, or quantity, or quality, or the place where. But generations—the physical or natural ones, I mean— are those, unquestionably, of which the generation is from Nature, and that from which they are generated is that which we denominate matter; but that by means of which they are generated belongs to some one of those things which have a subsistence by Nature; and that which is some particular thing is man or plant, or some one of the things of that sort which we affirm to be especially substances. Now, all things which are produced either by Nature or Art involve matter, for it is possible for each of them both to be and not to be; this capability, however, is the matter in each. And, in general, Nature is even that from which a thing proceeds, and that according to which entities are generated is Nature likewise: for that which is being produced has a nature; as, for example, a plant or animal, and that by means of which a thing is generated is Nature herself, which is predicated according to the species, and is of the same species; but this is inherent in another, for man begets man. In this way, therefore, are produced the things that are generated through Nature: and the rest of the generations are denominated productions or operations. All operations, however, are either from art, or from potentiality, or the understanding. But of these some are produced, also, from chance and from fortune in a similar way, as in the case of those things that are produced by Nature; for there also are produced some things that are the same both from seed and without seed. Respecting, indeed, these, then, we will subsequently institute an examination. From Art, however, are generated those things of whatsoever there is a form in the soul. But I mean by form the essence or very nature of each thing, 1032b and the first substance. For, also, of contraries in a certain manner is there the same form; for thus the substance of privation is the substance that is the one opposed, as health of disease; for by the absence of health is disease made apparent, and health constitutes the principle in the soul and in the science.

The salubrious, however, is produced when the physician reasons thus: since this is done for the sake of health, it is necessary, if this will be salubrious, that this particular condition should exist; for example, evenness, and, if this takes place, that the result be heat. And so he always reasons, until he conducts you to that which he himself can accomplish last. Accordingly, now the motion which begins from these is called the operation that tends towards becoming healthy. Wherefore, it happens that in a certain manner from health is generated health, and a house is constructed from a house; namely that which involves matter arises, or is generated, from that which does not involve a connection with matter: for the medicinal and the house-building arts are the form, the one of health, and the other of a house. Now, I mean by substance not involving any connection with matter, the essence or very nature or formal cause of a thing. Of generations, however, and of motions one is termed thought and another operation; that is termed conception or thought which arises from the first principle and the form, but that is operation which takes its rise from the thought or conception of what is ultimate. In like manner, also, is produced each of the rest of those things that are media; now, I say, for instance, if health is to be restored there must needs be a reduction to equality secured. What, then, is this reduction into a state of equality? It is this particular result. But this particular result will take place if heat shall have been promoted. And what is this? It is this particular effect. Now, this effect is inherent in capacity, but the former already lies in the power of the physician. Now, that which brings about the result, and whence the motion of restoring health derives its beginning, if it springs from art, such is the form that is in the soul; but if it arises from chance, it arises from that evidently which, for once, is the principle of bringing about the change to one that acts from art: as also, perhaps, in the case of restoring health, the first principle originates from the communication of heat; and this result it accomplishes by means of friction. Accordingly, heat is either a part of health (I mean, such heat as inheres in the body), or there follows it directly some such thing as is a part of health, or that is accomplished indirectly, that is, by means of many media. This last, however, is that which produces the result, and in this way is part of health, as stones are parts of a house, and something else a part of other things.

Wherefore, as it is said, it is impossible that there be a production of anything if nothing may preexist. That, certainly, therefore, a portion will exist necessarily is evident; for matter is that part, for this is inherent, and is itself produced. But then, as such, is it to be classed amongst those things that are contained in the definition. And in both ways we denominate the brazen circles what they are, speaking of both the matter that it is brass, and the form that it is such a figure, and this is the genus into which it is first posited. But a brazen circle involves matter in its definition.

1033a

But that from which, as from matter, some things are formed is styled, when it is so formed, not that from which they are formed, but is called something else that is of this; as, for example, a statue is called not a stone, but of stone or stony. And a man who is in a state of convalescence is not denominated that from which he recovers back his health; and a cause of this is the following, that that arises from privation and the subject which we call matter: as both a man and a person that is indisposed become healthy. Rather, however, is health said to arise from privation—as one in health from one that is indisposed—than from man. Wherefore, a sick person is not denominated as one that is sound in health; but this is affirmed of man, and a man who is in sound health. And in regard to those things of which the privation is obscure and nameless, as in the case of the brass, whatever be the figure, or in the bricks and timbers of a house, those things seem to arise from these: as, in the instance above adduced, one that is in health from a person that is indisposed. Wherefore, as neither that which is produced is called by the name of that from which it is formed, in the case of the instance above adduced, so neither in this instance is the statue called wood, but derivatively is classified as wooden, not wood, and as brazen, but not brass, and stony, but not stone; and a house also is spoken of as made of bricks, but not as bricks: since, if one carefully examines, he would not say absolutely that either is the statue produced from wood, or a house from bricks, on account of its being necessary that whatever is produced from anything should be changed from that from which it is produced, but should not continue as it was before. Therefore, on account of this, indeed, the thing is expressed in this manner.

8. Since, however, that which is produced is produced both by something (now, I mean that whence also originates the first principle of generation, that is, its efficient cause) and from something (but let this be not privation, but matter, for already has it been defined in what manner we have denominated this), also must there be that which is produced; and this is either a sphere or a circle, or whatever else of the other things that may chance to present itself; as neither the efficient cause produces the subject (I mean, the brass), so neither does it make the sphere, unless by accident, because a brazen sphere is a sphere; but it does not produce the sphere itself. For the production of a certain thing of this kind is the production of this particular thing from the entire subject. Now, I say, that to make the brass round is not to make the round or the sphere, but something different, such as this form in another thing. For, if the artist produces it, he would produce this from something else; for this 1033b would be the subject: as, for example, to make a brazen sphere; and this the artist makes in this manner because from this particular thing which is brass he forms this which is a sphere. If, therefore, also, he produces this very thing, it is evident that in like manner he will produce another; and the productions will go on in a process *ad infinitum.*

It is palpable, then, that neither form (or by whatever name we must needs term form, as it subsists in that which is cognizable to sense) is produced, nor is there a generation thereof, nor is this the essence or very nature of a thing; for this is that which is produced in another subject either from Art, or from Nature, or potentiality, and the efficient cause it is which produces the existence of a brazen sphere; for it produces it from brass and a sphere: for into this particular thing, which is the form, doth the efficient cause mold the brass, and this constitutes a brazen sphere. And if, in short, of the being or existence of sphere there exists a generation, it will be a something that is a generation from a certain thing: for it will be necessary that what is produced always be divisible, and that this should be this particular thing, and that should be something else: now, I mean that this should be matter, and that form. Therefore, if a sphere be a figure equal from the center to all points of its periphery, of this one part will be that in which that which produces will be inherent, and the other part that which resides in this part; but the whole is that which has been produced or generated: as, for instance, the brazen sphere. It is evident, therefore, from the statements that have been made, that what is denominated as form or as substance is not generated, but that the union which is said to take place according to this *is* generated, and that in everything which is being produced matter is inherent, and that one part is matter, but the other form.

Whether, then, is there any sphere besides these components, or is there a house besides the bricks; or shall we say that if this were the case neither would this particular thing ever have been produced, save that it signifies a particular thing of this sort? This, however, also, is not defined; but it produces and generates such a particular kind of thing from this particular thing, and, when it has been generated, it is this particular thing with such a quality. And the whole of this particular thing is Callias or Socrates, just as this is a brazen sphere, and man and animal are, in general, as the brazen sphere. It is evident, therefore, that the cause of forms (as some have been accustomed to denominate forms), if there are certain natures of this sort in existence besides singulars, in no wise is useful toward both generations and substances; nor would essential substances have a subsistence on account of these, at least. It is, accordingly, evident that in the case of some things, also, the generator is such as that which is being produced or generated, not, I admit, the actual thing itself, at least; not so numerically, but specifically, as may be observed to take place in natural phenomena; for man generates man, unless something abnormal or contrary to nature be produced, as when a horse begets a mule. And with these is it in like manner; for that which would be common to a horse and an ass, namely, the most proximate genus, would not have a name imposed upon it, but both, perhaps, would be as a mule. Wherefore, it is plain that it is in no wise necessary to provide a form as an 1034a exemplar or model (for in these, that is, in things sensible, especially, investigators from time to time have searched for them, for these same in an eminent degree are substances); but for the generator it sufficeth to have produced, and to be the cause of the subsistence of form in matter. And the entire now of such a form in these things, such as flesh and bones, is Callias and Socrates, and different, no doubt, is a thing on account of the matter thereof; for matter in each thing is different, but in form it is the same, for the form is indivisible.

9. Someone, however, may doubt, perhaps, why some things are produced by both art and from chance, as health, but other things are not produced in this way, as a house. Now, a cause of this is the following,—that the matter of these, which is the first principle of generation, consists in the accomplishing and the production of something of those things that are artificially formed, in which there is inherent a certain portion of the thing, which matter is partly of such a kind as is capable of being moved by itself, and partly is not so; and of this one part is it possible to move in this particular way, but the other it is not possible; for many things involve the capacity of being moved by themselves, but not in this way: for instance, to leap. As regards those things, therefore, of which the matter is of such a kind, as stones, it is impossible for them to be moved in this way, unless by something else,—yet in this way, assuredly,—and it is so with fire. On account of this some things will not be without that which is in possesion of art; whereas other things will be, for they will be

moved by those things which do not possess art, no doubt, but are themselves capable of being moved either by other things which do not possess art, or possess it partially. But it is evident, from the statements that have been made, that also all things, in a certain manner, are generated from things that are equivocal, as those that have a subsistence from Nature, or from an equivocal portion,—for example, a house from a house,—or by reason of intellect; for art is form, either from a part or from that which possesses a certain part, if it be not produced according to accident. For the cause of the production is an essential first portion.

For the heat (which is involved in motion) has generated heat in the body, and this is, unquestionably, health, or a part of health, or there follows it a certain part of health, or health itself. Wherefore, also, it is said to be a producer, because that produces health on which heat follows, and to which it is an accident. Wherefore, as in the syllogisms substance is the first principle of all things (for from the nature of a thing are syllogisms), so, also, in this instance, are generations. And, in like manner, also 1034b with these are those things that are by Nature constituted. For the seed produces as things that are constructed from art; for it involves form in capacity, and that from which the seed originates is, in a manner, equivocal; for it is not necessary to investigate all things in this way, as man is from man; for woman also is from man: wherefore, mule does not originate from mule, save unless there be an injury from mutilation. Thus as many things, however, as are being produced from chance— just as in that instance—are those the matter of which is capable, also, of being moved by itself with that motion which the seed effects; but those things the matter of which does not possess this capability, it is impossible can be produced in any other way except from themselves by generation.

Not only, however, does this reasoning concerning substance manifest the non-production of form, but, in like manner, concerning all that are primary natures there is involved the same reasoning in common, as of quantity, quality, and the rest of the categories. For as the brazen sphere is what is produced, but not the sphere or the brass, and as it is so in the case of brass, if it is what is produced (for always it is necessary that there preexist matter and form), so, also, must it be in the case of "the what anything is," or quiddity, and in the case of quality, and quantity, and similarly of the rest of the categories; for there quality is not produced, but such a sort or quality of wood, neither quantity, but such a measure or quantity of wood, or an animal of such a kind. But from these statements may we acquire what is a peculiarity of substance, namely, that there is a necessity that there should always preexist a different substance (I mean, one subsisting in a state of actuality), which produces: as, for instance, an animal must preexist if an animal is produced; but this is not necessarily the case with quality or quantity, unless in potentiality merely.

10. But since definition is a sentence or explanation, and every sentence or explanation has parts, and as a sentence is similarly related to the thing itself, as the part of the sentence to the part of the thing itself, the doubt now suggests itself whether it is necessary that the definition of the parts should be inherent in the definition of the whole, or not? In the case of some things they appear to be as things that are inherent; but in the case of others it is not so. For thus the definition of a circle does not involve that of its segments; but the definition of a syllable involves that of the letters of speech: notwithstanding that the circle, also, is divided into segments, as, likewise, is the syllable into letters or elements of speech. But, further, if the parts are prior to the whole, and if the acute be a part of the right angle, and the finger of an animal, the acute would be a thing that is prior to a right angle, and the finger to man.

Now, these do not seem to be prior; for in the definition they are denominated from them, and also are they prior in their being capable of subsistence without one another: or shall we say that part is denominated in many ways, of which one mode is the measurement according to quantity? Let, however, the mode of the subsistence of this be omitted; but into these things

of which substance is composed, as from parts, we must institute
an investigation. If, therefore, the one be matter, but the other
form, and the third that which is composed of these, and if
substance be both matter and form, and that which consists from
these, it is the case that also matter is termed in one respect a part
of something, but it is the case that such is not so in another
respect; but this is true as regards those things of which the
definition of form consists: as, for instance, of hollowness, indeed,
the flesh is not a portion, for this is matter from which hollowness
is produced; but it is a certain portion of flatness of nose, and of
the entire statue, no doubt, is the brass a part, but of that which is
denominated as the form of the statue it is not so; for by form
must we predicate, and so far forth as everything involves form:
never, however, is the material to be essentially predicated.

Wherefore, the definition of a circle does not involve that of
its segments; but that of a syllable does involve the definition of
the elements of speech, for the elements of the definition are
parts of form, and are not the matter thereof: but the segments
of a circle thus are parts—as matter—in which the circle is
ingenerated; they are, I admit, nearer to form than the brass
when roundness is ingenerated in the brass. But it will be the
case that neither all the elements of the syllable will be contained
in the definition of syllable; as, for instance, these waxen letters,
or those which are in the air, for now, also, are these a part of the
syllable as sensible matter. For, also, it does not follow that
because a line if divided into halves is corrupted, or a man when
divided into bones, and nerves, and flesh, that therefrom they
are in such a manner, on this account, composed as though they
were parts of the substance, but that they are composed from
them as from matter. And they are parts of the entire, so to be
sure; but they are not any longer parts of form, and of that about
which the definition is concerned only. Wherefore, neither are
they found in definitions. Of some definitions, indeed, therefore,
will there be inherent the definition of parts of this kind, and of
others it is necessary that it not be inherent, unless such be the

definition of that which is taken together; for, on this account, from these as from first principles do some things consist, into which they are corrupted, and others do not consist from these. Whatever things, indeed, therefore, are assumed together are form and matter; as a flat nose or a brazen circle: those are corrupted into these, and matter constitutes a portion of them; but as many things as are not assumed along with matter, but involve no connection with matter, as the definitions of form merely, these, however, are not corrupted either entirely, or by no means in this way, at least. Wherefore, things that fall not under these are the first principles and parts of those, but of the form are these neither parts nor first principles. And, on this account, a statue of clay is corrupted into clay, and a sphere of brass into brass, and Callias into flesh and bones; and, further, a circle is corrupted into its segments, for there is something which is assumed along with matter; for equivocally is the circle predicated, both that which is predicated simply, and those that are singulars on account of there not being a proper name for singulars. 1035b

Therefore, indeed, also, has the truth now been declared, yet, nevertheless, let us express ourselves more clearly on resuming the subject. As many things, therefore, as are parts of the definition, and into which the definition is divided, these are prior, either all or some of them. But the definition of a right angle is not divided into the definition of an acute; but that of an acute angle is divided into the definition of a right angle: for a person who defines an acute employs a right angle, for the acute is less than the right. In like manner, also, is it the case with a circle and semicircle, for the semicircle is defined by the circle, and the finger by the whole, for such a part of a man is a finger. Wherefore, whatsoever parts involve such a relation as matter, and into which, as into matter, the whole is divided, are things subsequent; but as many as belong to the relation of definition and of substance, which subsists according to the definition, are things that are prior, either all or some of them.

Now, since the soul of animals (for this is the substance of that which is animated) constitutes the substance according to definition, and their form and the very nature or essence of such a body, if, at least, the part of each thing be properly defined, it will not be properly defined without mention of its appropriate function; and this, in the present case, will not subsist without sense. Wherefore, the parts of this, that is, of soul are prior, either all or some of them, to the entire animal, and, doubtless, similarly is it with an individual thing. But the body and its parts are subsequent to this substance; and the substance is not divided into these as into matter, but the entire is. To the entire, therefore, these are, in a manner, prior, but, in a manner, are not prior; for neither are they capable of subsisting in a state of separation; for neither does finger belong to an animal when disposed in every way, but equivocally so termed is a dead finger. Now, some things perish along with the whole, and these are principal parts wherein, as first, are inherent the definition and the substance: as, for instance, the heart or brain, if such be the principal part, for it makes no difference which of these is of such a kind. But man and horse, and those that are so, are found in singulars. And an universal substance does not subsist; but there will be a certain entirety composed from this reason or formal principle, and this matter as an universal: but as regards a singular consisting from ultimate matter, this is Socrates, in the present instance, and the case is similar with other things. Therefore, also, is definition a portion both of the form (but by form I mean the essence or very nature of a thing) and of the universal that is composed from form and matter itself.

But the parts of definition are only the parts of form; but a definition is of that which is universal: for the being of a circle 1036a and a circle, and the being of a soul and a soul, are the same thing. And of that which is entire now, as of this circle,—of any of the singulars, either sensible or intelligible,—(now, I mean by the intelligible, for example, the mathematical, but by the sensible such as are made of brass and wood), of these, however, I say there is no definition, save that they are known by the intervention of the intellect or sense. And when they are removed away from actuality it is not evident whether they exist at all or do not exist, yet they are always expressed and made known by universal definition. But the matter is unknown in itself. Now, matter is partly sensible and partly intelligible; that which is sensible is such as brass and wood, and such as is movable; but intelligible matter is that which is inherent in things that are sensible: but not so far forth as they are sensible as mathematical entities. How, indeed, therefore, this is so respecting the whole and part, and respecting the prior and subsequent, has been declared.

But as to whether a right angle, and a circle, and an animal, are prior to the parts into which they are divided, and of which they are composed, my reply to this question, when anyone puts it, must necessarily be, that not simply or absolutely are the parts predicated. For if, also, soul is an animal, or that which is animated, every animal is each animal's own soul; and if the circle constitute the being of a circle, and the right angle, the being of the right angle, and the substance, also, the substance of the right angle, what particular thing, and belonging to what, as a substance, each of these is, we must state on a subsequent occasion; for instance, of those parts that are contained in the definition, and of a certain right angle; for both the angle of brass which subsists in conjunction with matter is a right angle, and that, also, contained within lines—I mean, singular lines. But a right angle that involves no connection with matter is subsequent to those parts that are contained in the definition, and prior to those parts that are contained in the singular. But this is not to be affirmed of part absolutely. And if soul be something that is different, and does not constitute an animal, in this case must we both assert some parts to be prior, and other parts we must assert to be not prior, just as has been declared.

11. But it is a matter of doubt, naturally, what is the quality of the parts of form, and what sort the parts are not, but what kind the parts are, which belong to a composite nature. Although, in case this is not evident, it is not possible to define each thing. For of

that which is universal and of form is there the definition; as to which, therefore, of the parts are related as matter, and which are not so, if these be not manifest, neither will be manifest the definition of the thing. As many things, indeed, therefore, as appear to be ingenerated in the form of different things, as a 1036b circle in brass, and stone, and wood, these, then, seem to be manifest, because neither the brass nor the stone is anything of the substance of the circle consequent upon its separation from them. But as many things as are not perceived to be separated there is no hindrance to their being similarly disposed with these, as if all circles were seen composed of brass; for, nevertheless, would the brass be in no wise a part of form, but it would be difficult in thought to abstract this: as, for instance, the form of man always appears in flesh and bones, and in such like parts— are these, then, also, parts of form, and of the definition, or are they not so, but matter merely? But, on account of its not being ingenerated in another also, we find it impossible to separate it. And, since this seems to be admissible,—yet as to the time when, this is obscure,—certain philosophers now are involved in doubt, in the case both of a circle and in the case of a triangle, as if it were not fitting for lines, and that which is contained with lines, also to be defined by continuity; but that all should be predicated in a similar manner with the flesh or bones of a man, and the brass and stone of a statue, and they refer all things to numbers; and the definition of a line, they say, is that of the dyad. Of those, likewise, who assert the existence of ideas, some make the actual line the dyad, but others, the form of the line; for, in regard of some things, they say that form, and that of which the form is compounded, are the same: as, for instance, a dyad and the form of the dyad. But in the case of a line it is not so.

There happens, therefore, to be one form of many things of which the species appears to be different, which consequence also ensued in their system unto the Pythagoreans; and it is possible, as a result from this position, to make one actual form of all things, and that other things be not forms at all, although on this supposition will all things be one. That, therefore, those things involve a certain doubt (I mean, those questions that have been started respecting definitions, and from what cause is it that they are thus attended with difficulty), this has been declared.

Wherefore, both to reduce all things in this way, and to abstract matter, would be superfluous; for in the case of some things, perhaps, this is in this, or these things are so disposed. And the comparison that is made in the case of an animal, which the junior Socrates was accustomed to employ, is not a good one, for it forcibly withdraws one away from the truth, and makes us suppose as possible that man should subsist without parts, as a circle without brass. But this latter instance is not similar to the former, for animal, perhaps, is something that is cognizant by sense, and which cannot be defined without motion; wherefore, neither can it be defined without the parts somehow disposed. For not altogether is the hand a part of a man, but that which is able to accomplish the proper function of a hand; wherefore, when it is animated it is a part, but when it is not animated it is not a part. Respecting, however, mathematical entities, why are not definitions parts of the definitions of such? For example, why are not semicircles parts of the definition of a circle? For these are not sensibles; or, shall we say that this makes no difference, 1037a for they will be the matter of certain things, and of those that are not sensible, and of everything that is not the very nature or essence of a thing? These, then, will not be the parts of universal circle, but of singulars, as has been stated previously, for matter is partly sensible and partly intelligible. And it is evident, also, that the soul is the first substance, and that body is matter, but man or animal is the compound of both as universal. If the soul, however, be the form of such, Socrates and Coriscus are twofold; for some regard Socrates as soul, but others as an entirety: but if they be considered as this soul regarded simply, this body also will involve the relation of the universal and of the singular.

Whether, however, beside the matter of such sort of substances, there is any other substance, and whether it is necessary to search for any different substance of these—as, for instance, numbers, or some such thing—must afterwards be examined into. For, on account of this, let us also endeavor to frame some distinctions respecting sensible substances, since, in a certain manner, the investigation regarding sensible substance is a work of the physical and second philosophy; for not only is it necessary for the natural philosopher to afford information respecting matter, but also respecting that substance which subsists according to the definition, even still more. In the case, however, of definitions, in what manner are those parts which are assumed in the definition, and why definition is one reason,—for it is evident that the thing is one, and that the thing is in a certain way one definite particular, which involves parts,—this must subsequently be inquired into.

What, therefore, is the essence of a thing, and how this subsists in itself, that is, absolutely, has been declared respecting everything universally, and why the definition of the essence of some things possesses the parts of that which is defined; but, in other things, why this is not the case, and why that in the definition, indeed, of substance the parts so constituted as matter are not inherent, this, likewise, has been declared. For they are not parts of that substance, but of the entire together; and of this there is at least, in a manner, a definition, and there is not so. For as involving a connection with matter there is not a definition (for it is a thing that is indefinite), but according to the first substance there is; as, for instance, the definition of man is the definition of his soul. For the substance constitutes form, that is, such as is indwelling, from which and from matter the entire substance is denominated; as, for example, hollowness or concavity: for from this and nose a flat nose, and flatness, are composed, for therein twice will the nose be inherent. In the substance, however, in its entirety, as a flat nose, or Callias, is matter also inherent. And that the essence or very nature of a

1037b thing, and a singular in the case of some things, are the same— as in the case of primary substances; for instance, a curvature, and the essence of a curvature, if it is primary—that these, I mean, are the same, this has been declared. Now, I mean by primary, or first, that which is not expressed in respect of one thing being inherent in another, and in a subject as matter. But as many things as subsist as matter, or as things involving a connection with matter, these are not the same, except that they are one according to accident, as Socrates and the musical, for these are the same according to accident.

12. Let us now, however, first discuss the subject so far forth as there has been no statement made concerning definition in the Analytics; for the doubt that has been expressed in those inquiries is of advantage to our present dissertations respecting substance. Now, this doubt which I allude to is as follows: "Why, pray, a thing that is capable of definition, of which the reason, we say, is a definition, is one thing, as the definition of man is a two-footed animal: for let this stand as a definition of him." Now, why is this one thing, but not many, animal and two-footed? For also, in the case of man and white, they are many things when they are not inherent, either in the other; but when the one is inherent in the other, and when the subject—viz. man—undergoes any passive condition, they are one, for then a white man becomes and is one thing. Here, however, either does not partake of the other, for genus does not appear to participate in the differences; for in such a case would the same thing at the same time participate in contraries, for differences are contraries wherein the genus differs. And if the genus does participate in the differences, the same reasoning holds good, even though the differences be many in number; for instance, having the capability of walking, biped, without wings. For why are these things one, but not many? For they are not one because they are inherent, for so, indeed, will there be one of all. But it is requisite that, at any rate, as many things as are contained in definition should be one, for definition in a certain single principle or reason, and belongs to substance. Wherefore, of one particular thing this must needs be a definition, for also substance signifies one certain particular thing, as we say.

And it is necessary, first, to examine respecting those definitions which subsist according to divisions. For there is nothing else involved in definition unless the genus that is denominated first, and the differences, but the other things are genera, both that which is first, and the differences comprehended along with this; as, for instance, the first genus is animal, and that next in order to this is two-footed animal; and, again, two-footed animal without wings; and, in like manner, will it be the case if the definition be expressed by means of many distinctive qualities. In general, however, there is no difference whether it subsists by many such, or by few, or by two of them: yet if a thing be defined by two distinctive qualities, the one will be difference, and the other genus, as, for instance, of two-footed animal, animal is the genus, and the other, two-footed, is the difference. If, therefore, genus, simply considered, is not anything different from the species, as it were, of that genus, or if, indeed, it is, yet it is as matter,—for voice is genus and matter, but the differences produce the forms and elements out of this,—it is evident, in such a case, that a definition is a sentence or discursus composed from differences. But, therefore, is it necessary, likewise, that the difference of the difference should, at least, be divided; as, for example, a difference belonging to animal, such as having the support of feet: again, it is requisite to know the difference of the animal that possesses the differential quality of being supported on feet, as far forth as it is such—I mean, such as has the support of feet. Wherefore, it is not proper to say that of an animal which has the support of feet, one sort we find with wings and another without them, if one is to express himself correctly; but on account of the impossibility of making a proper division of the distinctive qualities will one do this: but it is correct to say so if one kind has cloven, and another has feet that are not cloven; for these are the differences of foot, for a cloven foot is a certain quality of foot. And so always does one desire to go on making divisions of distinctive qualities, until we come to things that do not involve any difference. But then will there be as many species of foot as there are differences, and the number of animals with feet supporting them will be equal to the differences.

Now, if these things are so, it is evident that the ultimate difference will be the substance of the thing, and the definition of it, if it is not necessary to say oftentimes the same things in the case of definitions, for it would be superfluous. But this, at least, happens sometimes; for when one calls an animal that has feet supporting it a biped, he has said no more than this, viz., that an animal having the support of feet has two feet. And if he makes a division of this by an appropriate difference, he will say the same thing frequently, and in an equal number of times with the differences. If, indeed, therefore, a difference of a difference may be produced, one which is the ultimate difference will constitute form and substance; if, however, the division be made according to accident, as if one should make a division, in the case of the classes of that which has the support of feet, of one into white, and another into black, so many differences or distinctive qualities will there be as there may be divisions of them. Wherefore, it is evident that definition is a sentence that is composed from the things that are differences, and from the last of these that is drawn up in accordance with a correct classification, at least. And this would be plain, if one should transpose the arrangement of the term of definitions of this kind; as, for example, that of a man, saying,—instead of the ordinary definition,— animal biped having the support of feet; for superfluous would be the distinctive quality of having the support of feet, on the supposition of the thing defined being denominated a biped. An arrangement of terms, however, does not exist in substance; for how is it necessary to understand the one as subsequent, but the other as prior? Respecting, then, definitions that subsist according to divisions of the distinctive qualities of the things defined what sort they are, let thus much, in the first instance, be affirmed.

13. But since our present investigation is concerning substance, 1038b let us once more take a review of the matter. Now, substance is said to subsist as the subject and the essence or very nature of a thing, and that which is composed from these is termed substance, and that which is universal. Respecting, indeed, then, two of

them have we declared our opinions already; for also we have done so in the case of the essence or very nature of a thing, and the subject, observing that in two ways it is a subject, either as being this certain particular thing, as an animal is the subject of its passive states, or it is as matter in a condition of actuality. But to some speculators doth the universal in an eminent degree appear to be a cause, and the universal appears to be a first principle also. Wherefore, likewise, as regards this point must we institute an inquiry.

For it seems to be a thing impossible that substance should be anything whatsoever of those things that are denominated universal, for primary substance, to be sure, in everything is that which does not belong to another thing; that which is universal, however, is common, for that is said to be universal which by nature is fitted to be inherent in many things: of what, then, will this be a substance? For either it will be a substance of all things or of nothing; but of all things it is not even possible that it should be a substance: and if it be the substance of one thing, other things also will be this; for those things of which the substance is one, and the essence or very nature one, will themselves likewise be one. Further, is that denominated substance which is not predicated of a subject; the universal, however, is invariably predicated of a certain subject. But then shall we say that it is not possible, certainly, that it should subsist in such a way as the essence or very nature of a thing, but that it be inherent in this: for example, animal in man and horse. Therefore, is it evident that there will be a certain definition of it. But there is no difference either if there is not a definition of all those things that are contained in the substance; for this, nevertheless, will be a substance of something, as man is the substance of man, wherein man is inherent. Wherefore, the same consequence will again ensue, for substance will be substance of man: as, for instance, animal is substance in that species in which it is inherent as a peculiar property.

And, further, the thing would be both impossible and absurd, that this particular thing and substance, if they are composed from certain things, should not consist of substances, or of anything of the sort, but from quality. For that which is not substance and quality will be prior both to substance and this particular thing; an assertion that is impossible: for neither in definition, nor in time, nor in generation, is it possible, likewise, that the passive properties of a thing should be prior to the substance of it, for they will involve a subsistence separable from it. Moreover, in Socrates, who is a substance, will substance be inherent; wherefore, will Socrates be a substance in two substances. And in general the result following ensues—if man is substance, and as many things as are thus expressed—that one of those things contained in definition is substance of anything, and that it has not a subsistence separable from them, nor does it subsist in another: now, I mean, for example, that there is not any animal besides those certain particular ones, or anything else of those things that are contained in the definitions. Now, from these considerations, also, it is evident to persons examining into the subject, that nothing of those things that have an universal subsistence is substance, and that nothing of those things that are predicated in common signifies this certain particular thing, but a thing of such a quality.

And if this be not admitted, any other consequences also will ensue, and, amongst the rest, the consequence that there will be a third man. Further, also, it is evident that the case stands thus, 1039a from the following remark, for it is impossible that substance should be compounded from substances which are inherent in such a manner as to subsist in actuality; for two things thus would subsist in actuality, yet they never would be one thing in actuality. But if they may be two things in potentiality, they will be one; as the twofold is compounded of two halves, at least, in potentiality, for actuality in the case of other separates them. Wherefore, if the substance be one thing, it will not be compounded from substances that are inherent, and subsisting according to that mode which Democritus mentions correctly; for it is impossible, he says, that from two atoms should be generated one, or two from one, for he makes magnitudes that are indivisible to be substances. Therefore, is it is plain that also in the case of number this will take place in a similar manner, if number be a composition of monads, as is said by some speculators, for either the dyad is not one, or it is not the monad that is involved in this actuality.

But the result which ensues contains a matter of doubt; for if neither from the universals is it possible that any substance be compounded, on account of an animal's signifying a thing of such a sort, but not this certain particular thing, neither is it possible that there subsists any substance from substances, in actuality—I mean, that no composite nature can thus subsist; now, on such a supposition, every substance would be a thing that is uncompounded. Wherefore, neither would there be a definition of any substance. But, assuredly, it seems, at least, to all speculators, and has been laid down originally, that definition is conversant about substance, either solely or principally: but now the conclusion drawn is this, that neither is there definition of this, that is, of substance, nor will there be a definition of any one thing in such a case; or, shall we say that in a certain manner there will be, and in a certain manner there will not be, a definition of substance? What, however, that is which is affirmed will be more manifest from the sequel.

14. Now, from these very circumstances is evident the result which ensues, to those both who say that ideas are as well substances as separable substances, and who at the same time constitute form out of the genus and the differences. For if forms and animal exist in man and in horse, there is, undoubtedly, one and the same, or a different animal in number, for by definition it is evident that there is one and the same; for the same definition does he assign who says that they are inherent in each. If, therefore, there is some man—an actual thing subsisting essentially—that is this certain particular individual thing, and one which has a separate subsistence, it is necessary, also, that those things from which they are composed, as for example, animal and biped, should signify this certain particular individual thing, and should involve a separable subsistence, and be substances. Wherefore,

also, this will be the case with animal. If, therefore, animal will be the same and one thing in horse and man, as yourself in yourself, how will it be one in things that subsist separately, and why will not this animal subsist, likewise, apart from itself? If, in the 1039b next place, it will participate in the properties of two-footed and many-footed, something which is impossible ensues; for contraries, at the same time, will be inherent in this, which is one thing, and this certain particular thing. And if this is not the case, what is the mode of subsistence when one affirms that an animal is two-footed, or adapted for walking? Perchance, however, they are composites, and are in contact with one another, or have been mingled together. But all such suppositions as to the mode of subsistence in this case are absurd. Shall we say, however, that in each thing there subsists something that is different? Therefore, to speak the word, those things will be infinite of which the substance is animal; for not according to accident is man from animal: moreover, many things will animal itself be, for animal which is contained in each individual is substance, for it is not yet predicated of anything else. And if this not be admitted, from that will man subsist, and that will be a genus of man. And, further, all things from which man consists will be ideas; therefore, idea will not be an idea of one thing, but a substance of another, for this is impossible; for, in such a case, each of those things that are contained in animals will be an animal itself. Further, will it subsist from this certain particular thing? And how will it subsist from this actual animal? Or how is it possible that animal should subsist—which is substance—as this very thing beside animal itself?

Further, also, in the case of sensibles, both these consequences ensue, and consequences still more absurd than these; if, therefore, it is possible that this can be the case, it is evident that there is not an idea of them after such a mode as some would affirm.

15. But since both entirety and the formal cause are a different substance,—now, I say that the former is substance in this way as the formal cause that is comprehended along with matter, and

that the latter is the formal cause in general—in regard of as many things, then, as are so denominated, of these, truly, is there corruption, for of these also is there generation; with form, however, there is not a disruption of parts in such a way as for dissolution to ensue, for neither exists there generation in this case; for the being of a house is not generated, but the being of this particular house: but forms subsist without any connection with generation and corruption, and do not subsist in a state of dependence upon either; for it has been demonstrated that no one generates or produces these. And on this account, also, of sensible substances—I mean, such as are singulars—there is neither definition nor demonstration, because they involve matter the nature of which is such as to admit of the possibility both of being and not being; wherefore, all the singulars of such are things subject to decay or corruption. If, therefore, also, demonstration be of those things that are necessary, as well as that which is a scientific definition, and if it does not admit of being the case, as neither with scientific knowledge that at one time it should be scientific knowledge, and at another time should be ignorance (but a thing of this kind is opinion), so neither is it to be admitted that demonstration nor definition should subsist after this mode; but such is an opinion, in regard of that which admits of being disposed otherwise. It is evident, therefore, that 1040a there would not be either definition or demonstration of those things that may subsist differently; for, also, things that are subject to corruption or decay are obscure to those even that are in possession of scientific knowledge, when they pass away from under the notice of sense; and though the same reasons or principles be preserved in the soul, still will there not further exist thereof either definition or demonstration. Wherefore, as regards things relating to definition, when one defines any of the singulars it is right that he should not be ignorant that always is it possible to overturn this definition, for a thing of this sort does not admit of definition.

Neither, therefore, is it possible for any idea to be defined; for the idea ranks amongst singulars, as they say, and has, likewise, a separable subsistence. And it is necessary, also, that definition consist from names; but the person who is framing the definition will not create a name or nominative term, for it will be a thing unknown. The things, however, that are posited or acknowledged are common to all. It is necessary, then, that these also subsist in other things; for instance, even just as if one should define yourself, he would say that you are an animal which is attenuated or white, or something else that will be inherent also in another. If anyone, however, would say that there is no hindrance of all things being separately inherent in many, but that all collectively belong to this alone, we must, in the first place, say that also they would belong to both; namely, animal biped to animal and biped. And this must needs ensue, likewise, in the case of things that are everlasting; since, at any rate, they are prior existences, and are parts of that which is a composite. But, assuredly, also, are they separable, if the thing—man—be separable; for either nothing will be separable, or both will be so. If, indeed, then, nothing may possess the capacity of a separate subsistence, there will not exist genus besides species; but if both are separable, there will exist the difference likewise. In the next place, because they are prior existences in respect of being, these, also, on the contrary, will not be exposed to decay. And then, if ideas spring from ideas (for more uncompounded are those things from which other composites arise), it will be necessary that those things from which the idea consists should be predicated, further, of many; for instance, take the case of animal and biped. But if this be not admitted, how shall a knowledge of these be attained? For there will be a certain idea which it will be impossible to predicate in the case of more things than one. This does not, however, seem to be the case; but every idea appears to be participable.

As, therefore, it has been declared, it is overlooked by these persons that it is impossible to frame any definitions or distinctions in the case of things that are eternal, and eminently in the case of many things as are single; for instance, the sun and moon: for not only do persons err in the addition of things of this sort, in the event of which being taken away still the sun will continue as that body which revolves around the earth, or which is hid by night. For if the sun were to stand still in his orbit, or were to become apparent by night, in such a case no longer will he be the sun; but the thing would be absurd if he were not, for the sun signifies a certain substance. Further, such persons take for granted whatsoever points admit of being affirmed of another thing, just as if something else should become a thing of this sort, it is evident that it will be the sun. The definition, then, is

1040b common; but the sun was classed amongst singulars in such a way as Cleon or Socrates, whereas, why does no one of these bring forward a definition of idea? For it would become manifest, to those who would attempt to prove the existence of such, that what is now stated is true.

16. It is evident, also, that, likewise, the majority of those things which seem substances are capacities and parts of animals, for none of these involves a separate subsistence; but when they may be separated, then, also, are they all of them as matter—I mean, such as both earth, and fire, and air; for one of these is one thing, but each, as it were, a heap of immatured things before they be digested, and some one thing produced from their bring blended together. But particularly would one suppose the parts of animated beings, and those of the soul, to be both of them contiguous to an existence in this manner, as well in actuality as also in capacity, in respect of having the first principles of motion from something in their joints or flexures. Wherefore, some animals continue to retain life after being divided: but nevertheless, will all of them subsist in capacity when they may be one thing, and that which is continuous by nature, but not by force, or by connascence, that is, growth in conjunction with something else; for a thing of this kind is mutilation.

Since, however, unity is denominated as also entity is, and since the substance of unity is single, and those things of which there is one substance in number are one in number, it is evident that neither unity nor entity can possibly be the substance of things, as neither can the being of an element of first principle be the substance of things. But we are actually engaged in the inquiry, what, therefore, the first principle is, in order to conduct our investigation to that which is more known. The substance, then, indeed, of these is rather entity and unity, than both the first principle, and the element, and the cause; but by no means are these substances either, if there be not anything else which is in common with substance; for in nothing is the substance inherent but in itself, and in that which is in possession of itself, of which it is the substance. Further, unity would not subsist in many places at the same time; that which is common, however, does subsist in many places at the same time: wherefore, it is evident that nothing of those things that are universals can possess a subsistence separate from singulars.

But they who affirm the existence of forms, speak partly correct in assigning them a separable subsistence, if they be substances, but speak partly incorrect, because they assert unity to be a form in the case of many things. And the cause of this position with those Platonists is the following: that they have no rational account to render as to what are substances of this kind—I mean, such as are incorruptible, and have a subsistence independent of singulars and sensibles; therefore do they constitute them as the same in the species with things that are corruptible (for we know these), namely, ideal man and ideal horse, adding to sensibles the thing signified by the term ideal; although, indeed, if we had not beheld the stars, this would be no hindrance, I presume, to the existence of eternal substances, in addition to those which we had already attained a knowledge of. Wherefore, also, though even now we may not have it in our power to see what eternal substances are, yet, perhaps, it will be necessary that there be some eternal 1041a substances in existence, at any rate. That, indeed, therefore, neither any of those reputed universals is substance, nor that there is any substance composed of substances, is evident.

17. But what and what sort of a thing we ought to define substance let us again declare, just as if having made another commencement; for, perhaps, from these statements will be evident the

circumstances also concerning that substance which is separated from sensible substances. Since, therefore, substance is a certain first principle and cause, from this starting point must we pass onwards in our investigation.

But the inquiry why a thing subsists is invariably carried on in this way; namely, why one thing is inherent in a certain other; for the investigation why a musical man is a musical man, indeed, is to engage in the inquiry that has been mentioned, namely, why, or on what account a man is musical? Or it is to engage in the inquiry of something else. Therefore, in sooth, the investigation why this thing is the thing which it is, is no investigation at all; for it is necessary that the wherefore, and the existence of a thing, should inhere as manifest entities. Now, I say, for instance, the moon undergoes an eclipse: and of the inquiry why a thing is that thing which it is, there is one principle and one cause in the case of all things, as on what account a man is a man, or a musician a musician, except someone say that each thing is indivisible in regard to itself; but this would be to constitute unity: but this is both common in the case of all things, and is a thing that is concise. One, however, might inquire why man is that kind of an animal that he is. This, then, is evident, that such a one does not investigate why he who is a man is a man. Accordingly, he engages in the inquiry why a certain thing subsists, as what is common in the case of something; but that it does so subsist ought to be evident; for, if it be not thus, he inquires after nothing: as, to take an instance, why does it thunder? Why, because sound is produced in the clouds: for so one thing as the cause of another is that which is under investigation. And on what account do these things, as bricks and stones, constitute a house; it is evident, then, that he investigates the cause; but this is the essence or very nature of a thing (that is, if one is to express himself logically), which, in the case of some things, is that for the sake of which a thing subsists, that is, the final cause; as, perhaps, in the case of a house or a bed: but in the case of other things it is something that has imparted motion in the first instance; for this also is a cause. But a cause of this kind is such a cause as is sought for in the case of a thing that is being produced and destroyed; but the other cause also is sought for in the case of a thing already in existence. The subject of investigation, however, is in an eminent degree latent—I mean, such a one as is involved in the things that are mutually not predicated of one another; as, for instance, in the inquiry what man is, on 1041b account of its being asserted that he is simply so and so; but not from any definition being framed to the effect that he is this or that. It is requisite, however, if they conduct the inquiry correctly, to investigate such; but if not, it will be the case that nothing will be under investigation, and something under investigation in common. But since it is requisite to have in possession the being of a thing, and that it should subsist, it is evident that the inquiry is about matter, why it subsists; as, for instance, these particulars constitute a house—why? Because these subsist as that which is the being of a house.

Thus, too, is it in the inquiry why man is this particular thing, or why this body is in possession of this particular quality, the like inquiry is made. Wherefore, the cause of the matter is under investigation: but this is the form by which anything subsists, and this is substance. It is evident, therefore, that, in the case of simple substances, there is not any investigation in existence, nor any disciplinary teaching; but there is a different mode of investigation of things of this sort. Since, however, that which is compounded of something, and compounded in such a way as that the whole is one thing, but not as a heap, but as a syllable, yet a syllable is not the elements of speech, nor the same thing with the letters B and A; nor is flesh the same with fire and earth: for when a dissolution of these takes place, flesh and syllable no longer exist, as in the instance of the flesh and the syllable; but the elements subsist, that is, the fire and earth continue to subsist. The syllable in this case is something besides not only the elements of speech, namely, the vowel and the mute, but also something else; and the flesh not only is fire and earth, or the warm and the cold, but also something else. If, therefore, it is requisite that also flesh be either an element, or that which is compounded from elements—if it is an element—again will there be the same reasoning, for from this,—even from fire and earth,—will consist the flesh; and, further, from something else something different, so that the progression will go on to infinity: but if it be compounded from an element, it is evident that it will not consist of one, but many, or it will be that very thing itself. Wherefore, again, in the case of this, as in the case of the flesh or syllable, we shall put forward the same reasoning. Now, it would seem that there is something of this sort, and that it is not an element; and the cause, at least, of this thing being flesh, but that a syllable. In like manner, also, is it concerning other things. But the substance of each thing constitutes this, in truth; for this is the first cause of being or substance. Since, however, some things are not substances of things,—but this is the case with as many substances as according to nature are constituted as well as by nature,—to some, also, would this nature appear to be substance, or it is not an element, but a first principle. Now, an element is that whereunto as inherent in a thing, as matter, a compound is divided, as, for instance, of the syllable $A B$, A and B are the elements.

BOOK VIII

1. FROM the statements that have been now made it is necessary 1042a
to draw our inference, and, collecting together a summary of the
foregoing, to impose upon our remarks some termination or
conclusion. It has, therefore, been stated that the causes, and
the first principles, and the elements of substances, are the
subjects under investigation in the present treatise. Now, as to
substances, some are acknowledged to have a subsistence by all
philosophers; respecting others, however, certain speculators
have put forth from time to time certain peculiar opinions of
their own. Physical or natural substances are acknowledged to
have a subsistence; for example, fire, earth, water, air, and the
rest of simple bodies: in the next place, plants, and the parts of
these; animals, also, and their parts; and lastly, the heaven and
the parts of the heaven: but those certain philosophers, who
hold peculiar sentiments respecting substances, affirm that
both forms and mathematical entities or species are substances.
But, unquestionably, from the foregoing reasonings the consequence ensues of there being other substances—I mean, the
essence or very nature of a thing, and the subject. Further, in
other respects we may assume that the genus is substance in
preference to the species, and the universal to the singulars.
With the universal, however, and the genus, the ideas, also, are
connected, for they seem to be substances according with the
same process of reasoning.

Since, however, the essence or very nature of a thing appears to be substance, and the reason or principle of this is definition, on this account we have settled various points respecting definition, and respecting that which is essential. But since definition is a sentence, and since a sentence has parts, we found it requisite also to examine concerning a part, what sort are the parts of substance, and what sort they are not, and whether these ought to be the same with the parts of the definition likewise? Further, then, neither is the universal nor the genus substance. But concerning ideas and mathematical entities we will subsequently institute an inquiry; for, beside the substances of things cognizant by the senses, certain speculators assert these to have a subsistence. At present, however, let us treat of those substances that are acknowledged to have a subsistence; but these are sensible substances, or the substances of those things that fall beneath the notice of the senses.

Now, all sensible substances involve matter. But substance may be considered as those things that may be classed amongst subjects in one sense as matter, but in another as the definition; now, I mean by matter that which is not this certain particular thing in energy, but in capacity is this certain particular thing; and in a different sense definition and form are subjects. That which is this certain particular thing is separable from the formal principle of it, and third is that which is composed of these, of which alone there are generation and corruption, and which is a thing that simply has a separable subsistence; for of those substances which subsist according to a formal principle some are capable of a separate subsistence, but some are not so. But that matter is a substance is evident, for in all opposite changes is there something which is the subject of the changes; as, for instance, in place, that which is now here, but again is elsewhere; and according to increase, that which is at the present moment of such a size, and the next less or larger; and according to alteration, a person who is now healthy, and at another time indisposed: and in like manner, also, according to substance, a thing which now subsists in a state of generation is again, however, in a state of corruption, and that which is at the present time a subject, as this certain particular thing, yet is at some future period a subject as according to privation. And, doubtless, the rest of the changes follow upon this; yet this does not follow one or two of the other changes: for there is no necessity, should even anything involve local or topical matter, that this also involve matter, both such as is generable and corruptible. What, then, is the difference between simple production, and that which is not simple production, has been declared in our treatise on Physical Phenomena.

2. But since the subsistence of substance as a subject and as matter is admitted by philosophers, and this is that which subsists in capacity, it remains that we should state what that substance is amongst sensibles which subsists as energy. Democritus, therefore, assuredly seems to be a person who considered that, in regard of this, there are three differences; for he was of opinion that the subject-body and the matter were one and the same thing, but that the difference lay either in the rysmos, which is figure, or in the trope, which is position, or in the diathege, which is order.

But there appear many existing differences; as, for example, some things are termed substance from the composition of matter: as, to give an instance, whatsoever things are formed by mixture, such as mead, which is a mixture of honey and water; and others are termed so from a wooden fastening, as a chest; and others from a string, such as a bundle; and others from glue, as a book; and others from many of these; and others, again, are said to subsist from position, as a threshold and the lintel of a door: for these differ from circumstances of position in a certain respect; other things, however, derive their being from time, as dinner and breakfast, and some from place, as the winds. And some things are styled differences from the passive properties of sensibles; as, for example, hardness and softness, and thickness and thinness, and dryness and moistness: and some are so termed from certain of these qualities, and others from all of them; and, in general, some from excess, but others from defect.

Wherefore, it is evident that the fact of a thing's subsistence is denominated in thus many ways, for a threshold is a threshold because it is situated thus, and its subsistence signifies that it has this position in this way; and the subsistence of ice signifies the fact of its congelation in this form. And the subsistence of some things will be defined by even all of these circumstances; and this because some things consist from the mixture of some things, but others from their temperament, and some from their connection, and some from their condensation, and some from their employment of other differential qualities, as either the hand or foot. Therefore, must we take into consideration the genera of differences, for these will be the first principles of subsistence; as, for example, those things which have their subsistence in the more and the less, or the dense and the rare, and the other properties of this kind; for all these belong to excess and defect. If anything, however, has its subsistence in figure, or smoothness

1043a and roughness, all things will subsist in what is right-lined and curved. Now, to some things their subsistence will consist in their being mingled, and, in an opposite way, their non-subsistence will consist in not being mingled.

It is, therefore, evident from these foregoing statements, that if substance is a cause of the subsistence of each thing, that in these must be sought the solution of the question what the cause of the subsistence of each of these is. Substance, indeed, then, is not any of these, or a thing that is connected together; nevertheless, it subsists analogically in each thing. And as in substances whatsoever is predicated of matter is actual energy, this also in an eminent degree is the case with the other definitions; as, for example, if it be necessary to define a threshold, we will say that it is a piece of wood or stone situated in this way, and if a house, that it is bricks and timbers disposed in such or such a way; or, shall we further say that likewise the final cause exists in the case of some things? And if we are called on to define a lump of ice, we would reply, that it is water congealed or condensed in this form; and if symphony is to be defined, that it is a particular sort of mixture of the sharp and the flat; and we must proceed in the same manner with other things also.

It is evident, therefore, from these statements, that there is of different matter a different energy, and a different definition; for of some things composition is the energy and form, and of other things mixture, and of others something else of those particulars enumerated above. Wherefore, of persons engaged in defining things, those, on the one hand, who say what a house is, that it is stones, bricks, timbers, speak of the house in respect of potentiality or capacity, for these are matter; but those who say, in addition, that it is a receptacle preservative of goods and bodies, or that it is some other such thing, speak of the house in regard of its energy; and those who put both of these together, speak of the third substance—I mean, the substance composed of these, that is, of potentiality and energy. For the definition that subsists by means of differences seems to be that of form and energy, but that which consists from things that are inherent appears to be the definition of matter rather. In like manner, also, does this consequence result unto the definitions which Archytas admitted, for they are compounded of both together; as, for example, what is a lull? Stillness in a mass of air; the air in this case is matter, but the stillness is energy and substance. What is a calm? Smoothness of sea; the subject in this case, as matter, is the sea, but the energy and form are smoothness. Now, it is evident, from what has been stated, what sensible substance is, and how it subsists; for the one thing is as matter, but the other as form when it is energy: but the third is that which is composed of these.

3. It is requisite, however, that we should not be ignorant that sometimes it escapes our notice whether the name signifies the composite substance, or energy, or form; as, for example, a house, whether it is a sign of that which is common to all houses,—viz., that it is a shelter composed of bricks, and rafters, and stones, disposed in this way,—or whether it is a sign of energy and form, because it is a shelter? In the instance of a line, also, whether the name signifies that it is a dyad in length, or, because of its being the dyad, is a sign of energy and form? And, in the

case of animal, whether it is soul contained in body, or soul simply, for soul is the substance and energy belonging to a certain body? And animal, also, would be involved in both, not as what is predicated by one definition, but as in relation to one thing.

These, however, differ in relation to something else; but they in no wise contribute to the advancement of the present investigation about substance,—I mean that substance which is cognizant by sense; for the essence or very nature of a thing is 1043b inherent in the form and energy. For soul, I admit, and the being of a soul, are the same thing; but the being of a man, and the being man, are not the same thing; unless, likewise, the soul will be styled a man: and so the being of man will be the same, no doubt, in one respect, but not the same in another, with man. But the syllable does not appear to persons engaged in such investigations as consisting of the elements of speech and of composition, nor does a house seem to constitute both bricks and composition: and this supposition is made correctly, for the composition and the mixture of anything consist not from those things to which composition or mixture belongs. In like manner, also, it is not the case with anything else; as, for example, a threshold subsists from position, not position from a threshold, but the latter rather from the former; nor is a man animal and biped, but must needs be something which subsists besides these, if these are matter, and which is neither an element, nor from an element, but the substance; and the thing which they take away they denominate matter: if, then, this is a cause of existence, and if this is substance, they would term this actual substance. Now, it is necessary that this be either a thing eternal, or subject to decay without being reduced to decay, and be generated without going through a process of generation. But it has been demonstrated, and made apparent elsewhere, that no one produces form, nor generates it, but that this particular thing is produced, and that what is composed of these is generated. But whether there are substances of things corruptible capable of having a separate subsistence is in no wise evident as yet, save that thus much is plain, that it is not admissible with some things at any rate, such as cannot possibly subsist, even beside certain particulars, say a house or a utensil. Therefore, perhaps, indeed, neither such are substances—I mean sensibles—nor are these very things substances in any respect, nor anything else that does not consist naturally; for one may consider Nature as alone the substance in things that are liable to decay.

Wherefore, the doubt which the followers of Antisthenes, and persons similarly uneducated, indulged in, namely, that the nature of a thing cannot be defined, involves some opportunity of a solution at present; for what they say is, that definition is a long sentence: but, certainly, as to the quality of a thing, what it is, though we cannot frame any definition, yet we can even give instruction of some kind or other on such point; as, take the case of silver, you may not be able to tell what it is, to be sure, yet you may say that it can be assimilated in its appearance to tin. Wherefore, it belongs, in fact, to a substance of which it is admissible that there be a definition and formal principle; as, for example, of that which is a composite nature, whether it be cognizant to the sense or the intellect. But there cannot be such of those things from which these consist primarily, if the definitive reason has any signification in regard of anything, and it is necessary that the one be as matter, but the other as form.

Now, it is likewise evident, on the supposition that numbers are in a manner substances, why it is that they subsist after this mode, and not as certain philosophers say, because they are a multitude or aggregation of monads. For definition, also, is a certain number (for both it is divisible and resolvable into indivisible elements; for formal principles are not infinite), and number is a thing of this kind. And just as when any of those things whereof number consists has been either subtracted from number or added to it, no longer is there the same number, but a different one, even though ever so little be subtracted or added, so, in like manner, neither will definition, nor the essence or very nature of a thing, be any longer the same, when there is a subtraction or addition of anything. And it is necessary, further, as regards number, that there should be something 1044a

187

through which it is one, which in the present case they cannot assign—I mean something through which it is one—if number is one thing. For either it is not one thing, but is, as it were, a heap, or, if it is, it must be stated what that is which makes it to be one out of many things. Definition, also, is one thing, and similarly neither in regard of this which is compounded out of many things can they make assertions in this way. And this result naturally takes place, for it is a consequence from the same reasoning; and the substance in this way is one thing, but not in such a way as some would make out who say, for instance, that it is a certain monad, or point, but that each is actuality, and a certain nature. And as number involves neither the more and the less, so neither does that substance which subsists according to form; but, if this be the case, it is that which is connected with matter. Respecting, indeed, then, generation and corruption, in regard of the aforesaid substances, in what manner it is admissible, and how it is impossible that they should take place, and regarding the reduction of definition into number, let the foregoing distinctions be set down thus far.

4. As regards material substance, however, it is necessary that it should not escape our notice that, even though all things are from the same primary nature, or the same things as those that are primary, and though the same matter be as a first principle, for things that are generated, nevertheless, there is a certain peculiar matter of everything; for instance, the first matter of phlegm is the sweet, or the oily, and of bile, the bitter, or something else of this sort: but, perhaps, these, also, are from the same thing. And there are produced many substances of the same thing when one thing is the substance of another, as phlegm is from the fat and the sweet, if what is fat or oily be from what is sweet, and it is the case that it is from bile on account of the resolution of the component qualities into bile, as into their primary matter. For in a twofold way does one thing proceed from another, namely, either because it will be in the way of progression, or of analyzation into its first principle.

Now, on the supposition of the existence of one matter, it is possible for different things to be generated by reason of the cause which imparts motion, as both a chest and a bed are formed from wood: of some things, however, the matter is necessarily different, when the things themselves are different; as, for example, a saw can never be made of wood, nor does it belong to the cause imparting motion to accomplish this, for it can never produce a saw of wool or of wood. But if, then, it is possible to make the same thing of different matter, it is evident that art and the first principle, as one that originates the motion in a thing, are the same; for if matter were different from that which imparts motion, the thing made or generated would also be different. When, therefore, one may investigate what the cause of a thing is—since causes are denominated in many ways—it is necessary to mention all the contingent causes: as, for example, what is the cause of man as matter, that is, the material cause: is it the menstrual blood? And what is the cause, as that which imparts motion, or, in other words, the efficient cause: is it not the seed, then? And what is the cause as form, or the formal cause: is it not the essence, or very nature of the thing? And what is the final cause of his existence: is it not the end thereof? But, perhaps, both of these are the same. And it is requisite, also, to 1044b mention the most immediate or proximate causes. What is the matter of man? Not fire or earth, but that which is matter peculiar or domestic to the nature of man.

Certainly, then, respecting physical and generable substances, it is necessary to advance forwards in our investigations in this manner, if one will advance correctly; since, in such a case, both these causes, and causes of such a description, are in existence, and if it be requisite to have a knowledge of causes. Concerning physical or natural substances, however, but such as are everlasting, there is another mode of reasoning; for some of them, perhaps, do not involve matter, or do not involve matter of this kind, but only that which is movable in place. And, therefore, as many as possess a natural subsistence, but are not substance, these do not involve matter, but the subject to them constitutes substance; as, for instance, what cause is there of an eclipse? Say, what material cause is there, for no such can be assigned, save that the moon is that which is passive: and what is the cause of this phenomenon, as that which imparts motion and destroys light, that is, the efficient cause, the earth? The final cause, however, does not, perhaps, exist in this case: and the formal cause is definition; yet this is obscure, unless the definition be along with the cause: as, what is an eclipse? It is a privation of light. And if this addition be made, that this privation of light is occasioned by the earth intervening in the midst, this will be a definition in conjunction with the cause. But, in the case of sleep, it is obscure what is the first thing that is passive. Shall we say that it is the animal in its entirety? Yes: but in what part does this passive condition arise? And what organ is it that first undergoes this passive change? Is it the heart, or something else? Then, there is the inquiry, by reason of what agency does this passive condition ensue? And, in the next place, what is this passive condition—I mean, the condition that belongs to that particular organ, and does not belong to the whole body? Shall we say that it is such and such a kind of immobility? Be it so: but this is such because there is something to undergo an affection in the first instance.

5. And since some things are unconnected both with generation and corruption, and some are not so; as, for example, points—if they really subsist—and in general, species and forms (for it is not whiteness that is generated, but the white wood); or, if also everything which is generated is generated from something, in such a case all contraries would not be generated from one another; but in a different way would white man be from black man, and whiteness from blackness: nor of everything is there matter; but of as many things as there is generation and mutual change; and as many things as are without alterations, or are not, of these there is not matter. It involves, however, a subject of doubt, how matter—I mean, that which belongs to each thing—stands in relation to contraries; for instance, if the body be

healthy in capacity, and if the opposite thing to health be disease, whether shall we say that both subsist in capacity? Whether
shall we, also, say that water in capacity is both wine and vinegar?
Or shall we say that the body is matter of health according to its
habit, and according to form; but that it is the matter of disease,
according to privation, and according to corruption, such as is
contrary to Nature?

And another certain doubt is there, also, why wine is not the
matter of vinegar, nor vinegar in capacity, although vinegar is
produced from this; and, in respect of one that is alive, we may
doubt whether such is in potentiality a dead body, or is not; but
the corruptions subsist according to accident: the actual matter, 1045a
however, of an animal, subsists according to corruption, as the
capacity and matter of a dead body, and the water, also, of vinegar;
for from these are they generated, as night from day. And as
many things, therefore, as in this way undergo changes into one
another, ought to revert back into matter; as, for instance, if
from a dead body an animated one should be generated, it is
requisite that the dead body should first be resolved into matter,
in order that in this way an animated body might afterwards be
generated from it; and, in like manner, vinegar must be resolved
into water, then will wine in this way be produced.

6. But bearing upon the doubt mentioned above, both respecting
definitions and respecting numbers, is the question, what is the
cause of there being one? For of all such things as have many
parts, and of which the whole is not, as it were, a heap, but is
something else, namely, an entirety, beside the parts, there is a
certain cause, since also in bodies—in some indeed—contact is
the cause of their being one, and in others viscosity or some
other such passive quality. Now, definition is one discursus or
sentence, not by a bond of connection, as the *Iliad,* but in
respect of being of one thing. What, then, is it which makes man
to be one thing, and why is he one thing, but not many things; as,
for example, both animal and biped, and in the most eminent
degree also, if, as some say, any animal in itself, and biped in

itself, have a subsistence? For why is not man those very things, and why will men subsist, not according to participation of one man, but the participation of two things, both animal and biped? And, in general, therefore, man will not be one thing, but many things, namely, animal and biped. It is, therefore, evident that to persons treating the subject in such a way as they have been accustomed to frame their definitions and assertions, it is not possible to adduce a reason of this and solve the matter in doubt.

But if the case stands as we say, namely, that one thing, indeed, is matter, but another form,—and, again, that one thing subsists in capacity, but another in energy,—no longer would the matter under investigation seem a subject of doubt, for this doubt is the same as if the round brass were the definition of a garment. For this name would be a sign of the definition; where-fore, the object of investigation is what the cause is that the circular and the brass are one. No longer, however, does the doubt appear to remain, because the one is matter, but the other form. What, then, is the cause of this, namely, that what subsists in capacity should subsist in energy beside the producing cause—I mean, in the case of whatsoever things there is genera-tion? For there is no other cause of the sphere that subsists in capacity subsisting as a sphere in energy, but this was the essence in each thing. And as regards matter, there is one kind that is intelligible, and another that is cognizant by the senses; and as regards definition, one sort, indeed, is invariably matter, and another is energy, as a circle is a plain figure. As many things, however, as do not involve matter, either intelligible or sensible, 1045b forthwith is it possible that each of these be one certain particular thing, as that which is a certain particular thing is this particular thing as well as quality and quantity; wherefore, also, there does not inhere in definitions either entity or unity, and the essence or very nature of a thing is forthwith a certain unity, as also a certain entity; wherefore, also, there is not any different cause for any of these being one, or of there being a certain entity in them, for immediately doth each constitute a certain entity and a certain unity; yet they are not inherent in entity or unity as in the genus of these, nor have they a subsistence as though they were separable from singulars.

And, on account of this aforesaid doubt, some philosophers maintain that participation, to wit, is the cause; and what the cause of the participation is, and what the participation itself is, they are in doubt; but some assign the intercourse of the soul as the cause, just as Lycophron, who says that science is the union of the act of scientific knowledge and of the soul: but others affirm that the principle of vitality consists in the composition or conjunction of soul with body. Indeed, the same reasoning holds good as regards all things; for also the being in sound health will be either the union, or conjunction, or composition of soul with health. And for the brass to be a triangle will be a composition of brass and of triangle, and for a thing to be white will be a composition of superficies and whiteness; and a cause of their speaking in this way is because they are searching for the uniting principle and difference of capacity and actuality. But, as has been said, both the ultimate matter and the form are the same; and the one subsists in capacity, but the other in actuality. Wherefore, the investigation of what is the cause of unity is similar to the inquiry into the cause of a thing being one; for everything is one particular thing subsisting both partly in capacity and partly in energy, in a certain respect, as one thing. Wherefore, there is no other cause, except there be something that can be shown to subsist as a cause imparting motion from potentiality into energy. Now, whatever things do not involve matter, all of these are simply some certain particular thing.

BOOK IX

1. CONCERNING substance, then—I mean, concerning that which is primarily entity, and to which all the rest of the categories of entity are referred—we have declared our sentiments. For according to the definition of substance are denominated the other entities, viz., both quantity, and quality, and the rest of the things that are predicated in this way; for all such will involve the definition of substance, as we have asserted in our earliest dissertations. But since entity is denominated partly as quiddity, or quality, or quantity, but partly according to capacity and actuality, and according to work, let us frame certain distinctions and definitions as regards both capacity and actuality; and, in the first instance, as regards that capacity, or potentiality, which is spoken 1046a of as such with especial precision: not, to be sure, that this is of service towards the advancement of our present design, for potentiality and actuality extend further than things merely predicated according to motion. But when we have spoken our opinions concerning this in our definitions, as regards energy, we shall make matters plain concerning the other points likewise.

That, indeed, therefore, potentiality is predicated in many ways, and that the possession of potentiality is expressed in many ways, has been settled by us elsewhere. But as many of these as are styled potentialities equivocally may be omitted; for some capacities, or potentialities, are denominated capacities by reason of a certain similarity (as in geometry we speak of potentiality in this way), and things that are potential and impotential we call such in regard of their being, in a certain respect, endued with such a capacity, or not being so. As many potentialities, however, as are referred to the same form or species all are certain first principles, and are predicated in reference to one primary potentiality, which is a first principle of change in another body, so far forth as it is another. For there is a capacity, on the one hand, of being passive, which, in the actual subject of passion, constitutes a first principle of a passive state through the intervention of another body, so far forth as it is another. There is, on the other hand, the habit of impassivity, such as tends towards a condition which is worse, and the habit of corruption, which arises from the instrumentality of another body, so far forth as it is another—I mean, a first principle capable of bringing about a change. For in all these definitions is inherent the definition of the primary potentiality just mentioned. And again, these potentialities are styled either those of action merely, or passion, or subsistence in an excellent manner. Wherefore, also, in the definitions of these are inherent, in a manner, the definitions of the former potentialities.

It is, therefore, evident that there is, in a certain respect, one potentiality of action and passion,—for a thing that is potential is such in regard of itself having the potentiality of passiveness, and in regard of another thing having it by reason of this,—and, in another respect, there is a different potentiality. For one kind of potentiality resides in the patient; for, on account of its having a certain first principle, and on account of matter, also, being a certain first principle, the subject of the passion is passive, and one thing undergoes a change by reason of another; for that which is fat is combustible also: but that which yields in this manner is a thing that is bruised; and in like manner, also, is it with other things. But another kind of potentiality resides in the agent, as the hot, and the capacity of house-building, are involved severally, the former in that which is capable of making a thing warm, and the latter in a person who is qualified to build a house. Wherefore, as far forth as a thing is naturally connected with itself it in no wise undergoes a passive state itself, by reason of its own agency, for it is one thing, and not anything else.

And impotentiality, and that which is impotential (now, such is contrary to potentiality), is privation. Wherefore, every potentiality belongs to the same, and subsists according to the same subject with impotentiality. Privation, however, is predicated in many ways; for privation is to be found where a thing does not possess something else, and, though fitted by nature for the possession of such, may yet not have it either entirely or when it is fitted by nature: and we say either, after this manner, that it is privation, for instance, altogether so, or yet even in some certain respect or other. And, in the case of some things, if being by nature adapted to possess a thing, they may not yet have such by reason of violence, we say that these are subjects of privation in this respect.

2. Since, however, such first principles of potentiality are inherent partly in things that are inanimate, and partly in things that are animate and contained in soul, and in that portion of the soul 1046b which possesses reason, it is evident that also of potentialities some will be devoid of reason, whereas others will be accompanied with reason. Wherefore, all the arts, even such as are constructive, as well as the sciences, are potentialities; for they constitute first principles which are causes of change in another subject, so far forth as it is another. And all those potentialities, indeed, that are accompanied, or involve any connection with reason, are productive of contraries; each of these, however, that is devoid of reason is alone productive of one result: as, for instance, that which is hot is productive of the promotion of heat merely, and the medicinal art of disease and health.

And a cause of this is the following, that scientific knowledge is reason, and the same reason makes manifest the result produced and its privation, though not after the same manner; and in one way is this reason that which creates this knowledge for both, yet in another it affords greater knowledge of the thing in existence than of its privation. Wherefore, it is requisite that such sciences as these should involve a knowledge of contraries; but that of the one it should be thus essentially, and of the other not essentially; for also reason is a knowledge of the one essentially, but of the other, after a certain manner, according to accident, for by negation and ablation it makes manifest the contrary; for primary privation is that which is contrary, and this is an ablation of the other. Since, however, contraries are not inherent in the same thing—now, science is a capacity in respect of the possession of reason, and the soul also possesses a first principle of motion—hence the healthy or salubrious produces health only, and that which is capable of promoting heat—warmth, and of promoting cold—chilliness; but the scientific person produces both. For of both, no doubt, has reason a knowledge, but not in the same manner; and this reason subsists in a soul which possesses a first principle of motion. Wherefore, soul will move both from the same first principle, having effected coherence towards the same thing; wherefore, the things which are potential, or endowed with capacity according to reason, produce contraries to the productions of that which is potential without reason, for one principle is comprised in reason. But it is evident that also upon the power of action and passion in an excellent manner there follows the power merely of action or of passion: but in this latter the former is not invariably to be found; for he that acts well must needs also be an agent, but where a person only is an agent it is not necessary, also, that he should act well.

3. But there are some who say—for instance, those of the Megaric school—that where there is energy, there only is there potentiality, or capacity, but that where there is no energy, there is no potentiality; for example, that the person who does not actually build has not the capacity of building, but that he has the capacity of building when he actually builds, and that it is in like manner, also, with other things. Now, the absurdities which ensue with these speculators it is not difficult to discover. For it is evident that neither will he be a builder if he does not actually build; for the being of a builder consists in the possession of the

capacity of building; and in like manner, also, it is the case with the rest of the arts. If, therefore, it is impossible for one to possess arts of this kind, if he has not at any time received instruction in them, and acquired them, and not to be in the possession of them, unless at some time or other he lose them (for one may do so either through forgetfulness, or a certain affection, or time; for as to the thing itself, that, at any rate, has not fallen into decay, for it is in existence always); this being the case when there may be a cessation of operation on the part of such a one, he will not have in possession the art, and how will he again forthwith proceed to build in resuming the art which he had lost?

And in like manner will it be the case, also, with things that are inanimate; for there will be neither cold, nor hot, nor sweet, nor, in short, anything cognizable by sense, when such is not an object of sensation. Wherefore, it will happen with these philosophers that they should put forward the same theory with Protagoras. But, unquestionably, neither will a man possess any sense unless he perceives or energizes. If, therefore, that animal is blind which does not possess the power of vision, though naturally adapted to see, and when it is naturally adapted to see, and, further, as it is thus naturally adapted, in such a case the same individuals oftentimes during the same day will be blind, and in like manner deaf. Further, if that which is impotential be that which has been deprived of capacity, that which has not been generated, to be generated will be a thing that is impossible; but one who says that what is devoid of a capacity of being generated, either actually exists, or will do so, shall affirm what is false; for this would signify what is impotential. Wherefore, these assertions overturn both the existence of motion and of generation; for that which stands will not always stand, and that which sits will always remain in a sitting posture; for a man will not rise up if he be sitting down, for it will be impossible for that to rise up which would not possess the capability, at least, of rising up.

If, therefore, it may not be possible to affirm these things, it is evident that potentiality and energy are something different from each other; those theories, however, take potentiality and energy to be the same: and thus it is not a small thing which they are seeking to overturn. Wherefore, it happens that a thing admits of being, and yet may not be, and that a thing admits of not being, and yet may be. In like manner, also, is it with the rest of the categories: that which is endued with the capacity of walking yet may not walk, and that which does not walk may yet be able to walk. This, however, is a thing that is potential, in which, when the energy is present of that of which it is said to have the capacity, there will not be in existence anything that is devoid of potentiality. Now, I mean, for instance, if one is able to sit, and it so happens that such a one sits, if the sitting posture will have an existence in the case of such a one, nothing impossible or impotential will ensue. And if anything may be moved, or may impart motion, or remain at rest, or impede a body in its course, or be in existence, or be generated, or not be in existence, or not be generated, the case will be similar.

But the name, energy, which is combined with actuality, and tends towards other things, has proceeded forth from motions principally; for motion is an eminent sense appears to constitute the energy of a thing. Wherefore, also, to nonentities they do not attribute the having motion imparted to them, but certain other categories: as, for instance, things which are nonentities are intelligible and desirable objects, but are not in motion. And this is the case because nonentities in energy will, however, subsist in energy; for of nonentities some are nonentities in capacity, but yet have no existence because they 1047b do not exist actually.

4. Now, if the potential be that which it has been declared to be, upon which energy is consequential, it is evident that it is not possible that it be true to say that this particular thing is endued with a capability of being, but yet will not exist; so that, on this

supposition, what things impotential are would elude our search. Now, I say, for instance, this is just as if anyone affirm it to be possible that the diameter of a square be commensurate with its side, although this commensurability will never be established; not reckoning that it is a thing that is impossible, because nothing hinders anything that is potential, in regard of existence and of generation, from not being, nor being likely to exist. But that follows necessarily from the points laid down, if, also, we should suppose a thing may be, or may be generated, which is not in existence, I admit, but yet is a thing that is endued with the capacity of being; because there will be in such a supposition as this nothing that is impossible: but, at any rate, it will be admitted that this result will ensue; for, allowing the commensurability of the diameter, the inference must follow that even are equal to odd numbers, which is an impossibility. For what is false is not the same also with that which is impotential; for that you now are in a standing position is false, to be sure, but is not a thing that is impossible.

And at the same time, also, is it evident that, upon the supposition of the existence of A, B must needs exist likewise; and if A exist as a thing that is potential in regard of being, it follows that also B must needs be a thing that is potential in regard of being; for if there be no necessity for its being a thing potential in regard of being, nothing hinders that which is a thing possible to be from not being at all. Now, let A be a thing that is possible to be. Therefore, since A is a thing possible to be, if A be admitted as existing, nothing impossible to be would actually ensue. However, B, at any rate, must necessarily exist; but this was impossible. Grant, therefore, that it is impossible. If, then, it were impossible for B to exist necessarily, it is necessary that it should be impossible for A to exist. But then A was possible, therefore will B be so likewise. If, then, A be possible, B also will be possible, if they subsist in such a way as that in consequence of the existence of A, B necessarily exists also. If, therefore, on the supposition that the things signified by A B subsist in this manner, it may not be a thing possible for this to take place in reference to *B* in this way, neither will *A B* subsist in the manner that has been laid down; and if, on the supposition of the possibility of the existence of *A*, it is necessary that *B* also should exist as a thing that is possible to be, supposing, then, *A* to exist, it is necessary also that *B* exist. For that it is possible from necessity for *B* to exist, if it is possible for *A* to exist, signifies as follows, that if *A* exists, and when it exists, and as far as it is a thing that is possible to exist, that then, and in this way also, that is necessary in regard of the existence of *B*.

5. And whereas of all existing potentialities some are congenital, as those of the senses, but others are developed from habit, as the ability of playing on a flute, and some from discipline, as capacity in the arts, it is necessary that those that are developed from habit and reason should be acquired by repeated exercises of previous activity, but that those which are not of this description, and such as are concerned with passivity, should not necessarily be acquired in this way. Since, however, that which is endued with potentiality is able to effect something, both the term "sometimes" and the term "somehow" 1048a must one add in the definition, and as many things else as are consequential to this. And some things that subsist according to reason do not possess the potentiality of imparting motion, and their potentialities are accompanied with reason; whereas, as regards other things that are irrational, and their potentialities irrational, those, also, it is necessary should subsist in an animate creature, but these in both—now this being the case—in respect of potentialities of such a description as this, it is requisite, when, as far as they are endued with capacity in this way, the passive and the productive approximate towards each other, that one set of them should be active and the other passive; but it is not necessary that this should take place with those—I mean, with rational—potentialities. For, as regards all of these, each one is productive of one thing; whereas those are productive of contraries: wherefore, this will at the same time produce contraries—a thing, however, that is impossible.

It is necessary, then, that there be something else which may be predominant, and this I call propension, or free-will; for whatsoever is the object of a particular propension, this will that propension authoritatively or rightfully accomplish, when as far as it is endued with capacity, it may subsist, and approximate unto the passive. Wherefore, that which is endued with capacity according to reason must altogether encompass its object, when it feels an appetite after that unto which it has a capability of attaining, and so far as it has this capability. Now, the power to do or accomplish anything subsists when that which is passive is present, and is so disposed. And if this be not the case, there will be no power to accomplish it; for, in the event of none of those things that are extrinsic offering any obstruction, there is no further necessity for adding these words, "nothing extrinsic offering obstruction," into the definition, for it involves potentiality, as it belongs to a capacity of action; yet it is not so altogether, but when things are disposed in some such manner as that in their case will also external impediments be removed; for these are taken away—I mean, some of those distinctive terms that are contained in the definition. Wherefore, neither will an appetite accomplish two things, or contrary things, even though at the same time it may feel disposed or be actuated by an inordinate desire to accomplish them; for it does not involve power over their attainment in this way at the same time, nor is there present the power of the simultaneous accomplishment of such, since those objects of pursuit over which appetite has control it will accomplish in this manner.

6. But since we have spoken concerning potentiality, such as subsists according to motion, let us frame some definitions and distinctions regarding energy, both as to what energy or activity is, and what sort of a thing it is. For the nature of that which is potential, or endued with capacity, likewise, at the same time will be apparent to those who make a division in this matter, because we not only say that this is a thing endued with potentiality or capacity which is fitted by nature to impart motion to something

else, or to have motion imparted to itself by something else, either viewed simply or in a certain manner, but we also assert this as being the case after a different mode. Wherefore, in our investigations we shall also treat of these points.

The existence of the thing, however, as the energy, does not subsist in such a way as when we speak of a thing in potentiality; now, we mean by a thing subsisting in potentiality, for instance, [a statue of Mercury in a block of wood], and the half in the whole, because it can be taken away from the whole: and we term that a scientific person in capacity, even though not actually engaged in speculation, provided only such may be endued with a capacity for speculative pursuits; and we mean by a thing's subsisting in energy,—now, by an induction of singulars is the assertion evident which we wish to make, and it is not expedient that we should seek after a definition for everything; but it is sufficient to perceive at a glance that which is analogous,—now, I say, by a thing's subsisting in energy we mean that it should be a person engaged in building stands in relation to that which is fit 1048b for being built, and the wakeful to the sleeper, and one who sees to one whose eyes are closed, but who nevertheless possesses the power of vision, and as that which involves a separable subsistence from matter to matter, and as that which has been wrought by art to that which is unwrought. After this mode, then, is energy compared with capacity or potentiality. By one portion, however, of this difference let energy be distinguished, and that which is endued with potentiality by the other.

All things, however, are not said to subsist in energy in a similar way; but either analogically as this thing in this, or relatively to this; and that thing in this particular thing, or relatively to this particular thing. For some things are as motion in respect of potentiality; but other things are as substance in respect of a certain matter. But the infinite and the void, and such-like things, are said to subsist both in potentiality and energy after another manner different from many entities; as, for example, that which sees, and that which walks, and that which is seen. For sometimes do these things admit of being verified, and simply verified; for the one is an object to be seen, because it is seen, but the other because it is endued with a potentiality of being seen; the infinite, however, does not subsist in potentiality after such a mode as it is likely to be in energy when it involves a separable subsistence: but it does in knowledge, for infinite divisibility is the cause which these persons assign for the subsistence in potentiality amounting to this energy; not, however, in respect of its being made to involve a separate subsistence.

But since none of those doings of which there is a termination constitutes an end, but only some of those that are performed in regard of the end,—as the actual end of inducing emaciation is emaciation, and when these happen to induce or promote a state of emaciation they are in this way in motion, not being inherent as the things on account of which the motion subsists,— now, on such a supposition, these things do not constitute the method of doing a thing, or, at any rate, such a method as is perfect, that is, involves an end. For they do not constitute an end, but in that—I mean, the motion—are inherent the end and the method of doing a thing; as, for example, a man sees, but also he exercises thought, and employs his understanding, and has employed his understanding, but he does not receive instruction, and has received instruction, neither is he in a sound state of health, and has he been restored to health; he may live properly, and has lived properly; but also he enjoys the felicity of a regular life, and has enjoyed this felicity; and if this be not the case, he ought at some time or other to intermit, as when he may induce emaciation; he does not, however, produce this state at present, but he lives, and has lived.

Therefore, is it proper to denominate some of these afore-said conditions as motions, and some of them as energies or activities; for every motion is imperfect: as, for instance, ema-ciation, learning, walking, building; and these are motions, even imperfect ones at least. For a person does not walk at the same time that he has walked, nor does a builder construct a house at the same time that he has built one, nor is a thing generated simultaneously with its having been generated in time past, or is motion imparted simultaneously with the communication of motion in time past, but it is a different thing as regards the communication and the reception of motion. Now, a person—to give an illustration—has seen and sees the same thing at the same time, and exercises his understanding, and has exercised his understanding simultaneously in regard of the same thing: a thing of this kind, indeed, do I denominate energy and activity; but I call that motion. Therefore, as to the subsistence of a thing in energy—both what it is and what sort of a thing it is—from these and such-like statement let this point be evident to us.

7. And when it is that each thing subsists in potentiality, and when it does not, this point must now be determined by us; for a thing does not subsist in potentiality at any time whatsoever indifferently,—thus, for instance, earth, is it, pray, man in poten- 1049a tiality, or is it not? But is this the case rather when seed already is generated (nor even the case somehow, perhaps then); just, then, as neither by the medicinal art everything would be indifferently reduced to a sound state, nor from chance, but there is something which is endued with a capacity of health, and this is that which subsists in a healthy condition potentially. But the definition of that which by reason of an exercise of intellect is in a state of generation in a condition of actuality, from such a cause as exists potentially, such a definition may be discovered when the process of generation is accomplished by one in the exercise of volition, and in a case where no impediment is offered by external obstructions. Now, this takes place in the instance adduced in the case of a person being reduced to a sound state of health, when there is no obstruction offered by those things that reside in himself.

And the case is similar with a house also in potentiality, if there is no hindrance to its construction as a house from obstacles discoverable in the builder of that house or the matter of it; and if there is not that which it is requisite should be added, or subtracted, or changed, this constitutes a house in potentiality.

And this is the case, likewise, with the rest of those things of which there is a first principle of generation that is extrinsic, and in regard of as many things, doubtless, as are contained in the thing itself in possession of them, whatever will subsist by means of this, in the absence of external impediments offering any hindrance; for example, the seed does not as yet subsist in potentiality, for it is necessary that it also accomplish a change in another body. But when now, by means of its own first principle, it may subsist as a thing of this kind, it is now this thing in potentiality; and that requires a different first principle, just as earth is not yet a statue in capacity or potentiality, for when it is being changed it will become brass.

But what we are speaking of seems to be not this particular thing, but a thing composed of this or that material, just as a chest is not wood, but wooden, or is the wood earth, but earthy. Again, if earth, after this manner, is not anything else, but is termed derivatively, or a thing that is composed from that material, in such a case that which subsists invariably in capacity simply is that which is subsequent, just as the chest is neither earthy or earth, but wooden. For this amounts to the subsistence of the chest in capacity, and this is the matter of the chest, simply considered as of that which is viewed simply; but of this particular chest is this particular piece of wood the matter.

If, however, there is something primary that is not any longer denominated according to something else, as a thing composed from that material, this is primary matter; for example, if earth is of air, and air is not fire, but composed of fire, in this case fire is the primary matter of earth, as this certain particular thing and substance. For in this respect is the universal different from the subject in regard of being the one this certain particular thing contrasted with the other which is not; for, to give an example, man, and body, and soul, are each the subject of passive conditions,—the passive condition, however, is the being musical and white. But when the musical is ingenerated as a capacity, that thing is not styled a musical capacity, but a thing that is musical, and man is not termed whiteness, but a thing that is white, nor walking, or motion, but a thing which walks or is moved, just as a thing that is composed of something else. Now, as regards, then, as many things as are denominated in this manner, that which is last is substance; but in respect of as many things as are not styled in this way, but of which a certain species and this certain particular thing are predicated, that which is last is matter, and a material substance. And therefore it happens correctly that what is composed of the material of something else is not predicated according to its matter and its passive conditions, for both of these are indefinite. When, 1049b therefore, a thing must be styled as that which subsists in capacity, and when it does not subsist thus, has been declared.

8. Since, however, it has been determined in how many ways that which has a priority of subsistence is predicated, it is evident that energy, or activity, is prior to potentiality. Now, I mean by potentiality not merely a definite potentiality, which is styled an alternative first principle in another body, so far forth as it is another, but, in general, every first principle which is the originator of motion or of rest. For Nature, also, may be ranked in the same genus with potentiality; for she is a first principle which is fit to be the cause of motion, not, however, in another body, but in itself, so far forth as it is itself.

Therefore, prior to every principle of this sort is energy, or activity, both in definition and in substance; but it is, also, in a certain respect prior in duration, and in a certain respect it is not so. That, indeed, therefore, it is prior in definition is evident, for that which is potential in regard of its possibility of energizing, or assuming a state of activity, such is a thing that is primarily endued with capacity or potentiality; for example, I speak of one that is skilled in building—now, I mean one that has a capacity of building, and I speak of one that is able to see, and I mean one that possesses the capacity of seeing, and of a thing that may be seen, as that which involves the capacity of being seen: and the same reasoning, also, holds good as regards other things. Wherefore, the definition and knowledge of energy must needs preexist in the definition and knowledge of potentiality.

But energy, likewise, is in time prior to capacity after this mode: namely, the priority of that which actively accomplishes the same thing in species, but not in number. Now, I mean to say this, that, in the case of this particular man existing at present according to energy, and in the case of the corn, and the horse, and the person who sees, prior in time are the matter, and the seed, and that which is able to see, which in potentiality constitute man, and corn, and one who sees, but are not as yet these in energy. Prior, however, to these in time are those different things that subsist in energy, and from which these have been generated; for always for man entity in capacity arises, or is generated, an entity in energy by means of an entity in energy—as man is generated from man, a musician by means of a musician—on the condition of something that is primary in its nature always imparting motion: the moving power at present, however, subsists in energy, or activity. But it has been declared, in our disquisitions concerning substance, that everything that is generated is generated from something, and by something, and that this is the same in species. Wherefore, also, it seems to be impossible that a builder be a person not likely to have built anything, or a harpist to be one who has not harped anything; for one who learns to play upon the harp learns to play upon the harp by actually playing upon the harp: it is also the case, in like manner, with other artists.

Whence arose the argument, by refutation, of the Sophists, that one who is not in possession of scientific knowledge will accomplish the mastery of that about which such scientific knowledge is conversant, for the learner of a science is not in possession of it. But, in reply to this, we may observe, that from the fact that something of that which is being produced, or generated, has been produced, and that, in general, something of that which is being moved has been moved—now, this is evident, according to what has been proved in our disquisitions

concerning motion—the learner, also, in this case, must needs 1050a
possess something, perhaps, of scientific knowledge. But then,
also, by this it is, at any rate, evident that energy in this way,
likewise, is prior to potentiality in regard of generation and time.

But, unquestionably, it is also prior in substance, at least, in the
first place, indeed, then, because those things that are subsequent
in generation are prior in form and substance; as a man to a
child, and a human being to seed: for now the one possesses the
form, but the other does not. And, in the second place, this is so
because everything that is being produced advances towards a
first principle and an end; for the final cause is a first principle,
and the generation or production is on account of the end. But
energy is an end, and on account of this is potentiality assumed;
for not in order that they may have the power of vision do animals
see: but they have the power of vision that they may see.

In like manner, also, persons are in possession of the building
art, or capacity, that they may actually build, and of the speculative
art that they may devise systems of speculation; they do not,
however, devise speculative systems that they may have the
speculative capacity, unless those who do so for the sake of
meditation: yet these by no means speculate absolutely; but they
either speculate in this manner, or the fact is so that they have
not in any wise an occasion to speculate. Moreover, matter
subsists in potentiality because it may advance onwards to form;
but when, at least, it subsists in energy, then doth it subsist in
form. In like manner, also, is it the case with other things, and
those of which the end is motion. Wherefore, as those engaged
in teaching by showing, in the way of example, one energizing—
say their pupil—think that they have adduced the end, it is so
with Nature in like manner. For, if this be not the case, a circumstance, like the Mercury of Passo, will take place; for scientific
knowledge would be obscure as to whether it might be internal
or external, as was the case with Passo's Hermes likewise, for an
end is the work, and the work constitutes the energy. Wherefore,
the name energy is denominated according to the work, and
converges towards actuality.

And since of some things that which is ultimate is the use—as, for example, of the power of vision the act of vision, and besides this no other work is produced different from the power of vision—yet in certain things is there something else generated; for example, from the art of housebuilding a house is produced in addition to the act of building, notwithstanding that energy, nevertheless, will be the end of potentiality, in both instances, to be sure, though it is more the end of it in the latter than in the former. For building is contained in that which is being built, and is generated and exists at the same time with the house. Of as many things, therefore, as there is something different (namely, that which is being produced) from their use, of these doth there subsist the energy in that which is being constructed, just as both the building resides in that which is being built, and the weaving in that which is being woven; in like manner, also, is it the case with other things, and, in general, doth motion subsist in that to which motion is being imparted. Of as many things, however, as there is not some different work beside the energy, in these is energy inherent; as, for instance, the act, or power, of seeing resides in the person who sees, and theory in the theorizer, and vitality, or life, in the soul: therefore, also, is happiness resident in the soul, for it also constitutes a certain 1050b sort of vitality. Wherefore, is it evident, that substance and form are each of them a certain energy. And therefore, according to this reasoning, it is evident that in substance energy is prior to potentiality. And, as we have stated, one energy invariably is antecedent to another in time, up to that which is primarily and eternally the moving cause.

But, assuredly, also, in a more strict and important sense is energy prior to capacity; for the things that are eternal are in substance prior to things that are perishable, yet nothing subsisting in potentiality is everlasting. And a reason of this is the following: every potentiality is at the same time a potentiality of its contradiction; for that which is not endued with the capacity of existing will not subsist in anything: but everything that is endued with capacity admits of not energizing. Accordingly, that thing the existence of which is potential admits of both being and not being: the same thing, then, is that which is potential, or endued with a capacity of both being and not being. But that thing the nonexistence of which is potential admits of not being, and that which admits of not being is subject to decay, either simply, or it is not this very thing the admissibility of whose nonexistence is affirmed, either according to place, or according to quantity, or according to quality; but simply is a thing exposed to corruption according to substance.

None, then, of those things that are simply incorruptible is an entity in potentiality, simply considered; but in a certain respect there is no hindrance to this being so; for instance, according to quality, or the place where. All things, then, subsist in energy: nor, even on the supposition of things being from necessity, are these things, however, primary, for unless these were so there would be nothing so. Nor, therefore, again, supposing there is any eternal motion, does such a motion subsist in capacity; nor, supposing that there is anything that is being eternally moved, such a thing that is being moved does not subsist according to capacity, unless so far as it proceeds from a certain quarter, or towards a certain direction. There is no hindrance, however, to the subsistence of the matter of this.

Wherefore, the sun and stars, and the entire firmament, perpetually energize. No apprehension, also, is there lest at any time they may come to a standstill, which dread overwhelms some of the Natural Philosophers. For neither are the heavenly bodies wearied in this operation of revolving (for their motion does not happen to subsist in regard of the capacity of the contradiction of those),—as, for example, is the case with things subject to decay—so as to render the continuity of the motion a laborious operation; for substance, which is matter and potentiality, and does not subsist in energy, is the cause of this.

There is, however, an imitation between things incorruptible and those that are in a state of change; for instance, earth and fire: for these, also, invariably energize, seeing that they involve motion essentially and in themselves. But all the rest of the potentialities about which we have discoursed (from the distinctions and definitions that have been framed), it is evident are conversant about contradiction; for that which is endued with the capacity of imparting motion in this particular way can also do so in another way, and not in this way—I mean, as many things, at any rate, as subsist as potentialities according to a rational principle. Potentialities, however, that are devoid of reason, in respect of presence and absence, will as the same be conversant about contradiction.

If, then, there are certain natures of such a sort, or substances of such a description, as those speculators who have been engaged in such theories affirm ideas to be, something would there be which would be skilled in scientific knowledge in a greater degree than science itself, and something would be much more moved than motion itself; for the former rather are energies, but the latter are potentialities of the former. That, therefore, energy is a thing prior both to potentiality, and every alternative first principle, is evident.

1051a

9. But that also energy is both superior and more excellent than potentiality, however excellent, is evident from these statements. For as many things as are denominated according to the being potential, as far as these are concerned, it is the same thing the being what is potential in regard of contraries; for instance, that which is said to be endued with a capacity of health and sickness is the same thing, and that, too, at the same time, for there is the same capacity, or potentiality, of being in a sound state of health and being indisposed, and of being at rest and in motion, and of building and of demolishing what is built, and of being built and falling into ruin.

The capacity, then, of accomplishing contraries exists at the same time; but the actual subsistence of these contraries at the same time is a thing that is impossible: and it is a thing that is impossible that contrary energies be also present at the same time; for instance, in the case of being healthy and being indisposed. Wherefore, either of these must needs be that which is good, and it must in like manner be possible that this be the case with both or neither. Energy, accordingly, is the more excellent of the two. There is, however, a necessity that, as regards that which is bad, the end and energy should be worse than the potentiality; for that which is endued with capacity, as regards both the contraries, is the same thing.

It is evident, then, that what is evil is not anything independent of the things themselves; for that which is evil is by the constitution of Nature subsequent to that which we term potentiality. Accordingly, neither in those things which subsist from a first principle, and those that are everlasting existences, is there anything that is either evil, or anything in the shape of imperfection, or aught that has been actually reduced to decay; for a tendency towards decay or corruption belongs to things that are evil.

But mathematical figures are also discovered as subsisting in energy; for persons discover such in the act of division; and if such had been divided in twain, these mathematical figures would have been apparent: but now they are inherent potentially. Why, let me ask, has a triangle angles equal to two right angles? Because the angles about one point are equal to two right angles. If, therefore, the line about the side be produced, to one who merely glances at the figure the thing is at once obvious. Why, too, in a semicircle, is the angle universally a right angle? Because, if there are three equal right lines, or even two at the base, and one right line raised thereupon from the central point, the thing will be obvious to anyone at a glance, provided he be a person that has some knowledge of mathematics. Wherefore, it is evident that mathematical diagrams, subsisting as they do in potentiality, are discovered when they are being reduced to energy; and the cause of this is the following,—that understanding constitutes the energy: wherefore from energy springs potentiality; and, on account of this circumstance, persons engaged in doing anything are acquainted with that thing, for subsequent in regard of production is energy—I mean, such as subsists according to number.

10. Since, however, entity and nonentity are denominated partly in accordance with the figures of the categories, and partly in accordance with the capacity, or the energy of these, or in accordance with contraries, but since that which is entity, in the strictest sense of the word, is what is true or false, and this in the case of things consists in composition or division, so that one can verify his assertion who considers that which has been divided to be divided, and that which has been compounded to be compounded; but he speaks falsely who, when either things are or when they are not, makes assertions abut them in a contrary way to that in which they actually subsist: seeing, then, that this is the case, the thing is termed true or false; for it is fitting that we should take into consideration what this is which is termed true or false. For it is not on account of a true supposition, on our parts, of your being white that you are in reality white, but, on account of your being white, we who make this assertion as to your whiteness can verify our assertion.

If, therefore, some things are invariably compounded, and involve an impossibility of being divided, but if other things are perpetually in a state of division, and are not endued with a capacity of being put together again, and if some things are the recipients of contraries, in such a case actual existence is the being compounded and the being one thing, but nonexistence, the not being compounded, but the being more than one thing. Respecting, then, admissible or contingent natures, the same opinion becomes false and true; and this is the case with the same definition, or discursus: and they involve the possibility of true assertions being made of them in one instance, but false assertions in another. Regarding, however, things that are devoid of a potentiality of being disposed otherwise than they are, a thing in this case is not generated so as at one time to be true, but at another false; but these things are invariably true and false. And, therefore, in regard of incomposite natures, what, let me ask, is the being or not being, and what the true and the false in respect of these? For it is not a thing that is compounded so that it actually involves existence when it may be in a state of composition, but does not involve existence when it may subsist in a state of division,—as a piece of white wood, or the incommensurability of the diagonal of a square with its side,—neither will the true and the false, in like manner, be still inherent, also, in those things—I mean, incomposite natures. Or, shall we say that, as neither that which is true in regard of these, so neither is their actual existence the same; but the one is that which is true, while the other is that which is false? Contact and assertion give us that which is true, for not the same thing is affirmation with assertion; not, however, to pass into contact amounts to ignorance, for deception about the nature of anything has no existence, save by accident. In like manner, also, is it in the case of substances that are uncompounded; for deception in regard of them is not a thing that is possible.

And all such substances subsist in energy, not in potentiality; for if they subsisted in potentiality they would be generated, and in process of time would be corrupted; but in the present instance the actual entity is not generated, nor is it reduced into corruption, for it would be generated from something. And as regards whatsoever things, therefore, that amount to the existence of any certain particular thing, and its subsistence in energy or activity, as regards these, I say, there is no possibility of laboring under deception, but either one understands them or he does not. But the inquiry as to the nature of anything is being instituted by us in respect of these natures, as to whether there are things of this sort at all, or not; and the fact is, the existence of a thing is as that which is true, and its nonexistence as that which is false; in one way, if it is that which is compounded, it is true, whereas, in the other, if it is not a composite nature, it is false: and in another way, if we suppose it to exist in this way, it is 1052a true, but if not in this way, it is not true. Now, that which is true amounts to the intellectual apprehension of these, but that which is false does not exist, nor does it amount to deception, but ignorance; not, however, such as may be assimilated unto blindness, for blindness is just as if one, in short, did not possess the capacity of intellectually apprehending any subject. And it is also evident that, respecting things that are immovable, there is no deception as to the time when of their existence, supposing that one consider them as things that are immovable; for instance, the triangle—unless viewed as that which is subject to mutation—a mathematician will not consider as being at one time in possession of angles equal to two right angles, but at another not so, for it would undergo a certain mutation; yet he might consider one thing in this point of view, but not another: for example, that there be no even number, first, or that some are so, but that other numbers are not so. In regard, however, of one thing in number we cannot expect that he should entertain this opinion, for no longer would he do so as regards certain things, yet not as regards others; but he will speak truth or falsehood so far as he makes assertions of it as a thing that is invariably disposed in this way.

BOOK X

1. THAT unity is denominated in many ways has been previously declared in our divisions on its multifarious predications; and whereas it is denominated in many ways, there are summarily arranged four modes of things that are styled one, primarily and essentially, but not according to accident. For both that which is continuous, either simply considered, or especially what is so by nature, at least, and not by contract, or by a bond of connection, such is one thing; and that in a more eminent degree is one thing, and prior to these of which the motion is more indivisible, and simple, rather. Moreover, is unity a thing of this sort; and in a more eminent degree is that which is a whole one thing, and that which possesses a certain form and species: but particularly we look for unity if a thing of this sort subsists by the constitution of Nature, and not by violent or abnormal means; in like manner as whatever things are joined together by glue, or by a nail, or by a chain, are one thing, but contains in itself the cause of its own continuity. And it is a thing of this kind in respect of its motion being one and indivisible in place and time; so that it is evident if anything by the constitution of Nature involves a principle of the earliest motion—I mean, such a principle as is primary—that it is the first magnitude; as, for example, I speak of the circular motion of a body, for this is the earliest motion. Therefore, in this way are some things one either as what is continuous or entire; others, however, are one of which the definition may be one. And things of this sort are such as those of which the

217

intellectual apprehension is one, and such as those of which it is indivisible, and of which there is an indivisible apprehension of what is indivisible in form or number. In number, therefore, is the singular indivisible; but in form that is indivisible which resides in what is an object of knowledge, and in scientific knowledge itself: wherefore, that would be one thing primarily which is the cause of the subsistence of unity in substances. Therefore, no doubt, is unity denominated in such many ways, as both that which is continuous by the constitution of Nature, and is an entirety and a singular, and that which is universal. Now, all these are one in respect of the indivisibility—of the motion of some of them, but of the intellectual perception or the definition of others.

It is requisite, however, to understand that we should not assume that the same assertions should be made alike in the inquiries both as to what sort of things are styled one, and what is the nature of the existence of unity, and what is the definition of it; for unity is predicated in thus many ways, and each of those things will be one in which any one of these modes will be inherent. The being or existence of unity, however, sometimes will be in accordance with one of these, and sometimes with another which also is nearer to the name, but those are one in regard of capacity; just as, also, if it may be expedient to discuss the subject relating to element and cause, it would be necessary, in the treatment of these matters, both to frame distinctions and to assign the definition of the name. For fire, in one sense, is an element,—and perhaps, also, with the Infinite in itself this is the case, or it is something else of the sort,—and, in another sense, it is not so; for the essence of element is not the same thing with the essence of fire and of element; but so far forth as fire is a certain thing and a certain nature, so far is it an element; but the name signifies that this particular quality is an accident in this, because there is something subsisting from this as from a thing that is primarily inherent. So, also, is it in the case of cause and unity, and all things of this sort. Wherefore, also, the essence or existence of one consists in being indivisible; namely, in being this certain particular thing, and incapable of a separate subsistence either in place or form, or in the faculty of thought, or in that which is entire, and has been made the subject of definition.

But especially doth the nature or essence of unity consist in being the first measure of every genus, and the principal portions of quantity; for from this quarter, likewise, hath it proceeded to other things, for measure is that whereby quantity is known. But quantity, so far forth as it is quantity, is known either by unity or by number; for every number is known by unity. Wherefore, every quantity, so far forth as it is quantity, is discoverable by unity; and that by which as primary it is known, this itself is one. Wherefore, unity is a first principle of number, so far forth as it is number. And hence, also, in the case of other things, that is denominated a measure whereby as primary each thing is known; and the measure of everything is one in length, in breadth, in depth, in gravity, in velocity. For gravity and velocity are what is common in the case of contraries, for in a twofold sense may each of them be taken; as, for instance, gravity is both that which involves any momentum whatsoever, and that which possesses a superabundance of momentum: and velocity is both that which involves any motion whatever, and an excess of motion; for likewise is there a certain velocity even of that which is slow, and there is a certain gravity of that which is rather light.

Now, a measure and first principle in all of these is a sort of unity, and a thing that is indivisible; since—to give an instance— in lines, also, they employ that which measures a foot as a thing that is indivisible: for everywhere, or in every instance, do investigators search for measure as a certain unity, and as a thing that is indivisible; and this constitutes what is simple, either in the quality or in the quantity. Wheresoever, indeed, therefore, there does not appear to be anything subtracted or added, this is the most accurate measure. Wherefore, the measure of number is the most precise of all measures, for the monad they have 1053a posited as in every way indivisible; but, in the case of other things, they imitate a measure of this sort: for from a stadium and a talent, and that which is invariably greater, would anything that has been both added and taken away rather escape our notice, than from that which is less. Wherefore, that from which, considered as primary, a thing does not admit of subsisting according to sense, this all men constitute as a measure, both of things moist and dry, and of gravity and magnitude; and they imagine that they then know the quantity of a thing when they happen to know it by means of this measure. And, therefore, also, motion do they measure by a simple motion, and one which is the most rapid; for this involves the very smallest possible duration. Wherefore, in astronomy a unity of this kind is a first principle and a measure—for their hypothesis is, that the motion of the heavens is equable, and that it is of the utmost velocity; and, in accordance with this, astronomers adjust the other motions—and in music diesis is adopted as a measure, because it constitutes the least perceptible sound; and in the case of vocal sounds it is an element of speech that is such. And all these things in this way are a certain one, not in such a manner as that the one is a thing common to them, but in such a way as has been declared.

A measure is not, however, invariably one in number, but sometimes more than one; as, for instance, two dieses such as are not understood according to hearing, but are contained in the definitions; and the vocal sounds by which we measure are more numerous, and the diameter of the square, likewise, is measured by two things, and this is the case with the side and with all magnitudes. Thus, therefore, is unity a measure of all things, because we thereby know those things of which substance consists, by making a division of it either according to quantity or according to form; and on this account is unity indivisible, because the original of everything is that which is indivisible. But each thing is not indivisible in the same manner as a foot and the monad; but the latter is indivisible in every respect, and the former has a tendency towards things that are indivisible according to sense, as just now has been remarked; for, perhaps, everything continuous is divisible. The measure, however, is always a thing of a kindred nature; for of magnitudes is magnitude the measure: and, in regard of an individual thing, length is a measure of length, breadth of breadth, of vocal sounds voice is a measure, weight a measure of weight, a monad of monads. For in this way must we receive this assertion, but not to the effect that number is a measure of numbers. Although this ought to be the case, if measure, in like manner, in this case is to be kindred with what is measured; but he who entertains this opinion does not think similarly of this instance, but just as if one would suppose that monads are a measure of monads, but not a monad; number, however, is a multitude of monads.

And science we pronounce to be the measure of things and sense, likewise, for this very reason, because we attain unto some knowledge through the instrumentality of these, since rather are they measured than are they standards of measure. But it happens unto us just as if another were measuring us we should know how large we were by reason of the cubital measure being extended over us thus far. Protagoras, however, says that man is the measure of all things; just as if he should say that one who possesses scientific knowledge, or who goes through an act of perception by sense, is a measure, and that this is so with these because the one possesses sense, but the other scientific knowledge, which we affirm to be measures of those things that are subjects to either one or the other. Doubtless, such persons, in their assertion of nothing that is extraordinary appear to say something pertinent to the matter in hand. 1053b

That therefore, indeed, the being or essence of unity subsists in an eminent degree, according to the name which they determine upon, as a certain measure—and the most important measure—of quantity, and, in the next place, of quality, this is evident. Now, a measure of this sort will be of one kind, if it may be indivisible as far as regards quantity, but of another, if it be so as regards quality. Wherefore, unity is indivisible either simply or so far forth as it is unity.

2. But as regards Substance and Nature we must institute an inquiry how they are disposed, in like manner as in the doubts mooted in the earlier portions of this work we have taken a

review of what unity is, and how one ought to take up his opinions respecting the same,—whether as though this unity were to be considered as a certain substance (as both the Pythagorics affirm in the first instance, and Plato subsequently), or rather, whether some nature is subjected to it, and in what manner this ought to be more intelligibly discoursed of, and whether rather is it the case that we should look at unity from the point of view that some of the natural philosophers do? For of those a certain one says that unity is harmony, but another air, and a third the Infinite. Now, if it is not possible for any of the universals to be substance, as has been declared in our disquisitions concerning substance, and in those concerning entity, nor that this very thing be substance so as to be endued with the capacity of subsisting as a certain one thing separate from plurality for a thing of this kind is what is common, but alone may be ranked as a category, it is evident, if the foregoing be true, that neither is unity itself a substance, for entity and unity, in an eminent degree above other things, are predicated universally of all things. Wherefore, neither are genera certain natures and substances capable of a separable subsistence from other things, nor does unity admit of being a genus, on account of the same causes, through which neither does unity or substance admit of being a genus. And, further, in like manner it is expedient that the case stand in regard of all things. Now, unity and entity are predicated in an equal number of ways: wherefore, since in quantities there is a certain unity and a certain nature, and since, in like manner, both of these reside in quantities, it is plain that likewise, in general, we must investigate what unity is, as well as what entity is also; as if it were not sufficient to determine that this very thing is the nature of it.

But, unquestionably, in colors, at least, there is the one color,—for example, white,—afterwards the rest appear to be produced from this and black; but black is a privation of white, as darkness also is of light, but this is a privation of light. Wherefore, if entities were colors, entities would constitute a certain number—but of what, let me ask—without doubt, manifestly of colors; and unity would be a certain one thing, as, for example, white.

And in like manner, also, if entities were melodies there would be a number of dieses, however; but the substance of them would not be number, and unity would be something the substance of which would not be unity, but diesis. In like manner, 1054a also, in the case of the elements of sounds, if all entities were sounds they would constitute the number of the elements, and unity would be a vocal element; and if entities were right-lined figures they would constitute the number of figures, and unity would be a triangle: and the same reasoning stands good, likewise, in the case of the other genera of things. Wherefore, if also in passive properties, and in qualities, and in quantities, and in motion, there subsist numbers, and a certain one thing in all these, unity would be both a number of certain things, and it would constitute a certain entity; but by no means would this be the substance of that thing: and as regards substances the case must needs be the same; for in like manner is it in the case of all things. That, therefore, unity in every genus is a sort of nature, and that this very thing—namely, unity—is not the nature of anything, is evident; but as in colors there is one color to be sought for as unity itself, so, also, in substances is one substance to be sought for as unity itself.

But that somehow unity and entity are equivalent in their meaning is evident from the fact that unity follows upon the categories in an equal number of ways with entity, and yet does not subsist in any of them; as, for example, neither in quiddity nor in quality, but it subsists in like manner as entity. And from this fact it follows that there is not anything different from man additionally predicated in the predication of one man, as neither is entity anything independent of quiddity, or quality, or quantity, and that the being of unity is the same thing as the being of some individual thing.

3. Unity, however, and plurality are opposed in many ways; in one of which modes the unity and the multitude are opposed as what is indivisible and what is divisible: for that which has been divided, or is actually divisible, is styled a certain multitude; but

what is indivisible, or that which has not been divided, is styled one. Since, therefore, the oppositions are fourfold, and one of these is expressed according to privation, there would subsist what is contrary, and neither would they be denominated as contradictions, nor as things predicated relatively. But unity is predicated from its contrary, and thereby made evident,—viz. that which is indivisible from that which is divisible,—from the fact that multitude, and that which is divisible, are rather cognizable by sense than that which is indivisible. Wherefore, in the definition the multitude is prior to that which is indivisible by reason of perception by sense.

There also belong to unity—as we have likewise described in our division of contraries—sameness, and similarity, and equality; but to multitude belong diversity, and dissimilarity, and inequality. Seeing, however, that sameness is predicated in many ways, after one mode also—namely, according to number—subsists that which we denominate occasionally as this, and after another mode if a thing be one both in definition and in number; for instance, you are the same with yourself both in form and matter. Further, are those things said to be the same to the primary substance of which there may belong one definition; as, for instance, equal right lines are the same, and equal and equal-angled quadrangular figures, notwithstanding that they are many in number; but in these the equality is unity. And things are said to be similar if they be not the same simply considered, nor without a difference in regard of subject-substance, but yet may be the same as regards form; for example, the greater square is similar to a less: and so it is with unequal right lines, for these are similar, no doubt, but not the same absolutely. And some things are called similar if they possess the same form wherein reside the more and less, as properties ingenerated, while the things themselves are neither greater nor less. And other things are so styled if there belong to them the same passive condition, and such as is one in species; as, for instance, that which is exceedingly white, and what is so in a less degree, they say that such are similar because the form of them is one.

1054b

And other things are so called if they possess more of sameness than of diversity, either considered simply, or provided they be more obvious to perception as possessing such; for instance, tin is more similar to silver than to gold, and gold is similar to fire, so far forth as it is ruddy and brilliant.

Wherefore, it is evident that both diversity and dissimilarity are denominated in many ways; and that which is another thing is expressed in opposition to that which is the same. Wherefore, everything in relation to everything is either the same or different; but that is said to take place if the matter and the definition be not one: wherefore, you and your neighbor are different. But a third signification of the foregoing is when things subsist as in mathematical entities. Therefore, indeed, on this account, everything of those, as many as are denominated unity and entity, are so denominated in reference to everything as different or the same. For neither is there any contradiction of sameness. Wherefore, the assertion is not made in the case of nonentities, but of all entities,—the "not-same," however, is predicated of entities,—for sameness and diversity being constituted by nature an entity and one thing, are either one or not one. That, then, which is diversity, and that which is sameness, are in this way opposed. Difference, however, and diversity are something else; for it is not requisite that a thing which is diverse, and that in reference to, or because of which, a thing is diverse, should be a diverse thing by reason of something common; for everything whatsoever, in regard of its being an entity, is either diverse or the same. That, however, which is different from something is different by something, or in some respect, so that it is necessary that something wherein they differ should be the same, and this something which is thus the same is either genus or species; for everything that is different differs either in genus or in species; those things differ in genus of which neither the matter is common or their generation into one another—for instance, take the case of those things of as many as there is another figure of predication—but things are different in species of which the genus may be the same, and that is called a genus in respect of which both of the things that are different are styled the same according to substance. But contraries are things different, and contrariety is a certain difference.

And that we have made this foregoing supposition correctly is evident from induction; for all those things that are different their difference is even apparent: and not merely so when they are diverse; but some things are diverse in genus, but others are 1055a diverse which belong to the same coordination of predication. Wherefore, also, those same things that are contained in the same genus are also involved in the same species. Now, it has been determined in the case of other things what sort of entities are the same or different in the genus.

4. But since it is admissible that things which are different should differ one from another more and less, there is, likewise, a certain greatest difference; and I mean by this contrariety: and that there does exist this greatest difference is evident from induction. For some things that are different in genus do not possess a way one towards another, but are distant to a considerable extent, and are not things that may be compared together. To those things, however, that differ in species belong generations that take their rise from contraries as from extremes, but the last interval is the greatest. Wherefore, also, is this the case with that which lies between the contraries. But, surely, this which is the greatest in each genus, at any rate, is that which is perfect; for greatest is that of which there is no excess, or superabundancy, and finished is that beyond which there is no possibility of assuming anything, for the perfect difference involves an end: in like manner as other things are called perfect, or finished in respect of their involving an end. But to the end there is nothing extrinsic; for it is the ultimate thing in everything, and comprises those things of which it is the end. Wherefore, nothing is extrinsic to the end, nor does the perfect require anything of the sort. That therefore, indeed, contrariety constitutes a perfect difference is evident from these statements. And whereas contraries are denominated in many ways, subsistence in a perfect manner will follow in such a way as that the subsistence also of contraries

would be inherent in them. Now, seeing that these things are so, it is plain that there is no possibility of one thing involving many contraries; for neither could there be anything more ultimate, or final, than the extreme, nor of one interval would there be more than two extremes. And, in general, if contrariety be a difference, yet difference is the difference between two things: wherefore, also, this will be the case with the perfect difference.

It is necessary, however, that the rest of the definitions also of the contraries be correct; for likewise doth the perfect difference evince the greatest amount of difference: for of things that differ in genus and in species there is no possibility of assuming anything that is more external; for it has been demonstrated that, respecting things extrinsic to the genus, there subsists not a difference, and of these this is the greatest difference: and those things that belong to the same genus, and involve the greatest difference, are contraries, for the greatest difference of these is the perfect difference. And those things that involve the greatest amount of difference in the same recipient are contraries, for there is the same matter for the contraries; and things that rank under the same potentiality, and involve the greatest difference, are also contraries; for also the science is one concerning one genus of those things in which the perfect difference is the greatest.

The first or chief contrariety, however, consists in habit and privation; yet not every privation (for privation is predicated in many ways), but whatsoever such as may be perfect. And the other contraries will be denominated according to these, some, on the one hand, in respect of possession, and others from action, or from being fit subjects for action; and, on the other hand, some in respect of their being recipients, and rejections of these, or of other contraries.

Now, if they are opposed—I mean, contradiction and privation, and contrariety and relations—and if of these contradiction is the first, and of contradiction there is nothing intermediate but if of contraries this is admissible, it is evident that contradiction is not the same thing with contrariety, and that privation constitutes a certain contradiction; for privation belongs either to what is entirely devoid of a capacity of possessing, or to that which, even though adapted by nature for possession, may yet not actually possess either entirely or in a certain definite manner; for we now express this in many ways, just as the distinctions have been drawn by us elsewhere. Wherefore, privation is a certain contradiction, or a defined impotentiality, or one which is conjoined along with what is receptive. Wherefore, of contradiction there is not anything that is intermediate; but of a certain privation there is, for everything is either equal or not equal; but not everything is equal or unequal, but only if it be contained in that which is receptive of equality.

If, now, there are generations in matter from contraries, and these are produced either from form and the habit of the species, or from a certain privation of the species and of the form, it is evident that every contrariety would constitute a certain privation, but not every privation, perhaps, would constitute contrariety. And a cause of this is the following: that whatever is a subject of the privation admits of being a subject of privation in many ways; for those things from the extremities of which changes are generated, these are contraries.

And this is evident, likewise, from induction; for every contrariety involves a privation of either of the contraries. Not similarly, however, is it the case with all things; for inequality is a privation of equality, but dissimilarity of similarity, and vice of virtue. But there is the same difference as has been stated; for one thing is a subject of privation if it may happen to be deprived of anything, but another if it may be so at any time, or in any subject; as, for example, would be the case at a certain age either in that which is the principal age, or altogether so. Wherefore, of some contraries is there a medium, and there is a man who is neither good nor evil; but of others there is not a medium, but a number must needs be either odd or even: further, do some things involve a definite subject, but others do not. Wherefore, it is evident that invariably either of the contraries is denominated according to privation: it is sufficient, however, if there are in existence the primaries and the genera of contraries; as, for instance, unity and plurality are styled such, for the rest are referred or reduced to these.

5. But since one thing is contrary to one thing, a person would feel perplexed as to how unity and plurality are opposed, and how the equal is opposed to the great and the small. For there is the question whether invariably we speak of a thing in the way of opposition—for example, whether it is white or black, and whether it is white or not white—but we do not say whether such is a man or a thing that is white, unless hypothetically, and in such an inquiry, as, for instance, whether Cleon came or Socrates. But there is no necessity for this inquiry being found in any genus; but this, likewise, has proceeded from thence. For things in opposition do not admit of subsisting alone at the same time; which aforesaid mode of speaking of a thing one employs in the present instance,—I mean, in the inquiry, which of the two came first? For if both could do so at the same time, the question would be ridiculous. And if this were possible in this way also, in like manner would the person who makes the inquiry fall into 1056a opposition, viz. into unity, or plurality; as, for example, whether both came, or either of the two? If, therefore, in things that are opposed the question whether a thing "is so and so" is to be found invariably—now, we speak of a thing as to whether it is greater, or less, or equal—what opposition is there of equality in respect of these, for neither is it contrary to either only, nor to both? For why should it be contrary to the greater more than to the less? Further, is the equal contrary to that which is unequal; wherefore, it will be contrary to more than one. If, however, inequality signifies the same thing with both of these at the same time, it would be in opposition to both, and the doubt renders assistance to those who say that inequality constitutes the dyad; it happens, however, that one is contrary to two, which is impossible. Moreover, equality seems to be a medium between the great and the small; but no contrariety seems to be either of the nature of a medium, nor from the definition is it a thing possible that it

should; for it would not be perfect if it were a mean between anything: yet it rather invariably involves something that is a medium with respect to itself.

It therefore remains that equality be opposed either as negation or as privation. Now, certainly, it is not possible that it should be in opposition to either; for why should it be opposed to the large more than to the small? In such, then, there would subsist a privative negation of both. Wherefore, also, the question "whether" is predicated in respect of both, but not in respect of either; as we do not say whether a thing is greater or equal, or whether it is equal or less; but the question of "whether" invariably subsists in reference to three things. It does not, however, constitute privation from necessity; for it does not follow that everything is equal which is not greater or less: but that takes place in the case of the things in which those—I mean, the greater or less—are naturally inherent. Now equality is that which is neither great nor small, but that which by nature is adapted for becoming great or little; and as privative negation is it opposed to both. Wherefore, also, it is a thing that is a medium; and that which is neither evil nor good is in opposition to both, but without a name: for in many ways is each denominated, and that which is receptive is not one thing, bur rather that which is neither white nor black. Neither, however, is this styled one thing; but colors are somehow defined in respect of which this negation is affirmed privatively; for it is requisite that this be either a negation of white and black, or that it be a thing devoid of color, or something else of the sort.

Wherefore, those persons do not correctly reprehend our remark on this point who are of opinion that all things are expressed similarly: wherefore, there will be between a shoe and a hand something that is a medium which will be neither shoe nor hand; since, also, that which is neither good nor bad will be a medium between what is good and what is bad; as if there were likely to be something intermediate between all things. It is not, however, necessary that this result should ensue; for this co-negation of things that are opposed belongs to those of which there is a certain medium, and between which a certain interval has been fitted by nature to exist; but as regards these there is not a difference in existence, for in another genus are those 1056b things to be classed of which there are co-negations: wherefore, the subject of them is not one.

6. And, in like manner, also, concerning unity and plurality a person might express the following doubt. For if plurality be opposed to unity, absolutely or simply considered, there ensue certain consequences that are impossible; for unity will be a thing that is few in number, or will amount to few things, for plurality is likewise opposed to the few. Further, are two things many, since the twofold is manifold; and so also is two denominated twofold. Wherefore, unity is a thing that is few in number; for relatively to what are two things styled many, unless in reference to unity and fewness? For nothing else appears to be less. Further, must this be admitted, if as what in length are the long and the short, so in multitude are the much and the few; and whatever may be much is also many, and the many is also much: unless there is some difference, then, in a thing that is continuous and easily defined, fewness will be a certain multitude. Wherefore, will unity be a certain multitude, if, also, it be that which is few. And this must needs be so if two things are many.

But, perhaps, plurality is styled somehow also as the much, yet as being a thing that is different, as water, which is much, but not many. But in respect of as many things as are divisible therein subsists the many, or plurality, in one way, if the multitude involves superabundancy either absolutely or relatively to something— and, in like manner, it is the case with fewness, if the multitude should involve deficiency—but, in another way, plurality subsists as number, which also alone is opposed to unity. For in this way do we denominate unity, or plurality, just as if one should say unit and units, or a white thing and white things, and things that have been measured in respect of measure, and that which is capable of being measured. So, also, things which are manifold are denominated many; for each number is many because it is one, and because each is measurable by one, and as being that which is opposed to unity, not to fewness. So, indeed, then, two things are many, likewise; yet they are not so as a multitude involving superabundancy either relatively or absolutely, but primarily. And two things are simply what are few; for it is the first multitude which involves deficiency, and two is the first multitude in number.

Wherefore, Anaxagoras did not correctly withdraw his assent from the current opinion when he laid down that all things had a subsistence at the same time, and were infinite both in multitude and smallness; but he ought to have said, instead of this expression, that things were infinite both in smallness and paucity, for paucity or fewness does not constitute infinity, since fewness does not subsist on account of unity, as some philosophers would make out, but through duality.

Unity, therefore, and plurality, such as are to be found in numbers, are opposed in the way a measure is opposed to that which is measurable; and these things are opposed as those that are relative to something—I mean, as many things of those that are relative as do not involve an essential subsistence. Now, 1057a a distinction has been drawn by us elsewhere, to the effect that relatives are predicated in a twofold way,—partly as contraries, and partly as scientific knowledge is related to that which may be made an object of science, because something else is predicated with respect to them. But that the one may be less than a certain thing—as, for example, than two—there is no hindrance to this being the case; for though it be less, it does not follow that it also be what is few in number. Multitude, however, is, as it were, the genus of number, for number constitutes multitude, which is measurable by one: and unity and number are, in a manner, opposed,—not as a thing that is contrary, but, as has been stated, as some of those things that are relatives; for as far forth as unity is a measure, and number that which may be measured, thus far are they opposed to each other. Wherefore, not everything that may be one constitutes number; as, for example, on the supposition that there is anything that is indivisible.

But though science is denominated in like manner in relation to that which may be made an object of scientific knowledge, it is not yet similarly attributed as such; for science would appear to be a measure, but that which may be an object of science would appear as that which is being measured. It happens, however, that every science is a thing fit to be an object of scientific knowledge; yet everything that is an object of science is not a science, because, in a certain respect, is science measured by that which may be made an object of scientific inquiry.

But neither is multitude contrary to fewness; but the much is opposed to this as a multitude which is excessive is opposed to a multitude that is exceeded. Nor is multitude contrary to unity altogether; but in respect of unity the case stands just as has been stated, namely, that one sort is divisible, but another indivisible, and again, a third subsists as a relative, just as science subsists with respect to what may be made an object of science, on the supposition that science constituted number, and that unity were a measure.

7. And since between contraries there is a possibility of there being something that is a medium,—and of some there is a medium,—it is necessary that media should derive their being from contraries; for all media, and the things of which they are media, are contained in the same genus. For we denominate those things media into whatsoever a thing that is undergoing a change must needs be changed in the first instance; for example, if one should pass from the hypate to the nete, if the transition be made in a short space of time, he will previously reach the intermediate sounds; and the case is the same in colors,—if one will pass from white to black, he will come to the purple and that which is duskish previously to his reaching what is black: and in like manner is it with other things. But that a change should take place from one genus to another genus is not possible, except according to accident; as, for instance, in a transition from color into figure. It is requisite, then, that media, and the things of which they are media, should be contained in the same genus also with themselves.

But, unquestionably, is it the case that all media are, at any rate, media of certain things that are opposed; for from these alone is it possible should arise a change that is essential. Wherefore, it is impossible that there should subsist any medium of things that are not opposed; for otherwise would there be a change, and that not from things that are opposed. But there is no medium of contradiction in things that are opposed, for this constitutes contradiction, and amounts to antithesis or opposition; and to an opposition of which, in any respect whatever, one of the members is present, having no medium between that of which, in any respect, either of the members—the yes or the no—is present, or, in other words, not having any medium at all. But of the rest some are relatives, but others are privation, and some are contraries. But as many things belonging to those that are relatives as are not contraries do not involve a medium. And a cause of this is the following, inasmuch as they are not contained in the same genus; for what is there that is a medium between science and that which may be made an object of scientific knowl-

1057b edge? But there is a medium between the great and the small.

Now, if media are contained in the same genus, as has been demonstrated, and are media between things that are contrary, it is necessary that these, likewise, be compounded of these contraries; for either will there be a certain genus of them, or there will not be any such. And if there will be a genus of them in such a way as that there be something antecedent to the contraries, those contrary differences will be antecedent which may make the contraries as species of genus: for from genus and differences subsist species; for example, if white and black be contraries, and the one is a segregative color, but the other a congregative color, these actual differences—I mean, discretive and syncretive colors—will have an antecedent subsistence. Wherefore, these contraries involve a subsistence prior to one another; but, surely, contraries, at any rate, that are different are contraries in preference. And the other things and the media will arise from genus and differences; as, for instance, whatever colors are media between white and black, these it is necessary should be denominated as consisting from genus (but color is a genus), and from certain differences. They themselves, however, will not constitute primary contraries; and if this be not the case, everything will be either white or black. These, then, are other colors; accordingly, these will be the media between primary contraries: primary differences, however, are those which are segregative and congregative. Wherefore, in regard of these primaries (as many as are contraries not in genus), we must investigate the following point,—from what the media of these consist; for it is necessary that things contained in the same genus should be compounded either of things incomposite in that genus, or that they should be incomposite natures. Therefore, are contraries uncompounded one of another, so that they are first principles; but the media constitute either all things or not any at all: and from things contrary something is generated. Wherefore, there will ensue a change into this previously to a change into contraries; for of each thing will there be both less and more: accordingly, will there subsist a medium, and this a medium between contraries. And all the other things that are media are composites then; for that which is a medium is more than one thing and less than another, and is in a manner compounded of those things of which it is said to consist,—as greater than one of them and less than the other. And since, as regards contraries, things that have an antecedent existence are not homogeneous, all media would arise from contraries; wherefore, both all things to be found in the scale of existence downwards, and contraries and media, will consist from primary contraries.

That, indeed, therefore, the media are all contained in the same genus, and that they are media between contraries, and that these media are all composed of contraries, this is evident.

8. Diversity, however, in species is a something that is diverse from a certain thing; and this must needs subsist in both; as, for instance, if animal were a thing diverse in species, both would be animals: it is necessary, then, that in the same genus there be contained those things that are diverse in species. For by genus I

mean a thing of such a sort as that by which both are styled one and the same thing, not involving a difference according to accident, whether subsisting as matter or after a mode that is different from matter; for not only is it necessary that a certain thing that is common be inherent in them (for instance, that both should be animals), but also that this very thing—namely, animal—should be diverse from both: for example, that the one should be horse but the other man. Wherefore, this common characteristic simultaneously is found in things that are different in species from one another: therefore, this will be such a particular animal essentially, and that will be an animal essentially different; as that will be a horse and this a man. It is necessary, accordingly, that this difference should amount to a diversity of genus; for I term a difference of genus diversity which makes this very thing to be diverse: therefore, will this constitute contrariety.

And the same is evident from induction, likewise; for all things are distinguished by things that are opposite: and it has been demonstrated that contraries are contained in the same genus, for contrariety amounts to perfect difference, and every difference which is contained in a species is something belonging to a certain thing. Wherefore is this both the same and a genus in both: wherefore, also, all contraries are contained in the same coordination of predication, as many as are different in species and not in genus, and diverse particularly one from another; for perfect is the difference between them, and they are not generated simultaneously with one another. Difference, then, amounts to contrariety, for this constitutes what it is to be diverse in species; namely, for things to involve contrariety when they are contained in the same genus,—things, I say, that are individual. Now, things are the same in species—as many as do not involve contrariety—when they are individual existences; for in division and in media are contrarieties generated, before one comes to those things that are individual.

Wherefore, it is evident that respecting that which is said to be a genus, neither the same nor diverse in species is any of those things which are adapted for being species as of a genus;

for matter is made manifest by negation, and genus is the matter of that of which it is termed a genus—not as the genus of the Heracleids, but as that which subsists in Nature. Nor is genus denominated in relation to those that are not contained in the same genus, but in relation to those of which there will be a difference from them in genus; and things differing in species differ from those that are in the same genus: for the difference of that from which it is a difference in species must needs be contrariety, and contrariety belongs to those things that are alone in the same genus.

9. But, perhaps, one would raise the question, why woman does not differ from man in species, when the female and male are contraries, and when contrariety amounts to difference? But neither are female and male diverse in species, although they are the essential differences of animal, and are not as whiteness or blackness, but the male and female are inherent in animal, so far forth as it is animal. Now, the following doubt is almost the same as the foregoing—namely, why it is that contrariety partly makes things diverse in species, and partly does not so; for example, why does it make that which has the support of feet, and that which is furnished with wings so, but does not make whiteness and blackness? Is this the case because some things are the proper affections of genus, and other things are less so; and since the one is form and the other is matter, as many contrarieties as are contained in form create a difference in species, and as many as reside in form, when assumed together with matter, do not give rise to a specific difference?

Wherefore, whiteness does not give rise to a difference of man, nor blackness; nor are these the specific difference of a white man in relation to a black man, nor would one name be assigned to both; for man is as matter, but matter does not create a difference: for men are not forms of man. For this reason, although the flesh and bones are diverse from which this man and that are made, yet the entire compound is a thing that is diverse, to be sure, but not different in species, because contrariety does not exist in reason or form, but this entire compound is an individual thing. Now, Callias is form in conjunction with matter; and this, therefore, is the case with white man,—because Callias is white, therefore man is white according to accident. Neither, doubtless, do a brazen and wooden circle, nor a brazen triangle and wooden circle, differ in species on account of matter, but because contrariety is present in the form.

But whether shall we say that matter does not render things diverse in species, though being somehow diverse itself, or is it the case that it makes them so partly? For why is this horse diverse from this man in species, and yet the forms of these subsist along with matter? Is it because contrariety is inherent in the form? For there is obviously a contrariety subsisting between a white man and a black horse. And this, at any rate, is a specific difference, but not so far forth as the one is white and the other black; since even if both were white, nevertheless in species they would be diverse. But the male and female are appropriate affections of animal; but not according to substance, but in matter and body. Wherefore, the same seed, in consequence of undergoing the same passive condition, is generated either as female or male. What, indeed, therefore, constitutes diversity in species, and why some things differ in species, but others do not, has been declared.

10. But whereas contraries are diverse in species, and that which is subject to corruption, and that which is incorruptible, are contraries—for privation is a definite impotentiality— it is requisite that things corruptible be diverse in genus from incorruptible natures.

Already, indeed, therefore, have we declared our sentiments respecting these universal appellations. So that it would not appear to be necessary that anything whatsoever that is incorruptible and corruptible should be diverse in species; as neither white and black should be so. For it is admissible that the same thing at the sane time should be both corruptible and incorruptible, if there may be in subsistence aught of things that are universal, as man would be both white and black; and the case is similar with the mode of the subsistence of singulars, for the same man would not be white and black at the same time, although what is white is contrary to what is black. Of contraries, however, some according to accident are inherent in certain things; for instance, those that have been just now mentioned, and many others: but in the case of others this is impossible—I mean, those to which both that which is corruptible and that which is incorruptible belong; for nothing is corruptible according to accident: for that which is accidental admits of 1059a not being; but that which is corruptible belongs to those things which subsist of necessity in those things in which it is inherent, or that which is corruptible will be one and the same thing with that which is incorruptible, if what is corruptible admits of not being inherent therein. Either, then, substantially, or as inherent in substance, must that which is corruptible subsist in each of the things that are corruptible. But there is the same reasoning, likewise, applicable to the case of that which is incorruptible; for both belong to things that possess a necessary existence. So far forth, therefore, as one is primarily corruptible, and the other primarily incorruptible, so far are they in opposition to each other; so that they must needs be generically diverse.

It is evident, therefore, that it is not possible that there be such forms as some affirm; for in such a case, as regards man, there will be one who is corruptible, but another who is incorruptible, although forms are said to be the same in species with certain particulars, and not equivocal in respect of them: things that are diverse in genus, however, are at a wider interval from one another than those that are diverse in species.

BOOK XI

1. THAT, indeed, Wisdom is a certain science conversant about first principles is evident from the early portions of this work, in which doubts have been expressed respecting statements that have been put forward by others concerning first principles; one, however, would feel doubtful as to whether it would be requisite to suppose Wisdom or Ontology to constitute one science or many? For if it does constitute one science, there is, at any rate, one science invariably of contraries; but first principles are not contraries. If, however, it does not constitute one science, as of what quality must we posit these many sciences? Further, to speculate into demonstrative first principles, is it the province of one or of many sciences? For if of one science, why, let me ask, is it the province of this more than of any other whatsoever? But if such speculation belong to many sciences, what sort must we consider these to be? Moreover, whether is there one science of all substances, or not? For if there is not one science of all, it would be difficult to render an account of what sort of substances there is one science in existence; if, however, there is one science of all substances, it is an obscure point how it is admissible that there should be the same science of many substances. Further, the question arises as to whether demonstration is conversant about substances only, or also about accidents? For if demonstration be conversant, at least, about accidents, it is not conversant about substances. But if there is one demonstrative science about accidents, and another about

substances, what, may I ask, is the character of both, and which of the two constitutes Wisdom or Metaphysics? For demonstrative wisdom is that which is conversant with accidents; that, however, which is conversant with first principles is the wisdom that takes cognizance of substances.

Neither, however, must we consider the science at present under investigation as a science respecting the causes that have been already enumerated in our treatise on Physics. For neither should we act thus in regard of "the final cause"; for a thing of this kind is that which is good: and this resides in practical things, and in those entities that are in motion; and this imparts motion in the first instance, for the end is a thing of this sort: but the imparter of motion in the first instance does not inhere in those things that are incapable of motion.

And, in general, one feels doubtful as to whether the science now under investigation is conversant about sensible substances at all, or not about these, but about certain other substances? For if metaphysical science be conversant with substances different from those cognizable to the senses, it will be conversant either with forms or mathematical entities. As regards forms, then, it 1059b is evident that they have no existence. But nevertheless, one would feel doubtful, even though he should admit the existence of these forms, why, forsooth, as in the case of mathematical entities, the same truth does not hold good in regard of the things of which there are forms? Now, I say that they have placed mathematical entities, no doubt, as intermediate between forms and things cognizant by sense, as it were certain third natures beside both forms and those things that are here—I mean, sensibles—but there is no third man, nor a third horse, beside both actual man, and actual horse, and singulars. And if, on the other hand, these mathematical entities do not subsist in the manner they affirm, about what sort of entities are we to assert that the mathematician is engaged? For, surely, he is not engaged about those things that are here,—that is, about sensibles,—for one of these constitutes the description of entity which the mathematical sciences investigate. Neither, certainly, is the science now under investigation—I mean, Metaphysics—conversant about mathematical entities for no one of these possesses a separable subsistence. Nor, however, is it a science belonging to substances cognizant by the senses, for these are corruptible. And, in short, one would feel doubtful as to what sort of a science belongs the investigation of the matter of mathematical entities; for neither does it belong to physical or natural science, from the fact that the entire attention of the Natural Philosopher is engaged about those things that contain in themselves the first principle of motion and rest: nor unquestionably, is it the province of a science that institutes an inquiry respecting both demonstration and scientific knowledge; for respecting this very genus it creates for itself an investigation. It remains, therefore, that this proposed Philosophy of Ontology, or Metaphysics, should make these a subject of its inquiry.

And, again, one would feel doubtful as to whether it is requisite to consider the science under investigation in the present Treatise as conversant about first principles—I mean, such as by some speculators are denominated elements? These, however, have been regarded by all philosophers as things that are inherent in composite natures. But it would rather appear to be a thing that is necessary that the science of ontology, under investigation at present, ought to be conversant with universals; for every rational principle, and every science, are conversant about universals, and not about the extremes of things. Wherefore, in this case ontology would be conversant about primary general.

And these would constitute both entity and unity; for these especially would be supposed to comprise all existencies, and in the most eminent degree to be assimilated unto first principles, on account of their being classed in the category of things that derive their primary existence from Nature: for when these have been corrupted, other things also are corrupted at the same time along with them; for everything amounts to entity and unity. As far forth, however, as it is necessary that differential qualities participate of these, if one will admit the subsistence of these genera,—now no difference participates in the genus,—thus far, likewise, would it appear that we ought not to establish these either as genera or first principles. But, further, on the supposition that that which is more simple is more a first principle than that which is less simple, but the extremes of those things that descend from the genus are more simple than the genera,—for these are individuals, whereas the genera are divided into numerous species and such as are different,—hence species would appear to be a first principle more than genera. As far forth, however, as species are liable to corruption in conjunction with their genera, the genera rather would seem to be more similar to first principles; for that which brings about the destruction of other things in conjunction with itself is a first principle.

These, then, and other such points are some of those questions that involve matter of doubt. 1060a

2. Further, may the question be raised as to whether it is expedient to admit the existence of something besides and independent of singulars, or not? But the science now under investigation is conversant with these. These are, however, infinite. Those things, at any rate, which have a subsistence independent of and beside singular are, without doubt, either genera or species; but the science at present under investigation is not a science conversant about either of these; for the reason why this is impossible has been already stated. For in general, likewise, doth the following question involve a doubt—namely, as to whether it is necessary to suppose the existence of any substance separable from sensible substances and those which are here, or whether this is not the case? But shall we say that these sensible things are entities, and that Wisdom is conversant about these? For the fact is we seem to investigate some different science; and this stands forth as the point proposed by us for investigation. Now, what I mean is this, that our aim is to discover whether there is anything that essentially involves a separable subsistence, and which does not reside in any nature belonging to those objects that are cognizant by the senses?

But, further, allowing that there is beside sensible substances any different substance, what sort of sensibles are those beside which it is requisite to establish the subsistence of this substance? For why should one seek to establish its existence beside men rather than horses, or beside these in preference to the rest of the animal creation, or in general to inanimate things likewise? Notwithstanding, the providing of different substances eternal in duration, equal in amount to substances that are cognizant by sense and subject to decay, would appear, perhaps, to fall outside the province of the rational sciences.

If, however, the first principle now under investigation be not separable from bodies, what other would one admit as existing in preference to matter? This, however, does not involve a subsistence in energy, indeed, but in capacity. Rather would species and form seem to be a first principle in a stricter sense of the word than this. Now, this is a thing that is subject to corruption: wherefore, in short, there does not subsist an eternal substance that involves a separable existence as well as an essential subsistence. But such a position as this is absurd; for it appears to be the fact—and such are the subjects of inquiry at the hands nearly of all those that are most accomplished philosophers—that there is in subsistence a certain first principle and substance of this description; for how, let me ask, will there prevail order on the supposition that there is no subsistence of that which is eternal, and which involves a separable existence, and is permanent?

But, further, admitting that there is a certain substance, and first principle, naturally of such a description as we are at present investigating, and this one principle belongs to all things, and the same is the principle of those things that are eternal, and those that are corruptible, the question, in such a case, arises, why, on the supposition of the existence of the same first principle, some things are eternal amongst those that may be ranked under this first principle, but others are not eternal? For this constitutes the absurdity. If, however, there is one first principle of things that are corruptible, and another of those that are eternal,—if, indeed, the principle, likewise, of those that are corruptible be eternal,—we shall be involved in similar perplexity; for why, on the supposition of the existence of an eternal first principle, are not those things that may be classed as effects under this first principle eternal likewise? And, on the supposition of the existence of a corruptible first principle, there arises a certain other principle of this, and again a different one of that; and so this progression of causes goes on to infinity.

But if, on the other hand, one will seek to establish the existence of both entity and unity, as those things that appear in the most eminent degree to be immovable first principles, in the first place, unless each of them signifies this certain particular thing and substance, how will they involve a separate subsistence, and an essential one? But it is respecting those eternal and 1060b original first principles of this description that we are engaged in our investigations in the present treatise. Nevertheless, supposing both of them to signify this certain particular thing, and substance, all the entities will be substances; for entity is predicated of all things, and unity, also, of some. That all entities, however, are substances is an assertion that is false.

But, further, how can the position of those be true who make out that unity is *the* first principle, and that this constitutes substance, and who from unity and matter generate the first number, and say that it is the substance of these,—how, I say, does this assertion of theirs admit of being true? For how is it requisite intellectually to apprehend, as one, the dyad and each of the other compound numbers? For on this point they neither say anything, nor would it be easy to make any assertion on the subject. Suppose, however, that anyone will seek to establish, as first principles, lines, or the things that are connected consequentially with these—now, I mean, surfaces such as are primary—yet these are not substances, capable of a separate subsistence, but are sections and divisions; the former of surfaces, but the latter of bodies: but points are sections and divisions of lines; and, further, they are the limits of these very same things, and all these are inherent in others, and there is no one of them that is separable. Further, in what way is it necessary for us to conceive the existence of a substance of unity and of a point? For of every substance is there generation, but of a point there is not, for a point amounts to division.

And this, likewise, furnishes a subject of doubt; namely, that every science should be conversant about things that are universal, and about that which is of such and such a quality, but that substance should not belong to things universal, but rather should constitute this certain particular thing, and that which possesses a separable subsistence. Wherefore, if we admit that science is conversant about first principles, how is it necessary to consider substance as the first principle of things?

Further, the question may be asked, is there anything beside entirety, or not? Now, I mean by entirety, matter, and that which subsists in conjunction with this; for if, in fact, this be not the case, all things, at least, that reside in matter are subject to corruption. If, however, there subsists anything beside entirety, it would constitute the species and the form. In the case of what things, therefore, this would subsist, and in the case of what things it would not, it would be difficult to determine; for in the case of some things is it evident that the form is not a thing that is capable of a separate subsistence: as, for example, the form of a house is not separable from the house. And, further, there is the question whether first principles are the same in species, or in number? For if they are one in number, all things will constitute these.

3. Since the science of the philosopher, however, is conversant about entity, so far forth as it is entity, and this universally, and not as regards any one part, and since entity is multifariously predicated, and not in one way merely—this being the case if entity is predicated equivocally, and not according to anything that is common—it does not fall under the province of one science to inquire into it (for there is not one genus of things of this kind); but if it be predicated according to anything that is common, it would fall under the notice of one science.

Now, it appears that it is predicated after the same manner as both what is medicinal and salubrious; for, likewise, are both of these predicated multifariously. And in this way each is predicated in respect of the one being somehow referred to 1061a medicinal art, but the other to health, and a third to something else; yet each is referred to the same thing. For a medicinal discourse, and a small knife, are denominated in respect the former of proceeding for medicinal science, but the other because it is serviceable to this art of medicine; and in like manner it is so with that which is salubrious: for a thing is termed thus partly because it is indicative of health, and partly because it is productive of it.

And the same mode exists in the case of other things: in the same way, therefore, is denominated entity in its entirety; for each of them is styled entity in respect of being a passion, or habit, or disposition, or motion, or something else of this sort, belonging unto entity, so far forth as it is entity. Since, however, there is a reduction of every entity to a certain one thing, and something which is common, so of contrarieties, likewise, each will be reduced to the primary differences and contrarieties of entity, whether multitude and unity, or similarity; and dissimilarity, and the primary difference of entity, or whether there are certain other differences of such; for let these stand over as subjects for future discussion. But there is no difference whether the reduction of entity be made to entity or to unity. For even if they be not the same, but something different, they are, at any rate, convertible terms; for both unity, also, in a manner constitutes entity, and entity constitutes unity.

Since, however, it is the province of one and the same science to speculate into all contraries, and since each of those is predicated according to privation,—although, as regards some contraries, at least, of which there is a certain medium, one would feel perplexed as to how they are predicated according to privation; as, for example, of the unjust and the just,—this being the case, concerning all such contraries, I say, is it necessary, therefore, to posit privation as existing, not of the whole definition, but of the ultimate species; for instance, if one is a just man who, through a certain habit, has been from time to time obedient to the laws, the unjust man will not be altogether deprived of the entire definition of just man: but inasmuch as in respect of habitual obedience to the laws he is in some point or degree deficient, in this respect, likewise, will there be inherent in him a privation of this definition. And in the same manner is it the case with other things.

But as the mathematician institutes for himself an inquiry regarding abstract quantities,—for he conducts his speculations by removing out of his consideration all sensible natures, such as gravity and lightness, and hardness, and its contrary, and further, also, heat and cold, and other sensible contrarieties, but he merely leaves remaining quantity; and continuity—some of which pertain to one, but others are in reference to two, and others to three, dimensions—as well as the passive conditions of these, as far forth as they are quantities and continuous; and this being the case, the mathematician does not speculate into them in reference to anything else; and of some things he examines into their natures and positions, one in respect of another, and into those things that are inherent in these, but of others into

1061b their commensurations and incommensurations, and of others into their ratios or proportions: but we, nevertheless, have established one and the same science as being conversant about all subjects of this kind, I mean, the science of the geometrician,— in the same manner, therefore, is it the case in respect of entity likewise. For the things that are accidental in this, so far forth as it is entity, and the contrarieties of this, as far forth as it is entity, it is not the province of a different science from Philosophy, that is, Ontology, to investigate; for to Physical or Natural Science may one ascribe the speculation of these, not as far forth as they are entities, but rather as far forth as they partake of motion. As to the sciences of the Dialectician, however, and the Sophist, they are sciences of the accidents, I admit, that reside in entities, for not so far forth as they are entities; nor do they speculate about entity itself, as far forth as it is entity. Wherefore, it remains that the Philosopher, or Metaphysician, should be a person qualified for speculating into the points we have just stated, insofar as they relate unto entities.

Since, however, every entity is expressed according to some one thing, and something that is common, which is multifariously predicated, and as contraries are expressed in the same manner— for they are referred to the primary contrarieties, and differential qualities of entity—and since it is possible that things of this kind should fall under the notice of one science, hence the doubt expressed in the opening parts of this work respecting first principles would be dissolved in this way. Now, the doubt I allude to is that wherein the matter of perplexity is involved in the question as to how there will be one science about entities that are many in number, and which are generically different?

4. But since, also, the mathematician employs things that are common in a manner peculiar to himself, it would be the province of the First Philosophy, that is, of Ontology, to speculate into the original principles of these things. For that when from equals equals are taken away the remainders are equal is, indeed, a dogma that is common to all quantities. Mathematical science, however, speculates about a certain portion of matter, properly so called, appropriating it to itself; as, for instance, about lines, or angles, or numbers, or something else pertaining to other quanties: not, however, as far forth as they are entities, but so far forth as each of them is that which is continuous in one, or two, or three dimensions. Philosophy, however, does not institute an inquiry respecting those particulars that are contained in a certain portion of matter, as far forth as something amongst them is an accident in each of these, but it contemplates everything of this kind respecting entity, so far forth as it is entity. And in the same manner, also, does the case stand in regard of physical science as with mathematical; for physical or natural science speculates into the accidents or first principles of entities, so far forth as they are in motion, and not so far forth as they are

entities. But we have said that Ontology, or the First Science, is conversant about these in as far as the subjects of them are entities, but not so far forth as they are anything that is different. Wherefore, we may set down that both this and the science of the mathematician are parts of Wisdom or Metaphysical Science.

5. There is involved, however, in entities a certain first principle about which it is not possible to labor under any deception, but it is necessary invariably to do the contrary; now, I mean to speak conformably with truth: as, for instance, that it is not admissible that the same thing should be and not be in one and 1062a the same period of time; and the case is so with other things that are opposed to themselves in the same manner. And, respecting points of this kind, demonstration, indeed, has no existence absolutely speaking; but in respect of this principle it has (for it is not possible to construct a process of syllogistic reasoning from a more trustworthy principle than this very axiom just mentioned), and it ought to be so, at any rate, if it is possible that there should subsist such a thing as a demonstration in absolute terms.

As regards a person, however, who makes an assertion of opposite statements, for the purpose of proving wherefore it is false, must some such position be assumed, as that although the thing will actually be the same with the non-possibility of being the same thing, and not being so at one and the same time, yet that it will not appear to be the same thing with it; for after this manner only can a demonstration be brought about in regard of one who affirms the admissibility of opposite assertions being verified of the same thing. And, in the next place, those people who are likely to take their share in mutual discussion ought, in some degree, to understand themselves; for, in case this be not done, how will there subsist with these persons a community in regard of such mutual discussion? It is necessary, then, that each of the denominations should be known, and they manifest some one thing, and not many things, but only one; and if it is equivalent in its signification to many things, one ought to make it evident towards which of these significations the denomination conducts one. Now, as regards a person who affirms that this thing both is and is not, this which he in general affirms to be, he affirms not to be: wherefore, he asserts that the name signifies that which it does not signify; but this is impossible. Wherefore, if the assertion that the being of this particular thing involves any signification, it is impossible that contradiction concerning the same thing should be verified. Further, if a name has any meaning, and this be capable of verification, this also must needs be from necessity; but that which is from necessity it is not admissible at any time should not be: it is not for this reason, then, admissible that opposite assertions be true concerning the same thing.

Further, on the supposition that assertion in no degree is more true than negation, the person who makes the affirmation that one is a man will in nowise the rather make a true statement than if he were to affirm that he is not a man: and a person who affirms a man not to be a horse would appear to speak truth either in a greater or not in a less degree than if he affirms that man is not man. Wherefore, one who affirms, also, that the same is a horse will speak true; for, in a similar way, it would be possible that opposite assertions should admit of verification. Wherefore, the consequence ensues that the same creature should be man and horse, or something else belonging to the animal kingdom. There does not, therefore, subsist in regard of these any demonstration in absolute terms: as relates, however, to the person who is for establishing these foregoing points, demonstration has an existence.

And quickly would one, likewise, who after this manner had put the question to Heraclitus himself, force him to acknowledge that it is never a thing that is possible that opposite assertions should be verified of the same things; but at present, not comprehending his own theory in regard of what he says at all, he has embraced this particular opinion we have been just endeavoring to overthrow. And in general, if the statement made by Heraclitus be true, neither would this very position of his be true; now, I

mean the admissibility that at one and the same time the same
1062b things should be and not be. For as also, on the supposition of
these assertions having been divided, in no respect the more will
affirmation be true than negation, in the same manner, likewise,
will it be the case when both are conjoined and connected
together—just as if affirmation is regarded as being one certain
thing, in no degree the more will negation be true than the entire
of the assumption which is made in an affirmation. Moreover, if it
is possible to make no affirmation that is true, even would this
very position be false—I mean, the assertion that no affirmation is
true: if, however, there exists any assertion that is true, that point
which is put forward by these Heraclitics would be decided—
I mean, such philosophers as resist the truth of things of this
sort, and, in fact, altogether do away with rational discussion.

6. But similar to the statements that have been just made is that
which has been asserted by Protagoras; for likewise, he said that
man is a measure of all things,—in this way affirming nothing
else than that what appeared to every man, that this, also,
indubitably is that which it appeared to be: if, however, this is
admitted, the same thing will happen to be and not be, and to
be both evil and good, and the rest of those things that are
expressed in accordance with opposite assertions, from the fact
that frequently to some persons, indeed, this particular thing
appears to be fair, and the contrary to others, and from that
which is apparent to everyone constituting a measure.

Now, this doubt would be resolved if persons considered
whence the origin of this supposition has been derived; for to
some speculators, no doubt, it would appear to have originated
from the opinion of the Physiologists, or Natural Philosophers,
but to others from the circumstance that all men do not possess
the same points of knowledge in respect of the same subjects,
but that to some this particular thing seems to be sweet, and to
others the contrary. For that nothing is generated from nonentity,
but everything from entity, is almost a commonly received dogma
amongst all Natural Philosophers. Since, therefore, that which is

not white is generated from that which is perfectly white, and by no means not white, supposing now, that what is not white has been generated from that which is not a white entity, that which is being generated as not white would be produced. Wherefore, such would be generated from nonentity, according to their doctrine, unless that which is not white were the same with that which is white. It would not, however, be difficult to decide this doubt; for it has been declared, in our treatise on Physics, in what manner from that which is nonentity are generated the things that are being produced, and how it is that they are generated from entity. Notwithstanding the giving heed, in like manner, to both opinions, and to the fanciful statements of persons who doubt in opposition to themselves, this would be a silly proceeding; for it is evident that one party amongst these skeptics must needs labor under fallacies. And this statement is manifest from observing things that are generated according to sense; for at no time does the same thing appear to some, indeed, sweet, and to others the contrary, provided that the organ which 1063a has the power of perceiving and deciding the above-enumerated tastes has not undergone any corruption and injury in the case of these others. But, on the understanding of such a state of things as this, we may suppose that some of them are a standard of measure, and suppose that others are not so. And in like manner, I assert this to be the case as regards both what is good and evil, and what is beautiful and disgraceful, and other things of the sort; for to lay down this as a principle, or to affirm the reality of nothing save the apparent, is a course nowise different from those who place their finger beneath the organ of vision, and thus from the one object make two to appear, and who really believe that there are two objects before them, upon account of their appearing such, and again that there is but one in reality; for to those persons who do not move their organ of vision that which is one appears one.

In general, however, it would be absurd, from the appearance of things that are here as subject to change, and which never permanently continue in the same dispositions, from this to come to any decision as regards truth; for it is necessary that we should go in pursuit of that which is true from amongst those things that invariably *do* subsist according to the same dispositions, and that never are instrumental in bringing about their own change. Now, of this description are those bodies that are regulated according to the orderly system of the Universe; for these do not at one time appear of this particular sort, but at one time of a different kind, but invariably the same, and as participating in no change.

But, further, on the supposition of the existence of motion, and of something that is being moved,—now, everything which has motion impressed upon it is put in motion by something, and in the direction of something,—in such a case, that which is being moved ought to be found, moreover, in that from which it will derive its motion, and yet not be found therein, and that it should be moved towards this particular place, and yet should not be generated in this: but how can such be the case? For we must bear in mind, that, even according to their own doctrines, that simultaneous verification is not possible as regards contradiction. And if, according to quantity, things which are here are continuously in a state of flux, and are being moved,—and if one admits this, although it should not be true,—why are they not permanent as regards quality? For these speculators in no small degree appear to predicate those things of the same thing, according to their contradictions, from the supposition that quantity does not continue permanently in bodies. Hence with them the same thing is and is not of four cubits in its dimensions. Substance, however, subsists according to quality, for this is of a definite nature; but quantity belongs to one which is indefinite.

Further, why, let me ask, when the physician gives a prescription that his patients should take this particular food,—why, I say, do they take it? For why is this particular piece of food bread rather than it is not bread? Wherefore, there would be no distinction in eating from not eating. At present, however, as the physician makes a true assertion about this thing, and this food that has been prescribed being in reality in existence, the patients accordingly take this food—although they ought not, at least, to do so on the supposition that there is no nature that is firmly permanent in sensibles, but that invariably all things are in motion and in a state of flux. But further, if, indeed, we are always undergoing a change, and never remaining permanently the same persons, why is it surprising if things never appear at any time to be the same as they do to those that are sick? For to these, also, on account of their habit being not similarly disposed 1063b as when they are in a healthy state, the things that subsist according to the senses do not appear to subsist in a similar manner; though sensibles themselves participate in no change on account of this, at least, but produce different sensations in the sick, and sensations that are not the same. In the same manner, therefore, is it requisite, perhaps, that consequences be disposed as if the aforesaid change took place. If, however, we do not undergo a change, but continue to be the same, there would be something in existence that is permanent.

Respecting, to be sure, those persons, therefore, who entertain from principles of reason the doubts enumerated, it would not be easy to advance a refutation when they are not for admitting anything, and no longer demand a reason of those things, for all reasoning, and every demonstration, arise in this way; for when they are disposed to admit nothing, they overturn the thing in dispute, and, in general, all rational discussion. Wherefore, with such speculators, of course, there is no such thing at all as rational discussion; but in regard of those that labor under perplexity, from the doubts that have been handed down, it would be easy to reply, and to unravel the difficulties that create in them the doubt referred to; now this statement is evident from those that have been made.

Wherefore, it is evident from these things that it does not admit of being possible that opposite assertions about the same thing should be verified at one and the same time, nor that contraries should, on account of the denomination of all contrariety according to privation. This, however, will be evident to those who resolve into their first principles the definitions of contraries. And, in like manner, neither is it possible that any of those things that are media should be predicated of one and the same thing; for, on the supposition of the subject being white, when we assert that this is neither white nor black we shall make a false assertion, for it happens that this is white, and yet that it is not; for either of these connected together will be verified concerning this, but this amounts to a contradiction of what is white.

Neither, therefore, is it possible for one who makes an assertion, in accordance with the theory of Heraclitus, nor of Anaxagoras, to assert what is true; and if this be not admitted, the consequence will ensue that they predicate contrary things of the same subject: for when Anaxagoras says that in everything is contained a part of everything, he says that a thing is not more sweet than bitter, or anything else of the other contrarieties, if in everything all things subsist not merely in potentiality, but in energy or activity, and in a state of separation. And, in like manner, neither is it possible that all assertions be false, nor all true, as well on account of many other difficulties which would be uttered in consequence of this position, as also because as regards all assertions, supposing that they are false, neither will one who makes this very assertion speak what is true; but if all assertions are true, the person who says that all are false will not speak falsely.

7. But every science investigates into certain first principles and causes respecting each of those objects of knowledge that 1064a fall under its cognizance; as, for example, medicinal science, and that of the athlete, and each of the rest of the productive or the mathematical sciences; for each of these having been for itself descriptive of a certain genus, treats concerning this as a thing existing and as entity, not, however, so far forth as it is an entity: conversant, however, about this last-named inquiry is there beside these sciences this certain other science of the Ontologist, which is different from them; but each of the above-enumerated sciences, taking for granted the mode in

which the nature of a thing subsists in each genus, endeavors to explain the remainder of the points relating to this more feebly or more accurately. They, however, make an assumption as to quiddity, or the nature of a thing, some of them by means of sense, but others from hypothesis. Wherefore, it is also evident, from an induction of this sort, that there subsists no demonstration of substance and quiddity.

Since, however, there exists a certain science which is conversant about Nature, it is manifest that it will be different from both that which is practical science and that which is productive or effective. For of productive science the first principle of motion resides in the producing or efficient cause, and not in that which is being produced; and this either is some art, or some other potentiality. And, in like manner, does the case stand with practical science also; the motion does not reside in the thing done, but rather in those who are agents. But the science of the Natural Philosophers is conversant about those bodies that involve in themselves a first principle of motion. That, indeed, therefore, Physical Science must needs be neither practical nor productive, but speculative or contemplative, is evident from these statements; for there is the necessity of its falling under the classification of some one of these genera. And since, in a manner, it is requisite for each of the sciences to possess a knowledge of the nature of a thing, and to employ this as a first principle, we ought not to forget how a definition of this quiddity should be framed by the physical inquirer, and how the definition of substance is to be assumed, whether as the flat-nose, or rather as the hollow; for, as regards these, the formal principle, no doubt, of flat-nose is denominated along with matter—I mean, such as belongs to the thing itself; the formal principle, however, of hollow-nose is expressed without matter, the flatness of nose is generated in the nose. Wherefore, also, the definition or formal principle of it is inquired into along with this, for the flat-nose constitutes a hollow-nose. It is evident, therefore, that the definition both of flesh, and of the eye, and of the other parts of the body, is always to be assumed along with matter.

But since there exists a certain science of entity, so far forth as it is entity, and so far forth as it involves a separable subsistence, we must examine whether at all we are to consider this to be the same with Natural or Physical Science, or rather to be different from it. Physical Science, indeed, then, is conversant about those bodies that involve in themselves a first principle of motion; but the science of the mathematician is itself a certain science that is speculative, I admit, and that, too, in regard of things that are permanent, but which do not involve a subsistence separable from sensibles. Respecting, then, that which is an entity capable of separate subsistence, and which is immovable, there exists a certain science different from both of these, on the supposition, of course, that there is some substance of this description in existence—now, I speak of a substance separable and immovable; and it is the validity of this very position that we shall attempt to demonstrate.

And if we admit that there subsists any substance of this sort in entities, here also, in a manner, would there be found Divinity residing, and this would be an original and most dominant 1064a principle. It is evident, therefore, that there are three genera of the speculative sciences—namely, the physical or natural, the mathematical, and the theological. The most excellent, then, is certainly the genus of the speculative or contemplative sciences; and of these very sciences that one which is mentioned last of the three possesses the greatest amount of excellence, for it is conversant about that one amongst entities which is more entitled to respect than the rest. Each science, however, is termed more excellent, and more inferior, according to its appropriate object of scientific knowledge.

Now, a person might raise the question as to whether at all we ought to seek to establish universally the science of entity, so far forth as it is entity, or not? For each of the mathematical sciences, no doubt, is conversant about some one definite genus; the universal science, however, speculates in common respecting all things. If, indeed, therefore, we admit physical substances to be the primary substances of entities, Physical or Natural Science would also be the chief one amongst the sciences; but, on the other hand, if there exists a nature that is different, and a substance that involves a separable subsistence, and is immovable, it is necessary, also, that there belong to this a different science, and that this science should be antecedent to physical science, and universal in respect of its antecedence or priority.

8. Since, however, that which is entity simply considered is denominated in many ways, of which one is that which is spoken of as subsisting according to accident, in the first instance our examination must be instituted concerning entity in this point of view. That, indeed, therefore, no one of the sciences that have been handed down from former generations is employed about what is accidental is evident; for neither does that relating to house-building or architectural art investigate into what is likely to be accidental with those who will make use of the house; for example, as to whether they will dwell there sorrowfully or the contrary: nor is it so with the art of weaving, nor of shoe-making, nor the cooking art. Each of these sciences, however, examines into that which is peculiar to its own department only; and this is its appropriate end. Neither does it consider a person so far as he is a musician and a grammarian, nor does it assert that he who is a musician, should he become a grammarian, will at the same time be both, though he were not so previously. But that which is not always an entity, this was generated at some time or other; so that such a person would at the same time become a musician and a grammarian. This, however, no one of those that are confessedly sciences examines into, with the exception of the science of the Sophist; for this alone is employed about what is accidental. Wherefore, Plato has not inaptly expressed himself when he affirms that the sophist wastes his time in the consideration of nonentity.

But that is not a thing that is admissible that there should be in existence a science of the accidental, will be manifest to those who attempt to discern what an accident is at all. Therefore, as regards everything, we affirm one thing, indeed, to subsist always and from necessity—now, I mean by necessity not that which is denominated according to what is violent, but what we employ in cases pertaining to demonstrations—but another thing we affirm as subsisting for the most part, and another, neither as for the most part, nor always, and from necessity, but as may happen at any time to be casual; for example, cold might be prevalent when the sun is in Canis: but a thing of this sort would take place 1065a neither as always from necessity, nor as for the most part, but might, nevertheless, accidentally occur sometimes. Therefore, does that constitute an accident which is produced, not always, nor from necessity, nor as for the most part. What, indeed, then, an accident is, has been declared; but why there is not a science of a thing of this kind is evident: for every science is conversant about that which is an entity always, or as for the most part; but the accidental is not ranked amongst either of these.

But it is evident that of what subsists according to accident there are not causes and first principles of such a description as there are of that which is an entity that involves an essential subsistence; for, if this be admitted, all things will be from necessity. For, if on the supposition of this particular thing being a consequence of that particular entity, but this a result from that, and if this subsists not from its being casual, but from necessity, from necessity will be likewise that of which this was the cause, until that which is denominated the last effect; this, however, subsisted according to accident. So that all things will be from necessity, and the possibility for anything whatsoever casually to occur, and the existence of contingency, and the being generated, and the not being generated, will altogether be taken away from things that are being generated. For, although a cause may be supposed not to be an entity, but that also which is being generated the same consequences will ensue; for everything will be generated from necessity. For, to give an instance, tomorrow's eclipse will take place if this particular thing may happen, and this will happen if something else does, and this last if something else ensues; and, doubtless, in this manner, on the supposition that a portion of duration be taken away from that definite time which may be measured from the present moment until tomorrow, one will ultimately arrive at that which is in being. Wherefore, since this is the case, all things that are subsequent to this will be from necessity: wherefore, will it be the case that all things will be generated from necessity.

As regards, however, that which is entity in reality, and not according to accident, one kind, indeed, is that which is contained in the comprehension of the intellect, and is a passive condition in this. Wherefore, respecting that which constitutes entity in this way first principles are not investigated; but respecting that which is an entity external to this, and possessing a separable subsistence, they are; and that which subsists according to accident is not necessary, but indefinite—now I mean, what subsists according to what is accidental, is in a less degree; but the causes of a thing of this sort are inordinate and infinite.

But that on account of which a thing subsists, that is, the final cause, is classified amongst those things that are generated by Nature, or that spring from Intellect. It is chance, however, that generates them when any of these may be generated according to accident; for, in like manner, just as also entity constitutes in one respect that which is essential, but in another that which subsists according to accident, so also is it the case with a cause. But chance is a cause according to accident in those things that are being generated in accordance with free-will, for the sake of something. Wherefore, chance and intellect are conversant about the same object, for free-will is not devoid of a connection with intellect. The causes, however, are indefinite from which might be generated that which arises from chance: wherefore, obscure to human calculation is chance, even as a cause subsisting according to accident, but, absolutely considered, such is not a cause of anything; and chance is good and evil when what is good or worthless may happen to be the result: but mischance and misfortune are conversant about the 1065b magnitude of these. But since nothing that subsists according to accident is antecedent to those things that possess an essential subsistence, neither, then, are causes so. If, then, chance, or even spontaneity, be a cause of the firmament, prior as a cause will be Mind and Nature.

9. Now, one thing subsists in energy only, but another subsists in capacity, and a third in capacity and energy; and of these one constitutes an entity, but the other a quantity, and the third something else of the rest of the categories. There is not, however, any motion beside the things themselves; for the change invariably takes place in accordance with the categories of entity. But in the case of these there is not anything that is common, nor is there a thing of this sort in a single category. Everything, however, subsists in all things in a twofold manner; as, for instance, this particular thing: for this is the form of it, but that is its privation; and according to quality one thing is white, but another black; and according to quantity one is perfect, whereas the other imperfect; and according to motion this tends upwards and that downwards, or the one is light, but the other heavy. Wherefore, there are as many species of motion and of change as there are of entity.

But on account of there being a division in each genus, of the one into potentiality or capacity, of the other, however, into acutality, I style energy the motion of that which subsists in potentiality, so far forth as it does subsist in potentiality. And that we make a true assertion in this point is evident from the following circumstance; for when a material is fit for being built, so far forth as it is a thing of this sort, we say that this very thing subsists in energy, so far forth as it is being built; and this constitutes the structure, or the mode of building. In like manner stands the case with disciplinary learning, healing, and rolling, walking, leaping, growing old, advancing towards a state of maturity. It happens, however, that a thing is in motion when the actuality itself may exist, and when it is a thing neither antecedent nor subsequent to this. Therefore, *entelecheia,* or actuality, belonging to that which subsists in capacity, when subsisting in actuality it energizes either as that which it is, or something else, so far forth as it is movable—this constitutes motion. Now, I mean by the expression "so far forth" a subsistence whose mode I would illustrate as follows.

For brass is a statue in capacity; but, nevertheless, actuality of the brass, so far forth as it is brass, does not constitute motion. For it is not the same thing, the belonging to brass and to a certain capacity; since if it were the same, absolutely speaking, according to definition, the *entelecheia,* or actuality, of the brass would amount to a certain motion: it is not, however, the same. And this statement is evident as regards contraries; for the capacity of being in sound health, and the capacity of being indisposed, are not the same; for in such a case would the actual conditions of health and sickness be the same: but the subject that is capable of being made both healthy and diseased, whether it be moisture, or whether it be blood, is one and the same thing. Since, however, the being of a thing is not the same with the being of a certain capacity, in the same way as neither is color the same with what is visible, so the *entelecheia,* or actuality, of that which is potential, so far forth as it is a thing that is potential, constitutes motion.

That, indeed, therefore, motion actually exists, and that a thing happens to be moved at the same time with its being itself actuality, and that it is a thing that is neither antecedent nor subsequent to this, is evident; for everything admits of subsisting at one time in energy, but at another time not in this state: as, for example, that which is fit for being built, so 1066a far forth as it is fit for being built, and the energy of that which is fit for being built, so far forth as it is fit for being built, constitute the mode or act of building; for the energy of this amounts either to the mode of building or the house built. But when the house may be finished—that is, when it constitutes the energy—it will no longer be a thing that is fit for being built; but, on the other hand, that which is fit for being built is actually built. It is necessary, then, that the mode or act of building amount to energy: but the mode or act of building amounts, likewise, to a certain motion. And the same reasoning holds good in the case of other motions.

Now, that these assertions have been made correctly is evident from the statements which other philosophers have from time to time put forward in regard to motion; as also from the fact of its not being an easy matter to frame a definition of it in a different manner from the foregoing: for neither is one able to set it down as being contained in another genus. And it is evident from what these speculators say on the subject; for some of them, indeed, regard it as equivalent with diversity, and inequality, and nonentity; and yet not one of these necessarily should have motion imparted to it. But neither does there exist change or mutation into these either, nor from things of this kind more than from such as are opposed. But a cause of their setting down motion amongst things of this kind is as follows,—because motion appears with them as something that is indefinite. Now, the first principles of a different coordinate series, from the fact of their being private, are indefinite; for not one of these is either this particular thing, or any other of the rest of the categories.

But a cause of this view of motion—I mean, of its appearing to be a thing that is indefinite—results from the fact that it is not possible to set it down under the category of the potentiality of entities, or under that of their energy or activity; for neither that which involves a capacity of being quantity has motion imparted to it necessarily, nor that which subsists as quantity in energy. And motion appears to amount to a certain energy or activity, no doubt, but an energy or activity which is imperfect: and a cause of this is the following—that that which is potential to which the energy belongs is itself imperfect, and on this account it would be difficult, as regards this, to apprehend what it is; for it must necessarily be classed either into privation, or into capacity, or into simple energy; and not one of these does it appear admissible that motion should be considered. Wherefore, it remains that it be what it has been declared to be—namely, both an energy or activity; and yet not such an energy as has been mentioned, for this would be an energy difficult to discern, indeed; but, nevertheless, one which it is admissible should subsist.

And that motion is to be found in that which is capable of being moved is evident; for the actuality of this lies under the influence of that which is capable of being moved. And the energy of that which is movable is not different from this; for it is necessary, surely, that there should subsist actuality in both; for a thing is movable in respect of its involving a capability of having motion impressed upon it, and that which imparts motion does so from energy or activity, but it thus acts from this energy in regard of that which is adapted for motion. Wherefore, in like manner, there resides one energy in both, just as from one to two is the same interval as from two to one. And in regard of ascent and descent the case is the same; but the essence in this instance is not one. And the same remark holds good, in like manner, with the power that imparts motion, and that which has motion impressed upon it thereby.

10. But the Infinite either is that which it is impossible to pass through, in respect of its not being adapted by nature to be permeated, in the same way as the voice is invisible, or it is that which possesses a passage without an end, or that which is scarcely so, or that which by nature is adapted to have, but has not, a passage or termination. Further, a thing is infinite from subsisting by addition, or subtraction, or both.

It is, indeed, possible, therefore, that the Infinite should constitute a certain entity that involves a separable subsistence, 1066b but that it is cognizant by sense is not possible; for, if it constitutes neither magnitude nor multitude, and if the Infinite be a substance, and not an accident of this, it will be indivisible; for that which is divisible amounts either to magnitude or multitude: but if it be indivisible it will not be infinite, unless in the same way as the voice is invisible. They do not, however, say so, nor do we inquire into the subject; but we consider it as a thing without any passage, or, in other words, impermeable. Further, let me ask, how is it possible that what is essentially infinite should exist, unless there should happen to subsist number and magnitude, of which two the Infinite is a passive condition? Moreover, if the

Infinite subsists according to accident, it would not constitute an element of entities, as far forth as it is a thing that is infinite, in the same manner as neither is that which is invisible an element of speech although the voice is invisible.

And that it is not possible for the Infinite to subsist in energy is evident, for any part whatsoever of itself that is assumed will be infinite; for the being of the infinite and a thing which is infinite are the same, if the Infinite be substance and not that which is predicated of a subject. Wherefore, it is either indivisible, or divisible in a progression *ad infinitum,* if it be made up of parts that are or may be divisible. That many infinites, however, should be the same thing is impossible; for as air is a part of air, so infinite is a part of that which is infinite, if it is a substance and a first principle. The infinite, then, is devoid of parts and indivisible. But it is impossible that an entity that subsists in actuality should be infinite, for it must needs constitute quantity. It subsists, then, according to accident: but if this be the case, it has been declared that it is not possible that it should be a first principle; but this must be affirmed of that to which it happens that number or evenness should be such. The investigation, therefore, is itself universal.

That the Infinite, however, does not subsist in things that are cognizant by sense is evident from the following circumstances:— for, on the supposition that the definition of body amounts to that which is bounded by surfaces, body would not be infinite, either that which is cognizable by sense or by the understanding; nor will it be number as actually separated and infinite, for number is that which is numerable, or which involves number. That the Infinite, however, cannot subsist in things cognizant to the senses—regarded in a physical point of view—is evident from these following reasons:—for neither is it possible that it should be a composite nature, nor one which is simple. For if you admit that it is a composite nature it will not be a body, if the elements are limited in multitude; for it is requisite that we should equalize the contraries, and that one of them should not be infinite: for if in any degree whatsoever the potentiality of the other body fails, the finite will be corrupted by the infinite body. But it is impossible that each of the elements should be infinite, for body is that which in every direction involves an interval; but that which is infinite is that which involves an interval without end. Wherefore, if there is in existence an infinite body, it will be infinite in every direction.

Neither, however, can there be in existence one infinite simple body, nor—as certain philosophers would lay down—can it subsist as different from, or independent of, the elements from whence they generate these things; for there is not in existence a body of this description beside the elements, for all those things of which they are compounded are resolved into these. This, however, does not appear to subsist beside the simple bodies— either fire or any other of the elements; for without some one of 1067a them being infinite it is impossible that the Universe, if it may be finite, should either be or be generated from some one of the elements: as Heraclitus says that all things were originally fire. And there is the same mode of reasoning, also, in the case of unity, the existence of which Natural Philosophers introduce besides the elements; for everything undergoes a change from its contrary, as from heat into cold.

Further, a body cognizant by the senses is situated in a certain place, and there is the same place of the whole as of part—of the earth, for instance, as of one of its clods. Wherefore, if the Infinite be of similar parts, indeed, it will be immovable, or always will be impelled forwards. But this is impossible; for why, may I ask, should it be moved downwards in preference to upwards, or in any direction whatsoever? For instance, if it were a clod of earth, in what direction will this be moved, or in what place will it remain at rest? For the place of the body naturally adapted to this will be infinite. Will it, then, comprise the entire place? And how will this be so? What, therefore, will be its place of rest and its motion? Or shall we say that it will remain at rest everywhere? It will not then be moved; or, shall we say that it will be moved in every direction? It will not then stand still. If the Universe, however, be of dissimilar parts, places, likewise, would be dissimilar; and in the first instance, no doubt, the body of the Universe would not be one, save in respect of contact: in the next place, these things will be either finite or infinite in species. That they should be finite is not certainly, then, possible; for some, indeed, will be infinite, and some not so, on the supposition that the Universe is infinite— for instance, fire or water: and a thing of this kind will be corruption to contraries. If, however, they are infinite and simple, both the places will be infinite, and infinite will be the elements; but if this is possible, and the places be finite in number, the Universe, also, must needs be finite.

And, in general, it is impossible that there can be an infinite body, and a place for bodies, if every body that is cognizant by the senses involves gravity or lightness. For it will have an impulse either towards the center or upwards; it is impossible, however, that the Infinite—either the whole or the half, of any part whatsoever—should undergo a passive state; for in what way would you make a division of it? Or of the Infinite how will there be one portion tending in a direction downwards, and the other in a direction upwards? Or how will this constitute the extremity, and that the center? Further, every body that falls under the notice of the senses subsists in place; and there are six species of place: but it is impossible that these should subsist in a body that is infinite. And, upon the whole, if it is impossible that place should be infinite, it is likewise impossible that body should be so; for that which subsists in place is somewhere, and this signifies a direction either upwards or downwards, or some one of the rest of the categories; and each of these constitutes a certain limit.

But the Infinite is not the same in magnitude, and motion, and duration, as if it were a certain single nature; but that which is subsequent is denominated according to that which is antecedent: as, for instance, motion is denominated according to, or conformably with, the magnitude in regard of which the motion, or the alteration, or the increase, is brought about; time, however, is reckoned or computed in consideration of motion.

11. Now, that which undergoes a change is changed partly, 1067b indeed, according to accident,—as when we say the musician walks,—and partly when a thing is said simply to be changed in respect of something belonging to this undergoing a change; for example, whatsoever things are changed, are changed according to parts: for the body is reduced to a sound state of health because the eye is restored to a healthy condition. Now, there is something which primarily is moved in itself or essentially, and this is that which may have motion impressed upon it from itself. And there is also something of the same sort in the case of that which imparts motion likewise; for one thing imparts motion according to accident, and another according to a portion, but a third essentially or of itself: and there is something that is the primary source of motion, and there is something that has motion impressed upon it; further is there the time in which, and there is the place from which, and the direction towards which, a thing is moved. But the forms, and passive states, and place into which are moved the things that are being moved, themselves are immovable, as science and heat; but the heat does not constitute motion, yet the process of heating does. The change, however, that does not ensue according to accident does not reside in all things, but in contraries and media, and in contradiction. But a reliance upon this statement may be drawn from induction.

Now, that which undergoes a change is changed either from a subject into a subject, or from that which is not a subject into a subject, or from a subject into a non-subject, or from a non-subject into a subject: but I mean by a subject that which is made manifest by affirmation. Wherefore, changes must needs be three in number; for that which is from a non-subject into a non-subject is not properly a change, for it subsists neither between contraries nor between contradiction, because there is not opposition in the case of a transition from a non-subject into a non-subject. The change, indeed, therefore, from that which is a non-subject into a subject, according to contradiction, amounts to generation; and such a change, of course, when simply considered, is simple generation, and when it is partial, it is partial generation: but the change from subject into that which is non-subject amounts to corruption, which, when it is simply so, is simple corruption; but when it is partial, it is partial corruption.

If, therefore, nonentity is predicated multifariously, and that according to composition or division does not admit of being put in motion, so neither can it be so with that according to capacity, which is opposed to that which subsists simply; for a thing that is not white, or not good, nevertheless admits of being moved according to accident: for that which is not white may be a man; but this cannot by any means be the case with this particular thing which subsists simply: for it is impossible that nonentity should be moved; and if this be admitted, it is impossible, also, that generation amounts to motion; for nonentity would be produced if it did, for in such a case most especially would it be produced according to accident; yet, nevertheless, it is true to assert of that which is generated simply that a nonentity has a subsistence. In like manner, also, stands the case with the being in a state of rest. And, doubtless, such are the difficulties that attend on this hypothesis, even on the supposition that everything that is being moved is in place; but what is a nonentity is not in place, for it would be somewhere. Hence neither does corruption constitute motion, for motion or rest is a thing that is contrary to motion, but corruption is contrary to generation. Since, however, every motion amounts to a 1068a certain change, and there are three changes, as just now enumerated, and of these the changes that ensue according to generation and corruption are not motions—and these are those that subsist according to contradiction—it is necessary that the change from subject to subject should alone constitute motion. Subjects, however, are either contraries or media; and let privation be considered as a thing that is contrary: and it is made manifest by affirmation; for instance, that which is naked and toothless, and that which is black.

12. If, therefore, the categories are divided by substance, quality, place, action or passion, relation, quantity, there must needs subsist three motions of quality, quantity, and of place; but according to substance there does not subsist any motion on account of their being nothing contrary to substance; nor is there a motion of relation: for it is possible, when either of the relatives has not undergone a change, that a verification should take place in regard of the other, as having undergone no change. Wherefore, the motion of these will subsist according to accident.

Neither is there a motion of that which is active and passive, or of that which is the efficient cause of motion, and has motion impressed upon it, because there is not a motion of motion, nor a generation of generation, nor, in general, a change of a change. For in two ways is it possible that there be a motion of a motion; first, either as of a subject—for instance, as man is moved because from white he is changed into black; wherefore, thus also is it with motion, either a thing is made warm or cold, or undergoes alteration in place or increase: this, however, is impossible; for the change does not amount to any of the subjects;—or, secondly, there may subsist a motion of motion, in respect of some different subject from change being altered into a different form, as man is changed from sickness into health. Neither, however, is this possible, except according to accident; for every motion constitutes a change from one thing into another: and, in like manner, the case stands with generation and corruption, except that those changes, I admit, that are wrought from things that are opposed in this or that way are not motions.

At the same time, then, is man changed from health into disease, and from this very change into a different one. It is therefore, evident that when a man shall have become indisposed he shall undergo a change into a disease of some sort or other; for it is admissible for such to remain in a state of rest: and, further, it is evident that he will not be changed into that state which is invariably casual, and that will amount to a change from something into something else, so that health will be an opposite motion, but from accident; as, for instance, one undergoes an alteration from memory into oblivion, because that wherein oblivion is inherent undergoes a change, sometimes into scientific knowledge, and sometimes into health.

Further will the progression advance on to infinity, if there will subsist a change of a change, and a generation of a generation. Therefore, also, must there be the former on the supposition that there is the latter; for instance, if the simple act of generation 1068b take place at any time, that also which is being generated simply has been produced. Wherefore, not as yet in existence would be that which is being produced simply; but something does exist that is being generated or produced, or which already has been generated. If, therefore, also, this thing once was generated, for what reason was that not yet in existence which is being then generated? Since, however, as regards things that are infinite there does not subsist anything that is primary, there will not be that which is first generated, and for this cause neither that which is in order consequential. Therefore, that any of these either should be generated, or be moved, or undergo any change, is not possible. Further, contrary motion, and rest, and generation, and corruption, will belong to the same subject. Wherefore, a thing that is being generated, when it may become that which is being generated, is then undergoing a process of corruption; for neither is it immediately corrupted as soon as it is generated, or subsequently to this; for that must necessarily exist which is undergoing a process of corruption. Further, it is the case that matter ought to subsist under that which is being generated and undergoing a change. Therefore, what matter will there subsist in like manner as an alterable body or soul? In this way, also, anything that subsists on being produced constitutes either motion or generation. And, further, what is that into which the thing is moved, for it is necessary that something amount to the motion of this particular thing from this particular thing into that, and yet that it should not be motion at all. How, let me ask, then, is this to take place? For the generation of discipline does not amount to discipline; so neither is it true to say that there will subsist a generation of generation.

Since, however, there is not in existence motion either of substance, or of relation, or of action and passion, it remains that there should subsist motion according to quality, and quantity, and place, for to each of these doth there belong contrariety. Now, I mean by motion according to quality not that which is found in substance—for difference also constitutes quality—but that which is passive, in accordance with which a thing is said to be passive or to be devoid of passion.

With regard, however, to that which is immovable, and that which, upon the whole, it is impossible should have motion impressed upon it, and that which with difficulty, in a long portion of duration, or slowly, commences its motion, and that which having been by nature, no doubt, adopted for having motion imparted to it, yet does not possess the capacity or ability of being moved when it is naturally fitted for motion—both as to the place where and the manner how—this is what I term merely a condition of rest amongst those things that are immovable; for rest is a thing that is contrary to motion.

Wherefore, it would amount to a privation of that which is receptive or capable of motion; and things are said to be moved according to place at the same time as many as are to be found in one original locality; and those things are said to be moved separately as many as are to be found in a different place. And things are said to be in contact with each other the extremities of which subsist together. And that is a medium into which that is fitted by nature first to proceed which is undergoing a change, before it arrives at that into which it is ultimately changed—I mean, what is uninterruptedly undergoing a change according to the constitution of nature.

A thing is contrary in regard of place which in a straight line is at the greatest distance possible: and a thing is successive between which—when it is after its first principle, either in position or form, or some other definite mode of subsistence—and that to which it is consequent there subsists no intervening medium of things on the same genus; for instance, lines are successive to a line, or monads are successive to a monad, or a house to a house.

There is no hindrance, however, to there subsisting any other medium between them; for that which is successive belongs to something in succession, and is something that is subsequent: for one is not successive to two, nor are the Kalends to the Nones. And a thing is coherent which, being successive, is in contact. Since, however, every change takes place in those things that are opposed, and these are contraries and contradiction, and since of contradiction there is nothing that is a medium, it is evident that in contraries there subsists a medium. And that which is continuous is that which has something of the nature of the coherent, or of that which is in a state of contact. And a thing is called continuous when the extremity of either of the parts by which they are in contact, and in continuity, may be one and the same. Wherefore, it is evident that what is continuous is to be found amongst those things from which, as compounds, there subsists any one thing naturally adapted for being generated according to contact.

And that what is successive ranks as what is primary is evident likewise; for everything that is successive does not subsist in a state of contact; but this is the case with what is successive on the supposition that what is continuous subsists in a state of contact. Even, however, though they should subsist in a state of contact, they yet by no means amount to that which is continuous. Those things, however, in which there is not found contact there does not subsist natural coherence in. Wherefore, a point is not the same thing with a monad; for, indeed, in points may be found contact: but this is not the case with monads, but these are successive to each other, and between points there may be found a certain medium; whereas we cannot discover any such between monads.

BOOK XII

1. THE present speculation is concerned about substance; for the first principles and causes of substances are under investigation. For both if the Universe be as one whole, substance constitutes the earliest portion; and if things subsist in a consequent order, in this way, likewise, would substance be first, and next quality, then quantity. But at the same time neither, so to say, are these, simply considered, entitities, but qualities and motions, in the same manner even as that which is not whole and that which is not straight. Therefore, we say that these also are in existence; for instance, that such a thing is not white. Further, still no one of the others possesses a separable subsistence.

And to the truth of this statement bear witness also, in reality, the philosophers of antiquity; for they from time to time have investigated into the first principles, and elements, and causes of substance. Those, to be sure, that are philosophers, nowadays, have in preference sought to establish universals as substances; for the genera are universals—which they way are first principles and substances—rather on account of their examining them logically. The philosophers, however, of old regarded singulars as substances—for example, fire and earth—but not a common body.

Now, substances are three in number; one, indeed, is cognizant by sense, the existence of which all acknowledge; and one part of this is eternal, and the other subject to decay, as plants and animals: but of the eternal portion of it, it is necessary that we should admit as elements either one or many. But another substance is immovable; and this, some say, involves a separable subsistence; amongst whom some make a division of it into two; others, however, rank into one nature forms and mathematical entities: whereas others of these admit mathematical entities only as subsisting. The substances that are cognizant by sense belong, then, of course, to the department of physical science, for they involve a connection with motion; but the immovable substance belongs to a different science, on the supposition that this possesses no first principle in common with the others.

1069b

2. Substance cognizant by the senses, however, is susceptible of change. Now, on the supposition that change takes place from things that are opposed, or such as are media, and not from all things that are opposites—for the voice is not a thing that is white—but from that which is contrary, it is necessary that something, also, subsist capable of undergoing an alteration into contrariety; for contraries do not undergo a change. Further does this, no doubt, continue permanent; that which is contrary, however, does not continue permanent; and hence doth there subsist a something third beside contraries—namely, matter. If, therefore, changes are four in number, either according to quiddity, or according to quality, or quantity, or the place where; and if simple generation, indeed, and corruption be what subsist according to quiddity, and increase and diminution be what subsist according to quantity, and alteration be that according to passion, and motion be that according to place—allowing all this to be the case, the several changes would take place into contrarieties: I mean, such as are involved in singulars. Therefore, it is necessary that matter should undergo a change which can pass into both.

Since entity, however, is twofold, everything which undergoes a change is changed from that which is an entity in capacity into that which is an entity in energy; as, for example, from what is white in capacity, or potentiality, into that which is white in energy: and in like manner, also, does the case stand with increase and diminution. Wherefore, not only according to accident is it possible that all things be generated from nonentity, but likewise from entity do all things derive their generation—I speak of what is an entity in capacity deriving its generation from a nonentity in energy or activity.

And this is the unit of Anaxagoras (for it is better to maintain this than the tenet of certain speculators who are of opinion that all things subsist simultaneously); and it is tantamount to the philosophic dogma of mixture adopted by Empedocles and Anaximander; and resembles the theory of Democritus, viz. that all things subsisted in capacity simultaneously, and not in energy. Wherefore, in this case they would touch upon matter, that is, the material cause. All things, however, involve matter as many as undergo a change; but entities involve different matter from one another: and of the things that are eternal as many as are not generable, but movable by an orbital motion, possess matter, yet such matter as is not generable, but is merely moved from this place towards that.

Now, one might raise the question, from what sort of nonentity generation could arise? For nonentity subsists in a threefold way. If, therefore, there subsists aught in capacity, from this will generation subsist; yet, nevertheless, not from anything whatsoever without distinction, but one thing will be generated from another. Neither is it sufficient to say that all things subsist simultaneously; for entities differ in matter: since why would things infinite in number be generated, but not one thing? For the faculty of the human understanding is one. Wherefore, if likewise matter be one, that would have been generated also in energy the matter even of which would subsist in capacity.

Therefore are there three causes, and three first principles,—two, indeed, amounting to contrariety,—of which one sort constitutes the formal principle and the species, and the second privation; but the third cause is matter.

3. After these inquiries there remains for us to make our readers aware that neither matter nor form is generated. Now, I speak thus of the extremities of things; for everything that undergoes any change is changed both by something and into something— 1070a by something, of course, I mean that which is the first imparter of motion, and of something, that is, matter, and that into which the thing is changed; this is the form. Therefore, they go on in a progression to infinity, if not only the brass becomes spherical, but also the spherical or the brass is generated: therefore, must we sooner or later come to a standstill in the series.

After these inquiries we must show how that each substance is generated from one synonymous with itself; for those things that are being generated by Nature, as well as other things, are substances. For things are produced either by Art, or Nature, or Chance, or Spontaneity. Art, indeed, therefore, constitutes a first principle which subsists in another subject, whereas Nature constitutes a first principle which subsists in the thing itself; for man begets man: and the remaining causes are the privations of these. Substances likewise are three in number, and one of these is matter; which is this certain particular thing in consequence of its appearance as such; for as many things as are one by contact, and not by cohesion, constitute matter and a subject: but another of these substances is Nature, which likewise is this certain particular thing, and into Nature is there the transition of a certain habit. Further, the third substance is that which subsists from these, and is ranked as a singular; for example, Socrates or Callias.

As regards some things, therefore, this certain particular thing involves no subsistence independent of a composite substance, as the form of a house, unless art constitutes this form. Neither is there any generation and corruption of these, but after a different manner they are, and are not, both the house itself, which is unconnected with matter, and health, and everything that is produced according to art; but if forms subsist, they subsist in the case of those things that are generated by Nature. Wherefore, doubtless, not injudiciously affirmed Plato that forms belong to those things as many as involve a natural subsistence, on the supposition of the existence of forms different from, or independent of, these; as, for example, fire, flesh, the head, and so forth. For all these things are matter, and belong to substance especially—I mean, such a description of matter as is ultimate.

Some causes, therefore, that are those that impart motion subsist as entities that have been previously generated, whereas other causes which subsist as the formal principle are simultaneously generated with their results; for when a man is in sound health then also is there present with him sound health, and the form of the brazen sphere subsists simultaneously with the brazen sphere.

And whether, also, there remains anything subsequently to the separation of form from the subject of form, we must examine; for in the case of some forms there is no hindrance to this taking place; as if soul were a thing of this description: not, to be sure, every soul, but the understanding; for that this should be so with every soul is not, perhaps, a thing that is possible. It is evident, therefore, that there is no necessity that on account of these, at least, ideas should have an existence; for man begets man, the singular begets a certain individual. And in like manner does the case stand with the arts; for the medicinal art is the formal principle of health.

4. And as regards causes and first principles, in a manner are they different according as they belong to different things, and in a manner this is not the case. Supposing one to express himself universally, and according to analogy the causes and first principles of all things will be the same. For one might raise the question as to whether the first principles and elements of substances, and of things which subsist as relatives, are different or the same and, therefore, in like manner is it the case with each of the categories. But it would be absurd if there were the same principles and elements of all things, for from the same things will relatives derive their subsistence as well as substance. 1070b What, therefore, will this be? For besides substance and the rest of the things that are predicated there is nothing that is in common. Prior, however, is the element to those things of which

it is an element; but, assuredly, neither is substance an element of relatives, nor is any of these an element of substance. Further, how is it admissible that there should be the same elements of all things? For none of the elements can be the same with that which is a composite nature of the elements; as, for instance, neither B nor A can be the same with BA. Neither, therefore, is it possible that any one element of those natures that are intelligible—as, for example, unity or entity—can be the element of all things; for these are present with each of the compound natures likewise. No one of them, therefore, will have a subsistence either as substance or relation; but it will be a thing expedient, however, that they should subsist in some form or other. The elements, then, of all things are not the same.

Or, shall we say—just as we have already affirmed—that in one way this is the case, and in another that it is not? As, perhaps, in regard of sensible bodies that which is hot subsists in one way as form, and after another mode that which is cold subsists as the privation thereof: but matter subsists as that which primarily and essentially constitutes both of these in capacity; substances, however, are both these and such as consist of those things of which these are the first principles. Or, if any one thing is generated from what is hot and from what is cold, as flesh or bone, still that which is produced from thence must needs be different from these. The first principles and elements of these, I admit, then, are the same, yet there are different elements of different things and, without doubt, we cannot say that the case stands in this way with all things; but analogically are the elements and first principles of all things the same: just as if one should say that there are three first principles in existence—namely, form, and privation, and matter; each of these, however, is different according as it is conversant about every genus, as in color, white, black, surface, light, darkness, air; and from these emerge forth day and night.

Since, however, not only things that are inherent are causes, but also causes of things that are external—as, for example, in the case of what imparts motion—it is evident that a first principle is a different thing from an element; yet both are causes, and into these is a first principle divided: but what subsists as that which imparts motion or rest constitutes a certain first principle and substance.

Wherefore, there are in existence three elements, indeed, according to analogy, but four causes and first principles; and a different cause subsists where the subject is different, and the first cause constitutes, as it were, that which imparts motion, and is different according as the subject is different. Thus, health is as form, disease as privation, body as matter: that which imparts motion is the medicinal art. Again, a house is as form, this certain sort of confusion as privation; the bricks are as matter, and that which imparts motion, or the efficient cause, is the builder's art. And into these, therefore, is a first principle divided.

But since that which imparts motion in physical or natural things is a man, and in things springing from the understanding form, or the contrary, in one respect would there be three causes, and in another four; for the medicinal art constitutes in a manner health, and the building art the form of the house, and man begets man; further, beside these—as that which is the first of all things—is that which imparts motion, or is the efficient cause, to all things.

5. And since some things involve a separable subsistence, and some do not involve a separable subsistence, the former are 1071a substances; and on this account these are the causes of all things, because the passive states and motions of things do not involve a subsistence independent of substances. In the next place, perhaps, will these constitute soul and body, or understanding, and appetite, and body.

Moreover, in another manner analogically are first principles the same; for example, take the instances of energy and capacity. These, however, are both different according as the subjects of them are different, and they subsist in different ways; for in certain bodies the same thing subsists sometimes in energy and sometimes in capacity—as wine, or flesh, or a man. But also do these fall under the category of the causes above enumerated; for form constitutes an energy, no doubt, if it be that which has a separable subsistence, and which is compounded from both: and this is the case with privation,—for instance, darkness, or a creature that is sick; but matter subsists in capacity, for this is that which is endued with the capability of becoming both. But after another mode do those things differ in energy and capacity of which the matter is not the same, and of which the form is not the same, but different,—as a cause of man are both the elements fire and earth, as matter; and his proper form, and if there is anything else extrinsic—I mean, such as his father; and beside these the sun and the oblique circle, which constitute neither matter, nor form, nor privation, nor are of the same species, but are motive natures.

And, further, it is expedient for us to perceive that as regards causes it is possible to enumerate some that are universal and some that are not; therefore, the original first principles of all things are that which subsists in energy as this first thing, and something else which subsists in potentiality. Those, indeed therefore, that are universals have not any subsistence; for the singular constitutes a first principle of singulars: for man, to be sure, is the principle of universal man, yet there is no universal man; but Peleus is the cause of Achilles, and your father of you, and this particular letter *B* is the cause of this syllable *BA*, and, in short, *B* of *BA* absolutely.

In the next place, the forms of substances are first principles; but there are different causes and elements of different things, as has been declared: thus, of the things that are not contained in the same genus, such as colors, sounds, substances, quantity, the elements are not the same, except analogically: the causes, likewise, of those things that are contained in the same species are different, but they are not different in species, but because the matter of singulars is a thing that is different, both your matter and form, and that which imparts motion and the species, differ in number from mine, though, according to the formal principle of the universal, they are the same.

Therefore, as to the inquiry, what are first principles or elements of substances, and relations, and qualities, as to whether they are the same or different? It is evident that, if they are predicated multifariously, there are the same principles and elements belonging to everything; but, if they are divided, there are not the same, but different first principles of everything, unless that, also, in a certain respect there are the same principles of all things. Thus, they are the same analogically, I admit, because there is matter, form, privation, that which imparts motion: and in that way the causes of substances are as the causes of all things, because, on the supposition of substances being destroyed, all things are destroyed. Further, that which is first subsists in actuality, and in this way are these primaries different,—as many as are contraries,—seeing that they neither are predicated as genera, nor denominated multifariously; further likewise, are there different kinds of matter that are styled causes. What, 1071b therefore, the first principles of sensibles are, and what sort they are, and after what mode they are the same, and after what mode they are different, all this has been declared.

6. But since there have appeared three substances—two, indeed, that are natural or physical, and one which is immovable— regarding this immovable substance we must endeavor to establish that it is necessary that it should constitute a certain eternal substance, one which is immovable; for the first of entities are substances; and if we suppose all of them to be corruptible, all things are corruptible. It is impossible, however, that in such a case motion should be either generated, or that it should be corrupted, for it was always in existence; nor is this possible with duration; for it is not possible that there can be that which is prior and subsequent, on the supposition that time or duration has no existence: and motion, then, in this way is continuous, as also duration; for duration either is the same as motion, or it is a certain passive condition of motion. But there is not any motion that is continuous save that which is local or topical, and to this belongs the motion that is circular; but,

doubtless, if there is anything that is fit for being moved, or that is productive, but not anything that energizes, in this case motion has no existence; for it is admissible that what involves capacity should not energize.

There would, then, be no advantage gained, not even if we could make substances eternal, as those do who constitute as such the forms or ideas, unless there will be inherent some first principle capable of working a change. Therefore, neither would this be competent for such, nor would there be any other substance different from, or independent of, the forms; for, on the supposition that it will not energize, there will be no motion in existence. Further, neither will this be the case if the substance will energize, but if the substance thereof constitutes capacity; for there will not be in existence a perpetual motion, for it is possible that that which subsists in capacity should not exist. It is, therefore, necessary, that there should be a first principle of this kind whereof the substance constitutes an energy.

Further, therefore, it is necessary that these substances do not involve a connection with matter. For it is requisite that they should be eternal, if, in sooth, there is also, at least, anything else that is everlasting. It is, then, in energy that they subsist. Although this involves a matter of doubt; for it appears to be the case that what energizes should subsist entirely in a state of potentiality: but that everything that is endued with capacity should not altogether energize. Wherefore, we may assume that potentiality is a thing that is antecedent to energy. But, surely, if this be the case, no one of the entities will be in existence; for it is possible that a thing possess a capacity of existence, but that yet it should not be in existence.

If the case, however, stands as the Theologians affirm—I mean, those who are for generating all things from Night—or as the Natural Philosophers, who say that all things subsisted simulataneously, the same impossibility will ensue. For how, let me ask, will matter be put in motion if nothing that subsists in energy will be a cause? For the matter of a house, at least, will not itself move itself, but the builder's art will; nor does the menstrual blood move itself, nor earth, but seeds, and human seed.

Wherefore, some have recourse to an energy that is always in action, as Leucippus and Plato; for they maintain that motion is always in existence: but why, and in what way, they do not state, nor how this is the case; nor do they assign the cause of this perpetuity of motion. For nothing is put in motion at random; but it is necessary that there be something always in subsistence: as now, indeed, one thing is by nature moved in this way, and again is moved by force, either by Mind, or something else, after a different manner.

Then, what sort is the first motion? For this inevitably differs as much as possible. But, certainly, neither is it possible for Plato, at least, to call that a first principle which imparts motion 1072a to itself, and which he sometimes considers to be a first principle; for subsequent to, and yet coincident with, the heaven is the soul, as he says. Therefore, the supposition of the priority of potentiality to energy is in a manner a correct one, but in a manner is not so. And how this is correct has been declared.

But that energy may be a thing that is antecedent to potentiality Anaxagoras testifies (for the understanding subsists in energy), and Empedocles, in his theory about Harmony and Discord; and this is confirmed in the assertion of certain philosophers, as to the existence of perpetual motion, as Leucippus. Wherefore, not in an infinite time did Chaos or Night subsist; but the same things continually were in existence as are in existence at present, either in a revolutionary system, or otherwise, on the supposition that energy is a thing that is antecedent to poten-tiality. Supposing a thing, therefore, to be the same continually in a revolutionary system, it is necessary that something always should remain energizing in like manner. But if there is likely to ensue generation and corruption, it is necessary that there be something else which continually energizes at one time in one way, and at another in another. It is necessary, then, that it energizes in this way, no doubt, essentially, or from itself, but in a different way according to something else. It must in this case energize either according to something that is different, or according to what is primary or original. It is, therefore, necessary that it energize according to this; for again is that a cause of energy both to this and to that other. Wherefore, that which is primary is superior as a cause; for that, likewise, was a cause of a thing's subsisting continually after a similar manner, and something else would be the cause of the subsistence of energy in a different manner; but of its subsistence always in a different manner manifestly would both be a cause. Therefore are motions, also, in this manner disposed. Why, therefore, must we go in search of other first principles?

7. But since, as, the case stands thus—and, if it be not so, things will spring from Night, and from all things simultaneously, and from nonentity—these aforesaid questions may be decided, and something always would there be that is being moved with a motion that is incessant, but this is that which is circular; and this is evident not merely from reason, but from the fact itself. Wherefore, the first heaven would be eternal. There is, therefore, also something that imparts motion. Since, however, that which has motion impressed upon it, and which imparts motion, subsists as a medium, there is, therefore, something which, not having motion impressed upon it, yet imparts motion, which is a thing that is eternal, being both substance and energy. But in this way it imparts motion—I mean, that which is desirable and that which is intelligible impart motion, whereas they are not moved themselves.

But the originals of these are the same; for a thing that is the object of a propension is that which appears fair; but a thing which is originally selected from volition actually is fair. Now, we desire a thing because it appears fair, rather than that a thing appears fair because we desire it; for the perception constitutes a first principle: but mind is moved by that which is intelligible, and the other coordination constitutes essentially that which is intelligible; and belonging to this is the first substance; and of this is that substance which subsists absolutely and according to energy. Unity, however, is not the same with what is simple or absolute, for unity signifies measure; but what is absolute signifies the mode in which a thing itself subsists. But, certainly, both that which is fair, and that which is desirable for its own sake, belong to the same coordinate series, and that which is first is the most excellent invariably, or amounts to that which is analogous to it.

But that the final cause subsists in things that are immovable 1072b the division makes manifest. For the final cause of anything resides in those things of which the one is in existence and the other is not. Now, that which first imparts motion does so as a thing that is loved; and that which has motion impressed upon it imparts motion to other things. If, indeed, therefore, anything is being moved, it is admissible, also, that it should subsist in a different manner. Wherefore, if the primary motion constitute energy also, so far forth as the thing is moved, in this way is it likewise possible that it should subsist after a different mode in place though not in substance. Since, however, there is something that imparts motion, itself being immovable, and subsisting in energy, this does not by any means admit of subsisting in energy, this does not by any means admit of subsisting in a different manner; for the primary motion belongs to the changes, and of this that which is circular; but this First Mover imparts motion to that.

Of necessity, in this case, must this Immovable First Mover constitute an entity; and so far forth as it subsists necessarily, so far forth does it subsist after an excellent manner; and in this way constitutes a first principle. For what is necessary subsists in thus many ways: in the first place, by what is accomplished by violence, because it is contrary to free-will; and, secondly, as that without which a thing does not subsist in an excellent manner; and, thirdly, as that which could not be otherwise from what it is, but involves an absolute subsistence. From a first principle, then, of this kind—I mean, one that is involved in the assumption of a First Mover—hath depended the Heaven and Nature.

Now, the course of life of this First Mover—in like manner with our own, for a limited period of time—is such, also, as is the most excellent; for, in the present instance, doth that First Mover continue in the enjoyment of the principle of life forever: for with us, certainly, such a thing as this would be impossible; but not so with the First Mover, since even doth the energy or activity of this First Mover give rise unto pleasure or satisfaction on the part of such; and on this account vigilance, exercise of the senses, and perception in general, are what is most productive of pleasure or satisfaction; and with hopes and recollections is the case the same for these reasons. Now, essential perception is the perception of that which is essentially the most excellent; and that which is most essential perception is the perception of that which is most essential. The mind, however, is cognizant of itself by participation in that which falls within the province of the mind as its object; for it becomes an object of perception by contact, and by an act of intellectual apprehension. So that the mind and that which is an object of perception for the mind are the same; for that which is receptive of impressions from what is an object of perception, and is substance, constitutes mind: and when in possession of these impressions it energizes, or subsists in a condition of activity. Wherefore, that seems to belong to the First Mover rather than to the mind of man; and it is a divine prerogative which the mind appears to possess: and contemplation constitutes what is most agreeable and excellent. If, therefore, God in this way possesses such an excellent mode of subsistence forever, as we do for a limited period of duration, the divine nature is admirable; and if he possesses it in a more eminent degree, still more admirable will be the divine nature.

In this way, however, is the deity disposed as to existence, and the principle of life is, at any rate, inherent in the deity; for the energy or active exercise of Mind constitutes life, and God—as above delineated—constitutes this energy; and essential energy belongs to God as his best and everlasting life. Now, our statement is this,—that the deity is an animal that is everlasting and most excellent in nature; so that with the deity life and duration are uninterrupted and eternal: for this constitutes the very essence of God.

As many philosophers, however, as adopt the supposition—such as the Pythagoreans and Speusippus—that what is best and most fair is not to be found in the principle of things, from the fact that though the first principles both of plants and animals are causes, yet that what is fair and perfect resides in created things as results from these—persons, I say, who entertain these sentiments do not form their opinions correctly. For seed arises from other natures that are antecedent and perfect, and seed is not the first thing, whereas that which is perfect is; as, for 1073a example, just as if one were to say that a man is antecedent to seed; not the man that is being generated from seed, but another from whom the seed flows.

That, indeed, there exists a certain Eternal Substance, and a Substance that is Immovable, and possesses actually a subsistence separable from sensibles, is evident from the statements that have been made above. But it also has been demonstrated that it is not possible for this substance to involve any magnitude, but it is devoid of parts and indivisible. For it imparts motion throughout infinite duration; and nothing that is finite involves infinite potentiality. Since, however, every magnitude is either infinite or finite, for this reason such a Substance as the above would not involve a finite magnitude, and therefore it cannot involve an infinite magnitude, because, in short, there is no infinite magnitude in existence. But, unquestionably, also, it has been demonstrated that such is impassive and unalterable, for all other motions are subsequent to that motion which is local or topical. These statements, therefore, make it evident why it is that the deity is disposed as to existence after this manner.

8. Now, whether are we to admit that there exists one Substance of this description or many? And if so, how many such there are ought not to escape our notice; but we should call to remembrance also the assertions of other Philosophers, because, regarding the multitude of these substances, they have not spoken aught which amounts to even anything that is clear in the expression. For,

indeed, the opinion in regard of ideas does not involve any peculiar investigation, for the persons who affirm the existence of ideas affirm that these ideas are numbers; and, as regards numbers, at one time they speak of them as of things that are infinite, and at other times as of things that are limited as far as to the decade. As to the cause, however, why it is that there subsists a multitude of numbers of this kind, nothing is expressed by them with demonstrative certainty.

This, however, must we declare from principles that are taken for granted, and that have been determined. For the first principle, and the original existence of entities, is a thing that is immovable both essentially and according to accident, and it imparts motion with an original and eternal and single motion. But since that which is being moved must needs derive its motion from something, and that which first imparts motion is essentially immovable, and an eternal motion derives that motion from what is eternal as a moving cause, and a single motion its motion from what is single, and since we see that beside the simple revolutionary motion of the Universe—which we say derives its motion from the first substance and that which is immovable—there are other motions that are everlasting—namely, those of the planets (for eternal and unstable in its movement is a body that is circular; but we have furnished demonstrations in regard of these in our Physics);—now, I say, since the foregoing is the case, each of these motions must needs derive its motion from that which is both immovable essentially and is an Eternal Substance. For the nature of the stars consists in being a certain eternal substance, and that which imparts motion is eternal, and is antecedent to that which has motion impressed upon it; and that which involves priority of subsistence to a substance must needs also be a substance. It is evident, therefore, that it is expedient that there should be in existence substances of this kind, such as are both naturally eternal, as well as essentially immovable and devoid of magnitude, and that, too, on account of the cause that has been stated previously.

That, indeed, therefore, these substances are in existence, 1073b and which of these is primary, and which of them is secondary, according to the same order with the orbital motions of the stars, is evident. But at present must we discover the multitude of these orbital motions from that department of the philosophy of the mathematical sciences which is most appropriately devoted to this purpose—I mean, from astronomy; for this science institutes an investigation respecting a substance that is cognizant by sense, no doubt, but such as is eternal: the rest of the mathematical sciences, however, are not concerned about any substances whatever; for example, take the case of the science respecting numbers and geometry. That, therefore, there are numerous orbital motions belonging to the stars that are being moved across the arch of heaven is evident to those who have even moderately busied themselves in such inquiries. For more motions than one do each of the planetary stars assume. But as to how many these happen to be let us, likewise, now declare the statements which some of the mathematicians make on this subject, for the purpose of understanding the point under investigation, in order that it may be possible to apprehend a certain multitude of these when mentally defined. But as to what remains we must ourselves investigate into some points, but we must make inquiries into others from persons engaged in investigations into these subjects; if, haply, anything beside the statements that already have been made may appear to those who are busied in these speculations: and if so, we should bestow affection upon both, yet yield our assent only to those who are more accurate.

Eudoxus, in his system, therefore, laid down the orbital motion of the sun and moon to be severally in three spheres; the first of which he maintained was that of the fixed stars; and the second was that which accords with the circle which passes through the central signs of the zodiac; and the third, with that circle which is situated obliquely in the latitude of the zodiacal signs. Now, that oblique circle through which the moon is carried is situated in a wider latitude than that through which the sun is carried. But of the devious, or erratic, stars he makes a disposition of each in four spheres; and of these, likewise, he considers the first and second to be the same with those of the sun and moon. For the sphere of the fixed stars, according to him, is the same with that first sphere which carries along all the orbs; and that which has been arranged under this, and possesses a motion corresponding with the circle that passes through the central signs of the zodiac, he considers a sphere common to all these heavenly bodies. He is of opinion, however, that the poles of the third sphere, which is common to all, are situated in that circle which passes through the central signs of the zodiac, and that the motion of the fourth sphere is in an orbit declining towards the center of the third, and that the poles of the third sphere are the proper poles of the other spheres, but that Venus and Mercury have the same poles.

Calippus, however, sets down the same disposition of the spheres with Eudoxus, that is, the same arrangement of their mutual distances; but, with respect to their multitude, he ascribed to the star of Jupiter, as well as to that of Saturn, the same number with Eudoxus; yet still he thinks that to the luminary of the sun, and to that of the moon, there should further be annexed two spheres—that is, supposing one likely to furnish a solution of the phenomena. And in regard of the other spheres of the planets, he adds one sphere to each.

It is necessary, however, on the supposition that all, when 1074a collected together, are likely to furnish a solution of the phenomena, that according to each of the erratic stars there should be different spheres revolving, less by one than those which carry along the planets, and, in regard of position, restore into the same place the first sphere invariably of the star which is ranked in an inferior order; for in this way only is it possible that by the orbital motion of the planets should be produced all the phenomena that may be observed. Since, therefore, as regards the spheres in which the planets are carried along, some of them are made to amount to eight, but others to five-and-twenty, and of these it is not necessary that those merely should have revolving spheres in which a star arranged lowest down is carried, those, accordingly, that impart a revolutionary motion to the spheres of the two first will be six in number, while those to the spheres of the four subsequent stars will be eleven: the total amount of all the spheres, however, as well those that carry along the stars, as also those that make them revolve, will be fifty and five. But if one were not to add the motions of the moon which we have mentioned to the sun also, all the spheres will be forty and seven.

Let the number, then, of the spheres amount to so many; wherefore, it is reasonable to suppose that both the substances and the first principles which are immovable, and are cognizant by the senses, should be so many in number as we have enumerated; for that there must necessarily be such a number as this, let it be left to those to decide who are endued with greater ability to declare their sentiments on such points. If, however, it is not possible that there should be any orbital motion which does not contribute towards the orbital motion of a star, and, further, if it is requisite to suppose that every nature and every substance ought to be regarded—provided it be devoid of passion, and be essential—as having attained the most excellent end, in this case there would not be in existence any other nature independent of these: but it is necessary that this should constitute the total amount of substances; for whether there should be others, they would impart motion, as being an end of orbital motion.

But, at any rate, it is impossible that there should be other orbital motions beside those that have been enumerated; and this supposition it would be reasonable to arrive at from observing the bodies that are being moved along the surface of the heavens. For on the supposition that everything that is borne along the firmament subsists by the constitution of Nature, on account of that body which is borne along, and that every motion belongs to something that is carried forward, there would not exist any orbital motion on account of itself or of another motion; but on account of the stars would it exist. For if we admit that orbital motion will subsist on account of motion of the same sort, it will be requisite that this latter, likewise, should subsist on account of other orbital motions. So that, since it is not also possible to go on in a progression to infinity, and end of every orbital motion will be some one of those divine bodies that are borne along the surface of the heaven.

That, however, there is one heaven is evident; for if there were many heavens—as there are men—in regard of each will there be such a first principle as is one in species, but in number many, at least. Such things, however, as are many in number involve a connection with matter; for there is one and the same mode of reasoning applicable to the case of many—take the instance of a man—yet Socrates is one. But that which ranks as first amongst formal causes does not involve a connection with matter, for it subsists in actuality. Accordingly, in both reason and number, that which primarily imparts motion is immovable, and that which has motion impressed upon it in this case is always and uninterruptedly one thing merely; such being true, there is consequently in existence one solitary heaven.

1074b Traditions, however, have been handed down from our predecessors, and the very ancient philosophers, and left to their posterity in the form of a myth, to the effect that these many heavens—supposing them to exist—both are gods, and that the divinity encompasses the entire of Nature. And the remainder of these traditions, in the present day, have been brought forward, clothed in a fabulous garb, for the purpose of winning the assent of the multitude, and enforcing the utility that is urged in favor of the laws, and of general expediency.

For they speak of these as subsisting in the form of the human species, and as being like in appearance to certain of the rest of the animal kingdom. And other statements consequential upon these, and similar to those that have been declared, do they put forward.

Now, if as regards these traditions anyone having separated this form amongst the others may receive merely the first assertion—namely, that they supposed the First Substances to be gods—he would consider that this statement had been made after a divine manner; and in accordance with what is to be expected in the discovery—as frequently as is consistent with possibility—as well of every art as of every system of philosophy, and in the loss of these, again, he must conclude that likewise these opinions of those very ancient philosophers, as relics, have been preserved up to the time of the present day. This opinion, therefore, of our forefathers, and that which has been traditionally handed down from the very earliest speculators, is evident to us thus far, and no more.

9. There are points, however, respecting Mind which involve certain subjects of doubt; for it seems, certainly, to constitute the most divine existence amongst phenomena: but after what manner it is disposed, so as that it should be a thing of this sort, is attended with certain difficulties. For whether it be void of the faculty of understanding anything, but is like one who is sleeping, what, may I ask, would there be reverential in such a condition of being? Or, supposing that it possesses the faculty of understanding, and yet that there be something which is dominant over this faculty—for in this case that which is its substance is not intelligence, but capacity—should the foregoing be true, we could not say that Mind would be the most excellent substance; for it is through the faculty of the understanding that that which is entitled to reverence is inherent in the mind.

But, further, whether understanding constitute its substance, or whether perception does, what, may I ask, does it understand? For either it is itself that it understands, or something else. And supposing that it understands something else, either it will invariably be the same, or something different; whether, then, is there any difference, or no difference at all, between its understanding what is fair, and understanding what is casual; or, also, would it be an absurd idea to imagine that it exercises the faculty of cognition in regard of certain things? It is evident, therefore, that that which understands is most divine, and most entitled to reverence, and that it undergoes no change; for change would presuppose a transition into something that is worse: and a thing of this sort would, in the present instance, amount to a certain motion. In the first place, then, of course, supposing that the mind were not perception or intelligence, but capacity, it is reasonable to infer that continuity of perception would be a laborious operation for the mind; and, in the next place, it is evident that there would be in existence something else that is more entitled to reverence than Mind,—namely, that which is an object of perception to the mind: for both the faculty of understanding and actual perception will be present to the mind even in its understanding that which is most inferior.

So that we must avoid this consequence; for also would it be better not to see some things than to see them: hence, perception would not constitute that which is most excellent. Accordingly, may we assume that Mind is cognizant of its own operations, if it really is that which is most superior, and if perception amounts to the perception of a perception.

Now, scientific knowledge invariably appears, as well as perception by sense and opinion and the faculty of thought, to be conversant about something different from itself, and to be conversant about itself only in a secondary or subordinate sense. Further, if we suppose that understanding is different from being an object of perception to the understanding, according to which of these will subsistence in an excellent way be inherent in Mind? For neither is it the same thing the being inherent in an act of perception by the understanding, and in an object of perception to the understanding: or, shall we say that in the case of some things the science constitutes itself that which is the object of the science?

In the case, I admit, of the productive sciences, the substance and the essence do not involve a connection with matter; whereas in the case of the speculative sciences the definition or formal 1075a principle is the object of the science, as well as is the perception exercised by the mind. Inasmuch, then, as the object of the understanding is not a different thing from the understanding itself, in the case of as many things as do not involve a connection with matter they will be the same thing; and the act of perception by the mind will be identical with the object of perception.

Moreover, therefore, a doubt remains whether an object of perception is a composite nature or not; for, if this be the case, the object of perception, as a compound, would undergo a change in the parts of the entire; or, shall we say that everything is indivisible which does not involve a connection with matter,— as the human mind? Or, are we to take for granted that the perception of compound objects involves a connection with matter during a certain portion of duration? For an excellent condition of subsistence does not always reside in this particular thing or in that; but that which is most excellent subsists in a thing, viewed as a certain entirety, being something different from itself. And, therefore, the first and actual perception by mind of Mind itself doth subsist in this way throughout all eternity.

10. But we must also consider in what manner the nature of the entire creation involves what is good and what is most excellent; whether there exists something that has been separated in point of fact, and which actually subsists essentially, or whether we are to assume the existence of order, or make both of these assumptions together, just as we might illustrate our meaning by the case of an army.

For the good or excellent condition of an army depends upon the order that is enforced; and the commander who aims to promote this subordination, even this person in a more eminent degree may be regarded as a cause of such an excellent condition: for this officer is not set over the army on account of the order that is found to prevail there, but that order is found to exist on account of the command exercised by this officer. All things, however, are coordinated after a certain mode, but not after a similar mode,—take the classification, for example, of aquatic and winged animals, and of plants. And they are not disposed after such a way as that there should not subsist anything in common to either in relation to the other, although in respect of some point do they involve some resemblance. For, indeed, in regard of one characteristic are all things ranked under coordinate series; but as in a house it is allowable, least of all, for the free to do anything whatsoever they please, but all things, or most things, have been reduced into a state of orderly arrangement, so to slaves, likewise, and wild beasts, only in a small degree belongs a desire to do what may contribute to the general advantage; but for the most part their operations are confined to whatsoever chances to fall in their way, for the nature of each of them constitutes to them a first principle of this description. But I say, in this instance, that it is requisite for all to attain unto a condition where distinctions will be drawn; and other things subsist in this way, of which all participate, for the constitution or preservation of the entire.

But whatever impossibilities or absurdities ensue to those who make assertions in a different way, and what sort of theories those put forward on the subject who express themselves in a more elegant or accomplished manner, and in the case of which of these there prevail the least number of doubts, we must not allow such inquiries to escape our observation. For all philosophers are for producing all things from contraries; neither, however, is the expression "all things," nor the expression "from contraries," correctly employed by these speculators; nor do they declare, as regards those things in which the contraries are inherent, in what manner they will consist of contraries, for contraries are mutually impassive.

But by us is this controversy decided rationally by the introduction of a certain third nature. Some, however, constitute some one of the contraries as matter, just as those do who make the odd subject for the even, or plurality for unity. And this, likewise, is decided in the same manner; for the matter which is one is not what is contrary to anythings. Further, all things except unity will participate in what is worthless; for the evil itself constitutes one or other of the elements.

The other speculators assert, however, that neither what is good and what is evil are first principles at all, notwithstanding that what is good is in a most eminent degree a first principle in all things. And some, I admit, correctly make this assertion of what is good—I mean, that we must consider it a first principle;

after what mode, however, it is that what is good constitutes a first principle they do not state: whether it is to be regarded as an end, or as a moving cause, or as a formal principle.

Now, Empedocles also forms his opinions absurdly upon this point, for he makes Harmony to constitute what is good; and this Harmony, in his system, subsists even as a first principle that imparts motion, for it has the power of congregating entities; and it subsists as matter, for it is a portion of the mixture. Now, even on the supposition that to Harmony has it happened in this same system that it should subsist as matter and a first principle, and as a power that imparts motion, yet the essence of this is not the same with the essence of these; according to which of them, therefore, will Harmony subsist? And that Discord should be a thing that is incorruptible would be absurd likewise; and yet this very things constitutes the nature of what is evil. 1075b

But Anaxagoras regarded what is good as a first principle, so far as it is a power that imparts motion, for Mind, in his system, imparts motion; it imparts motion, however, for the sake of something else. Wherefore, that is different from that for the sake of which it subsists, except it subsists as we say it actually does; for the medicinal art in a manner constitutes health. But it was also an absurdity contained in the Anaxagorean philosophy, the not having produced a contrary to what is good as well as to Mind. But all who assert contraries to be first principles do not employ contraries as such, unless one is disposed to handle the subject in a careless vein.

And why it is that some things are corruptible, and some things incorruptible, no one declares; for they produce all entities from the same first principles. Further, some of these speculators produce entities from what is nonentity; but some, that they may not be forced to this, make all things to be one. Further, no one lays down a reason why generation will always exist; and what the cause of generation is nobody declares. And for those who create two first principles will it be necessary to have a different first principle which would be more dominant, as well as for those Philosophers who introduce forms, because there really exists another principle more dominant than these; for why has matter participated, or why does it participate, in these ideas?

And for others it is necessary that there should be something that is contrary to Wisdom, and to that which is the science most entitled to reverence; but to us this is not necessary, for there is nothing contrary to what is primary. For all the contraries involve matter, and these subsist in capacity: but contrary ignorance is opposed to what is contrary, yet nothing is contrary to what is primary.

Further, on the supposition that there do not exist other things beside those that are cognizant by the senses, there will not subsist a first principle, and order, and generation; and the celestial bodies will have no existence: but there is always a first principle of the principle, just as we find in the systems of Theologians and all Natural Philosophers.

Now, admitting that there will be forms or numbers, they will not constitute a cause of anything; and, if they are not a cause of anything, neither will they be a cause of motion at any rate. Further, how, let me ask, will magnitude and continuity arise from things that are devoid of magnitude? For number will not produce a continuous quantity, either as that which imparts motion or as form. But, certainly, there will not be anything, at least, belonging to the contraries which is both productive and motive, for it would admit of nonexistence; but, surely, the energy or producing cause is subsequent to the capacity, and in such a case eternal entities do not exist—but yet they do exist. Accordingly, some one of these hypotheses must be rejected; and this has been declared in the above statement that capacity antecedes energy—as to how it must be accomplished. Further, in what way numbers may be one, or soul and body, and, in general, form, and the thing itself, no one says anything on this point; nor is it possible that one should declare his sentiments thereupon, unless he express himself as we do—namely, to the effect that it is the cause which imparts motion that is the agent of production.

But they who say that mathematical number is the first, and in this way continually suppose the existence of another substance adhering thereto in succession, and of different first principles belonging unto each, these make the substance of the Universe 1076a to be adventitious; for in no wise does one substance contribute anything towards another, as to whether it exists or does not exist—and besides this they introduce many first principles.

The entities, however, do not choose to submit to injudicious government. "The government of many is not a good thing—let there be one ruler."

BOOK XIII

1. RESPECTING, indeed, therefore, the substance of things that are cognizant by the senses, it has been declared what it is, in the mode of inquiry adopted by Natural Philosophers in their theories concerning matter, and subsequently in our own Treatise in regard of matter in a condition of energy or activity. Since, however, our present investigation has for its object to ascertain whether beside sensible substances there is in existence a certain Substance that is Immovable and Eternal, or there is not; and on the supposition of the existence of any such, what it is: in the first place we must take a glance at the assertions made by other speculators, in order that if they happen to make any assertion not after a correct manner, we may not become entangled in the same errors, and that if there subsists any dogma in common between ourselves and them, we may not be indignant with it, as a thing peculiarly in opposition to our present design; for it is a thing that we should remain content with, if one should make some statements with more propriety, but others in a way no wise inferior to ourselves.

Now, there are two opinions respecting these subjects; for certain Philosophers affirm that mathematical entities are substances: such, for example, as numbers, and lines, and those things that are kindred to these: and, again, that ideas are existences of this description. Since, however, some speculators constitute these as two distinct genera—I mean, both the ideas and the mathematical numbers—and others maintain, in opposition, that there is one nature of both, and certain other Philosophers say that mathematical entities are alone substances, in the first place we must institute an investigation respecting mathematical entities, without annexing to them any other nature—as, for instance, might or might not be the case, according to whether they happen to be ideas or not, and whether these are first principles and substances of entities or not; but, as regards mathematical entities, attending to this point merely, whether they possess a subsistence or do not, and if they do, after what mode they subsist? In the next place, after these inquiries, we shall, apart by itself, institute an investigation concerning the ideas themselves, simply considered, and as much for the sake of usage as anything else; for most of the tenets of what relates to these inquiries have been divulged even by exoteric discourses respecting them. Further, also, in regard of that particular form of investigation, it is necessary that we encounter a more enlarged philosophic discussion, when we come to be engaged in our inquiries as to whether the substances and first principles of entities are numbers and ideas. For after the investigation relating to ideas this one remains as a third subject for inquiry.

But it is requisite, on the supposition of the existence of mathematical entities, that these should reside either in objects that fall under the notice of the senses, as certain affirm, or that they should involve a subsistence separable from sensibles; and some make a statement in this way: or, if they are not inherent in either one or the other, they either have no existence at all, or exist in some different manner. Wherefore, the question with us will not be concerning the existence of mathematical entities, but concerning their mode of existence.

2. That, indeed, therefore, it is impossible that these mathematical entities should reside in objects that are cognizant by the senses, and that at the same time the reason assigned for this position is a fictitious one, has been declared also in the doubts, where we have proved that it is impossible that there should be two solids 1076b in the same place at the same time. And, further, also, it depends

on the same course of reasoning, both that other potentialities and natures should reside in sensibles, and that no one of them should possess a separable subsistence. These things, then, have been already declared.

But, in addition to these statements, it is evident that it is impossible that any body whatsoever should be divided; for it will be divided according to a superficies, and this according to a line, and a line according to a point. Wherefore, supposing that it is impossible to divide a point, it is also impossible to divide a line; and if it is impossible to divide a line, the case is the same with the other mathematical quantities likewise. What, therefore, is the difference in allowing either that natures of this description should exist, or that these do not exist at all, but that such natures should be found in sensibles? For the same consequence will ensue; for, on the supposition of a division of the sensibles, they also will be divided, or they will not be of the nature of sensibles. But the fact is, neither is it possible that such natures should be actually, at least, separated; for if independent of such as are cognizant by the senses, there should exist other solids that are actually in a condition of separation therefrom, and which are antecedent to those that are cognizant by sense, it is evident that it is also necessary that beside surfaces there should exist other surfaces that involve a separable subsistence; and in like manner other points and lines, for this deduction rests upon the same reasoning.

And if these points be admitted, again, in addition to the surfaces, and lines, and points of a mathematical solid, there will be different ones subsisting in a separate condition. For incomposite natures are antecedent to those that are composite. And if antecedent to sensibles there exist bodies which do not fall under the notice of the senses, by the same reasoning those very surfaces which subsist essentially will likewise be antecedent to those surfaces that are to be found in immovable solids. Wherefore, those surfaces and lines are different from those which at the same time are inherent in separated solids; for the latter, indeed, are capable of consubsistence with mathematical solids, but the former are antecedent to mathematical solids. Again, therefore, there will be lines belonging to these surfaces prior to which there will needs be different lines and points for the same reason. And of those points contained in the lines that have an antecedent subsistence to those cognizant by sense there will be other prior points to which there will no longer belong different ones that have this prior subsistence.

Wherefore, also, such an accumulation as the foregoing would be absurd; for it happens that independent of such as fall under the notice of the senses there subsist single solids, no doubt, yet that there are three ranks of surfaces beside those that are cognizant by the senses, and that one of these subsists beside those that are sensible, and that the second resides in mathematical solids, and that the third subsists beside those sensibles that are inherent in these, and that there exists a fourfold classification of lines, and that there are five ranks of points. Wherefore, let me ask, respecting which of these will the mathematical sciences be conversant? For, undoubtedly, they are not conversant respecting the surfaces, and lines, and points that are resident in an immovable solid; for a science is always conversant about subjects that involve a priority of subsistence.

And the same reasoning holds good respecting numbers also; for beside each of the points will there exist other monads, and beside each of the entities that fall under the notice of sense; next in order will subsist those that are objects of perception for the mind: wherefore, there will exist infinite genera of mathematical numbers.

Further, how is it possible that we should decide the questions of controversy which we have taken a review of in the doubts enumerated above? For the objects about which Astronomy is conversant will in like manner be different from those that are 1077a cognizant by sense; and this will be the case, too, with those particulars about which Geometry is concerned. But let me ask the question how it is possible that Heaven, and the parts thereof, subsist, or any other thing whatsoever that involves motion? And the case stands the same in regard of those objects that pertain unto Optics and Harmonics; for there will exist both voice and a power of vision in addition to the things that fall beneath the notice of our senses, and to singulars. Wherefore, it is evident that there will be in existence both other senses and other objects of the senses; for why, may I ask, should these exist rather than those? If, however, these do exist, there will also be in existence other animals, if the truth be that also there are other senses.

Further, are some things described by the mathematicians as universal in addition to these substances. Therefore will this also constitute a certain other separated substance intermediate between both ideas and media, and which will be neither number, nor points, nor magnitude, nor duration. But if this is impossible, it is evident that it is impossible that those natures, also, should be separated from sensibles.

Now, the short of the matter is this, that the very contrary takes place, both to what is in fact true and habitually supposed to be true, if one will in this way seek to establish the existence of mathematical entities as certain natures possessed of a separated subsistence. For it is necessary, from the fact of the subsistence of these in this manner, that they should be antecedent to magnitudes that are cognizant by the senses, when yet in reality they are subsequent to them. For an imperfect magnitude is prior in generation, but subsequent in substance, in the same way as what is inanimate is prior to that which is animated.

Further, in what way also at all will these mathematical magnitudes be one, and when will this be the case? For the things, of course, that are here reside in the soul, or a portion of the soul, or in something else that is endowed with reason. And if this be not the case, many things are exposed to dissolution. But now, what is the cause of those things which are divisible and pertaining to quantity being one, and remaining in conjunction with one another as such?

Further, do generations make this evident; for in the first place, no doubt, such make a transition into what pertains unto length, in the next place, into what pertains unto breadth, and lastly, into what relates to depth, and has reached an end. If, therefore, that which is subsequent in generation may be antecedent in substance, corporeity would be antecedent to a surface and a length, and will be both perfect and an entirety in this way in preference, because it is rendered a thing that is animated; but how, one may ask, would a line or a surface become animated? For such an axiom as this would be above the grasp of our senses.

Further, it is true, corporeity constitutes a certain substance, for already doth it in a manner involve that which is perfect; but how are lines said to be substances? For neither are they substances in the same manner as species, and a certain form—for example, if in such a case we should admit that soul were a thing of this sort,—nor are they substances in the same way as matter—for instance, take the case of body as a thing of this description,—for nothing appears as endued with a capacity of consisting either from lines, or surfaces, or points. But supposing that it were a certain material substance, this would appear as one that is endued with capacity of assuming passive states.

In definition, then, granting that mathematical natures will 1077b be antecedent to sense, yet it does not follow that all things whatsoever that are prior in definition should be prior also in substance. For those things that are prior in substance, indeed, are whatsoever things which, involving a separate subsistence, are transcendent in their essence; but all those things are prior in definition of which these are definitions compounded of definitions. These, however, are not inherent at the same time. For if there are not in existence passive conditions, independent of the substances to which they belong—as, for example, a something that has motion imparted to it, or which is white—whiteness will be prior to a white man, and will be prior in accordance with the definition, but not in accordance with the substance; for it does not admit of a separate subsistence, but it always subsists in conjunction with a thing in its entirety—now, I mean by entirety a man, for instance, who is white. Wherefore, it is evident that neither is that prior which subsists by abstraction, nor is that subsequent which subsists by addition, for by addition is a man styled white by reason of whiteness.

That, indeed, therefore, neither are mathematical entities in a greater degree existences than bodies, and that they are not antecedent in their essence to those objects that fall under the notice of the senses, but are so merely in point of definition, and that it is not possible that they should be made to involve a separate subsistence in any place, has been declared with sufficient clearness. Since, however, neither in sensibles is it possible for these to subsist, it is evident that either, in short, they have no existence at all, or they subsist after some mode or other; and on this account not simply do they exist, for existence we predicate multifariously.

3. For in the same manner also as universals in mathematics are not conversant about things that have been separated, and in this condition of separation subsist independent of magnitudes and numbers, but are concerned about these—but not so far forth as they are things of such a kind as to involve magnitude, or to be divisible—it is evident that there is a possibility of there likewise being in existence both definitions and demonstrations respecting those magnitudes which fall under the notice of our senses; not, however, so far forth as they are things cognizable by sense, but so far forth as they are universals.

For in like manner as, also, so far forth as things are in motion merely, there are many formal principles of them independent of the essence of each of the things of this sort, and of their accidents, and since there is no necessity, on account of these things, either that there should exist anything that is being moved in a condition of actual separation from sensibles, or that there should be in things that are such as these any separated nature at all, so, therefore, likewise, in the case of things that are being moved, will there be rational principles and sciences; not, however, so far forth as they are things that are in motion, but so far forth as they are bodies merely: and, again, so far forth as they are surfaces merely, and so far forth as they are lengths merely, and so far as they are divisible, and so far as they are indivisible and things which involve position, and so far forth as they are indivisible merely.

Wherefore, since it is absolutely true to affirm, not only that things capable of a separate subsistence exist, but also things that are not capable of this separable subsistence—as, for instance, that things in motion exist—so, as regards mathematical entities, it is absolutely true to affirm, that such mathematical entities exist, and that, at any rate, they are such as they are asserted to be. And, likewise, as it is absolutely true to affirm, in respect of the rest of the sciences, that there are sciences conversant with this particular thing, and not with that which is accidental to it— for instance, that there is one of what is white, if that which is salubrious should be what is white, but so far forth as it is 1078a salubrious—yet they are not conversant with that, I say, which is salubrious, but with that to which each science of it belongs, if it is salubrious, that is, in this case, with the salubrious, and if so far forth as such is a man it is conversant with man, so also that this is the case with Geometry. It does not, however, follow, even though sensibles happen to belong to those objects about which Geometry is conversant, and though it may not be conversant with them so far forth as they are sensibles, that the mathematical sciences will be concerned with objects that fall under the notice of the senses. And they will not, certainly, be conversant with these while there are in existence other separate natures.

But many things are essentially accidental in things, as far forth as each peculiar quality of such is inherent in each. Since both as far as an animal is female, and so far forth as it is male, these are its peculiar affections, although there is not anything that is female, or anything that is male, which involves a subsistence separable from animals: wherefore, also, the case is the same so far forth as there are lengths merely, and so far as there are surfaces.

And by so much the more as Geometry is employed about those things that are prior in definition, and which are more simple, by so much the more does it involve the consideration of what is accurate; but the accurate is what is simple. Wherefore, Geometry speculates into things that are without magnitude, rather than into those that are connected with magnitude, and especially are without motion. But if it contemplates motion, especially will it contemplate that motion which is primary or original, for this is most simple, and of this is that motion which is equable.

And there is the same mode of reasoning both in the case of the sciences of Harmonics and Optics; for neither are the speculations of either carried on as far forth as the power of vision, or as far forth as voice is concerned, but as far forth as lines and numbers are the objects of inquiry; for these, of course, are the appropriate affections of those: and this is the case with mechanical science in like manner.

Wherefore, if anyone, admitting the existence of those things which involve a separate subsistence from accidents, makes any inquiry respecting these so far forth as they are such, he will not for this reason utter any falsehood; just as neither does he do so when he describes anything on the earth, and says that that is the measure of a foot which is not the measure of a foot; for not in the propositions doth the falsehood lurk. But thus would each particular be investigated in the most excellent manner, if anyone, having effected, as he thought, a separation, should regard as such that which does not in reality possess a separate subsistence, as is done by the arithmetician and geometrician.

For one, indeed, and indivisible is man, so far forth as he is man; but the arithmetician has established an indivisible one; and next he considers whether there is anything that is an accident in man so far forth as he is indivisible. The geometrician, on the other hand, carries on speculations relative to man neither as far forth as he is man, nor as far forth as he is indivisible, but as far forth as he is a solid. For what things, even though he were not indivisible anywhere, would be inherent in him is evident, because, even without these, that which is endued with capacity admits of being inherent in this very man. Wherefore, on this account, geometricians, with correctness, make assertions, and discourse concerning entities, and entities have an existence (for twofold is entity), the one subsisting in actuality and the other materially.

Since, however, that which is good is different from that which is fair—for the one is always in conjunction with the method of doing a thing, but that which is fair also resides in things that are immovable—those who assert that the mathematical sciences make no affirmation about what is fair or good make a false assertion; for they *do* speak of these, and frame demonstrations of them, in the most eminent sense of the word. For if they do not actually employ these names, they do not exhibit even the results and the reasons of these, and therefore they can hardly be said to make any assertion about them. Of what is fair, however, the most important species are order and symmetry, 1078b and that which is definite, which the mathematical sciences make manifest in a most eminent degree. And since, at least, these appear to be the causes of many things—now, I mean, for example, order, and that which is a definite thing—it is evident that they would assert, also, the existence of a cause of this description, and its subsistence after the same manner as that which is fair subsists in. We will, however, declare our sentiments in regard of these points, in a more intelligible form, elsewhere.

4. Respecting, indeed, therefore, mathematical natures, that they are entities, and how far they are entities, and how, in one respect, they are not antecedent to sense, and how, in another, they are antecedent, let thus much suffice to have been said on this subject. Concerning ideas, however, we must, in the first instance, examine into the actual opinion in regard of the idea which would not in any degree connect it with the nature of numbers, but in accordance with the hypothesis that has prevailed from the earliest age amongst those who originally were the first to affirm the existence of ideas.

The opinion, however, in regard of forms, happened to be adopted by those who make assertions in this way, on account of their being persuaded, respecting the reality of this dogma, by the arguments adduced by Heraclitus, to show that all entities that fall under the notice of the senses are in a state of continual flux. Wherefore, if there are systems of science and of practical wisdom, conversant about anything, we affirm that some different natures, in a condition of permanence, must necessarily exist beside those that are cognizant by the sense, for it is plain that a science of those things that are in a state of flux has no existence.

Now, seeing that Socrates was engaged in forming systems in regard of the ethical or moral virtues, and was the first to institute an investigation in regard of the universal definition of these—for, to be sure, Democritus to a small extent merely busied himself in physical inquiries, and defined after what mode that which is hot, and that which is cold, subsisted, but the Pythagoreans, previously to his time, brought forward definitions in respect of some few things, the formal principles of which these philosophers connected with numbers, as, for example, take the instance what opportunity constitutes, or justice, or marriage—Socrates, notwithstanding, I say, from time to time investigated into quiddity or what a thing is, and this, too, on rational grounds. For his aim was to form syllogisms, and we know that quiddity is a first principle of syllogisms. For dialectical strength not as yet had at that time any existence; so that they were able even without the possession of quiddity or the substance of a thing, to institute inquiries into those things that are contraries, even though we should suppose that there would be the same science of contraries. For there are two improvements in science which one might justly ascribe to Socrates; now, I allude to his employment of inductive arguments, and his definition of the universal: for both of these belong to a science that is conversant about a first principle.

Socrates, however, did not, it is true, constitute universals as things involving a separable subsistence, nor did he regard the definitions as such; the other philosophers, however, invested them with a separate subsistence, and, in addition, they denominated things of this sort as the ideas of entities.

Wherefore, it occurred to them, almost for the same reason, that there exist ideas of all things which are predicated universally; and this assumption is just as if one desirous of reckoning a particular sum, when, in fact, the component parts were fewer in number, should consider it an impossibility to do so, but when he had made them more numerous should succeed in counting them. For more numerous, so to say, are forms than singulars that fall under the notice of sense: from an investigation into the causes of which did these speculators advance from sensibles to 1079a ideas; for a form is a thing that is of the same import with a sensible singular, and it subsists independent of substances; and forms are there in the case of many other things—namely, both in these particular things and in those that are eternal.

Further, in the modes in which it is demonstrated that forms exist, according to none of these is it apparent that they really do exist; for from some of them it is not necessary that a syllogism should arise, but from certain others: and in the case of things where they do not suppose that there are forms in existence, of these are there generated forms. For, according to the rational principles that may be adduced from the other sciences, there will subsist forms of all things of whatsoever there are sciences; and according to the notion of the unity that is involved in plurality will there subsist forms also of negations, and according to the perception of something belonging to what has been corrupted will there be forms of things subject to corruption, for of these is there a certain impression on the mind.

But, further, with respect to the most accurate of the arguments that have been brought forward in favor of the Ideal Theory, certain speculators, no doubt, make ideas to belong to relatives, of which they do not affirm that there is an essential genus, whereas others assert the existence of a third man. And, in general, the arguments concerning forms overturn the very things which those persons who maintain the existence of these forms would desire to exist, in preference to the existence of the forms themselves. For it happens that the dyad is not first, but that the number is; and prior to this is that which is relative, and that which involves an essential subsistence is prior too; and this will be the case with all those things whatsoever which certain philosophers, in their adherence to these opinions respecting forms, have put forward in opposition to first principles.

Further, according, indeed, to that supposition by which these speculators affirm the existence of ideas, not only will there be forms of substances, but of many other things besides; for there is not only the one concept about substances but also concerning those things that are not substances, and there will be systems of scientific knowledge conversant not about substance merely. But there are innumerable other consequences that ensue unto this hypothesis. In accordance, however, with what is necessary, and with the opinions that are prevalent concerning the Ideal Theory, on the supposition that the forms are participants, it is expedient that there should be ideas of substances merely; for these do not participate according to what is accidental, but it is requisite that they should participate of each thing so far forth as there doth not exist a predication of it of a subject. Now I say, for example, if anything participates of the twofold itself, this also participates of what is everlasting, but according to accident, for it is an accident for the twofold to be everlasting. Wherefore, forms will constitute substance, and these here and there are in their signification equivalent to substance; or, can we say that there is any existence of anything independent of these? Take the case, for instance, of the notion of unity involved in that of plurality.

And, surely, if one establish that there is the same form of the ideas as of those things that are participants of them, there will subsist something that is in common to both; for why, may I ask, in the case of corruptible dyads, and of dyads that are many, I admit, in number, yet everlasting—why, I say, in the case of these is the dyad one and the same thing, rather than in the case both of this and a certain particular dyad? If, however, there is not the same form of these, the result would be that entities would be homonymous, and the case would be just as if one should call both Callias and a piece of wood a man, though at the same time unable to discern any point of communion between them.

1079b

If, however, we shall establish that other things—now, I mean common reasons—are capable of adaptation to the forms, as, for instance, a plain figure to the circle itself, as well as the other portions or the definition of the circle, and if that, also, to which it belongs will be annexed in addition—if all this be done, we ought to institute an inquiry as to whether or not this may be entirely an ineffectual proceeding? For, also, to what, it may be asked, will the addition be made—whether to the center, or to the surface, or to all the parts? For all things that are involved in substance constitute ideas; for instance, animal and biped. Further, it is evident that it is necessary that a thing itself should be something—in the same way as a surface must be some nature or other which will be inherent in all the forms—as is the case with the genus.

5. But most especially might one raise the question as to what at all it is that forms contribute either to the things that are eternal amongst those that fall under the notice of our senses, or to things that are being generated and corrupted? For neither are these a cause to them of any motion, or of any change whatever. But, certainly, neither do these forms render any assistance towards the advancement of the science of other things. For neither are those the substance of these—for, in such a case, they would be inherent in them—nor do they contribute to the existence of anything at all, inasmuch as they are not, at least, inherent in those things that are participants; for if they were so they might perhaps seem to be equivalent with causes, as in the case of what is white when it has been mixed with what is white.

But, undoubtedly, may this reason be very easily overturned—a tenet, to be sure, which Anaxagoras, in the first instance, and, subsequently to his age, Eudoxus, and certain other speculators, from time to time, maintained whilst laboring under doubts: the theory itself, however, I say, is capable of refutation; for it would be easy to collect together many antagonistic arguments as well as many impossible consequences in reference to such an opinion. But the fact is, that neither do other things subsist from the forms according to any of the modes which are accustomed to be put forward by the advocates of the Ideal Hypothesis.

And the assertion that ideas are models or exemplars, and that other things participate in these, is to speak quite at random, and to assert what is tantamount with mere poetic metaphors. For what, allow me to ask, is that which operates having an eye, so to say, or looking towards the ideas? For anything whatsoever admits of coming into existence, and of being generated; and yet there is no consequent necessity that it should be a thing that is modelled after some form or image. So that, even though we should suppose Socrates to exist, and not to exist, there yet would be generated some such thing as Socrates actually is. And in like manner is it evident that this would be the case even though Socrates were eternal. Also will there subsist many paradigms or models of the same thing; so that this will hold good of the forms, likewise: as, in the instance of man, animal and biped will subsist as forms in conjunction also with ideal man. Further, not only will the forms constitute the paradigms of sensibles, but also those of themselves; as genus might be regarded a paradigm of species that are generic. Wherefore, the exemplar and the image will be the same thing.

1080a   Further, it would appear an impossibility that substance and that to which the substance belongs should be separate. Wherefore, how would ideas which are said to constitute the substances of things involve a separable subsistence? In the Phaedo, however, is an assertion made to this effect—I mean, to the effect that forms are the causes both of existence and of generation. Nevertheless, on the supposition of the existence of these forms, entities, notwithstanding, are not being produced, if also there should not subsist something that is likely to be an efficient cause; and to this we may add that different other things are generated, as a house and a ring, of which they do not say that there are forms at all.

Wherefore, it is evident that those things, also, of which these advocates of the Ideal Theory say that there are ideas, may both exist and be generated on account of such causes as we may consider the things, also, to be that have been just now mentioned, but not on account of forms. But, certainly, as far as regards the subject of the Ideal Hypothesis, it is possible, both in the manner now adopted, as well as by means of arguments that are more logical and accurate, to collect together many similar points with those that already have been made subjects of inquiry.

6. Now, since we have thus far arrived at some settlement of the controversy concerning these upholders of the Ideal Theory, it is well once more to examine into the consequences in respect of numbers, that happen in the systems of those who assert that they are substances that involve a separable subsistence, and the primary causes of entities.

It is necessary, however, on the supposition that number constitutes a certain nature, and that there is not any other substance of it, but this very thing, as certain affirm—it is, I say, undoubtedly necessary in this case that something belonging to it should be classed as what is primary, whereas that something as consequential to this be in every instance different in form. And this directly resides either in monads, and then every monad whatsoever is incapable of comparison with any monad whatsoever, or all of these are directly in order consequent, and any whatsoever are comparable with any monads whatsoever, as scientific men affirm to be the case with mathematical number.

For in mathematical number there is no difference as regards any monad one from another: or, shall we say that, as far as the monads are concerned, that some of them are capable of comparison with one another, whereas some are not, just as if the first dyad were to subsist after unity, and next in order the triad; and so, therefore, another number? But the monads in each number are capable of being compared one with another, as the monads contained in the first dyad are with themselves, and those in the first triad with themselves; and so, therefore, is it in the case of the rest of the numbers. Those monads, however, that are contained in the dyad itself are incapable of comparison with those that are contained in the triad itself; and the case is the same with the other consecutive numbers.

Wherefore, also, the mathematician reckons two after the one, along with the one before, another one; and after the numeration of the three, in addition to these two, he subjoins another one, and the rest in like manner. But this philosopher—I mean Plato—after the one reckons two others without the first one, and the triad without the dyad; and the case stands the same with the other number: or shall we say that one sort of numbers should subsist as that which has been mentioned first, but another, such as the mathematicians put forward, and a third which has been spoken of as last?

1080b   Further, it is evident that these numbers are either separable from things or are not separable, but are resident in objects that fall under the notice of our senses; yet not in these in such a manner as we have considered at the first, but as subsisting in sensibles through inherent numbers; or, at any rate, one kind of these must have a subsistence thus, and another not so, or all of them must exist thus.

The modes, indeed, therefore, according to which it is possible that these should exist are necessarily only these. In general, however, those philosophers who affirm unity to be a first principle, and a substance and element of all things, and that number derives its existence from this and from a certain other one, almost each of them has declared his adherence to some one of these modes, with the exception of that one where all the monads are assumed as being incapable of comparison one with another. And this has happened consistently with rational principles, for it is not admissible that there should be further another mode of the subsistence of number beside those that have been enumerated.

Some, therefore, assert that both are numbers, and that one of these modes which involves what is antecedent and what is subsequent accords with ideas, but that mathematical number is different from ideas and sensibles, and that both ideas and mathematical number possess a separable subsistence from sensibles; whereas others assert that mathematical number only it is that is the original of entities, and that it has been actually separated from sensibles.

And the Pythagoreans say that there exists the mathematical unit, but not one which has been separated; but they affirm that sensible substances consist from this. For the entire heaven they construct out of numbers—with the exception of those that are not monadic numbers—but they suppose that the monads involve magnitude; yet as to how the first unit consists, possessed of magnitude, they seem to be involved in perplexity. A certain other philosopher, however, affirms that the first number is that one which ranks amongst forms; and others say that mathematical number is this first number.

And in like manner, also, is it the case in regard both of lengths and surfaces, and in regard of solids; for some say that those which are mathematical are different from those that subsist after ideas. But, in the case of those who say otherwise, some, it is true, speak of mathematical natures even mathematically—as many, I mean, as do not constitute the ideas as numbers, or say that the ideas exist; but others speak of the mathematical number, yet not mathematically, however; for what they maintain is this, that neither is every magnitude divided into magnitudes, nor that any monads whatsoever can compose a dyad.

All speculators, however—with the exception of such of the Pythagorics as assert that unity constitutes, as it may be said, an element and first principle of entities—seek to establish the dogma that numbers partake of the nature of monads; yet those, undoubtedly, speak of monads as involving magnitude, as has been stated previously. In what number of ways it is admissible, therefore, that statements should have been made respecting numbers, and that all such methods have been enumerated, is evident from these foregoing assertions: all these assertions, however, are, to be sure, impossible, but perhaps one more than another.

7. In the first place, then, we must examine whether monads are capable of mutual comparison, or are incapable of such comparison; and, on the supposition of their being incapable of comparison, whether they are to be viewed in the manner that we have divided. For, indeed, it is possible that any monad whatsoever should not admit of being compared with any whatsoever; and it is possible that those monads that are resident in the actual dyad should not be capable of a comparison with those that are in the actual triad; and so, therefore, that those be incapable of comparison with one another which are contained in each primary number.

1081a

If, therefore, all the monads are capable of comparison, and devoid of any mutual difference, mathematical number, and one number alone, come into being, and it is not admissible that ideas should constitute number. For what sort of a number will an ideal man be, or an ideal animal, or any other species whatsoever? For there is one idea of each, as one idea of man himself, and of animal itself there is another one. Numbers, however, that are similar and devoid of difference are infinite. Wherefore, in no respect will this triad constitute ideal man more than any other one whatever.

On the supposition, however, that the ideas are not numbers, neither is it possible that these exist at all; or from what first principles, may I ask, will the ideas be derived? For number is derivable from unity and the dyad, which is indefinite; and these are said to be the first principles and the elements of number, and it is not admissible to arrange them in classes either as prior or subsequent to numbers.

If, however, monads are incapable of comparison, and incapable of comparison after this mode, so that everything whatever is different from everything whatever, neither is it admissible that this can constitute mathematical number—for, in fact, mathematical number is derived from monads which are devoid of difference, and things that are demonstrated thereby are found to harmonize with monads of this description—nor yet can this number belong to forms, for the first dyad will not be derived from unity and the indefinite dyad. In the next place, the consecutive numbers, as it is affirmed, are dyad, triad, tetrad; for at the same time are the monads produced which are contained in the first dyad, whether after the same manner as the Philosopher was for maintaining who first made the assertion of their subsistence from unequal monads—for from things reduced to a state of equality they have been actually produced—or whether they have a subsistence in another way.

In the next place, on the supposition that there will be one monad that is prior to another, it will also be prior to the dyad that is derived from these. For in case of the subsistence of anything, there is something prior, and something subsequent; likewise will that which subsists from these be a thing that is antecedent to the one, but subsequent to the other. Further, whereas this actual unity is first, then doth there belong a certain first unit to the others, and a second after that, and again a third; there will be a second, of course, after the second, and a third after the first one: wherefore, the monads would be antecedent to the numbers of which they are composed; as, to give an instance, in the dyad there will reside a third monad antecedent to the existence of the number three, and in the triad a fourth, and in the tetrad a fifth, before the existence of these numbers.

No one, indeed, therefore, of these aforesaid philosophers hath asserted that the monads are incapable of comparison after this mode. But, in accordance, to be sure, with the principles of those speculators, it is reasonable that the case should be even 1081b so; though, according to reality, such is impossible. For also that monads should be prior and subsequent is reasonable enough, provided there may be in existence both a certain first monad and first unit; and that in like manner, also, this should be the case in regard of dyads, on the supposition that there is a first dyad likewise. For after that which is first it is rational and necessary that there should be a something that is second, and if a something that is second, a third, and so, therefore, of the rest in order. At the same time, however, to assert the existence of both—even the existence of a first monad, and of a second after unity, and of a first dyad—this is impossible. But they introduce a monad, I admit, and a first one, but no longer do they bring forward a second and a third; and they introduce a first dyad, but no longer do they bring forward a second and a third. But it is evident, also, that such is not admissible on the supposition that all the monads are incapable of comparison—I mean, that an actual dyad, and a triad, and so the other numbers, should have a subsistence. For whether the monads be devoid of difference, and whether they are severally different one from another, it is necessary that number be reckoned according to addition; as, for instance, the dyad by the addition of one to another one, and the triad by the addition of another one to the two, and the tetrad in like manner.

Inasmuch as these things, however, are so, it is impossible that there should be a generation of numbers after this mode, that is, in the same manner as certain speculators generate them from the dyad and from unity. For the dyad becomes a portion of the triad, and the triad of the tetrad; and in the same manner does it happen in the case of those numbers, also, that follow next in order. But from the first dyad, and from the dyad that is indefinite, is formed the tetrad, being two dyads in addition to the actual dyad; but, on the supposition that the actual dyad is not a portion, there will exist still another single dyad, and the dyad will be derived from unity itself, and another one. And, if this be the case, it is not possible that also an indefinite dyad should constitute the other element, for it produces one monad, but not a definite dyad. Further, beside the actual triad, and the actual dyad, how, may I ask, will there exist other triads and dyads, and in what manner are they compounded of prior and subsequent monads? For all these assumptions are even fictitious, and it is impossible that there be a first dyad, then an actual triad; and it would be necessary that this should be the case on the supposition that unity and the indefinite dyad will constitute elements of numbers. If, however, consequences that are impossibilities ensue, it is likewise impossible that these should be first principles.

If, indeed, therefore, the monads are different, any one whatsoever from any one whatsoever, these and such other results necessarily ensue.

But if the monads that are resident in another number are different, and others that are inherent in the same number are alone devoid of any such mutual difference, even in this case not a whit the less do consequences ensue that are attended with difficulty. As, for instance, in the decade itself are involved ten 1082a monads, and the decade is composed both of these and of two pentads. Since, however, the decade itself is not an ordinary number, and since it is not compounded of ordinary pentads, as neither of ordinary monads, it is necessary that the monads should involve a mutual difference—I mean, those that are contained in this decade. For, if they do not involve this difference, neither will the pentads be different of which the decade is composed; yet, since they do involve this difference, the monads, likewise, will differ. And, on the supposition that they differ, whether does it follow that there will not be inherent different other pentads, but merely those two, or that there will be inherent such? And if we do not suppose this to be the case, namely, that they will be inherent, it is absurd; or, if they will be inherent, what sort will be the decade that is composed of those? For there is not another decade resident in the decade beside itself. But, assuredly, also it is necessary that the tetrad, at any rate, be not compounded of the ordinary or casual dyads; for the indefinite dyad, as they say, receiving the definite dyad, has produced two dyads, for it causes the dyad it has received to become two.

Further, the existence beside the two monads of the dyad as a certain nature, and of the triad beside the three monads, how, may I ask, is such admissible? For one will either partake of the other, as a white man beside white and man—for he partakes of these—or will do so when the one amounts to a certain difference of the other, as man beside animal and biped. Further, some things are one in contact, and others by mixture, and others by position; not one of which is it admissible should be inherent in the monads from which the dyad and the triad are compounded;

but just as two men are not one certain thing beside both, so it is necessary, also, that the case should stand with the monads. And they will not be said to differ because they are indivisible, for on this account, also, are points indivisible; but, nevertheless, the dyad of them will not be anything different from the two. But, undoubtedly, neither should this escape our notice, that it happens that there will exist prior and subsequent dyads; and in like manner doth the case stand with the rest of the numbers. For, indeed, even allowing the dyads to rank in the tetrad one along with another, yet these are antecedent to those in the octade: and they themselves have produced—as the dyad has these—the tetrads that are contained in the octade itself; so that if, also, the first dyad be an idea, these likewise will constitute certain ideas.

And there is the same reasoning applicable to the case of the monads also, for the monads in the first dyad produce the four monads that are in the tetrad. Wherefore, all the monads become ideas, and an idea will be compounded of ideas. Wherefore, it is evident that those things of which the ideas themselves happen to be compounded will be composite natures, just as if one were to say that animals are compounded of animals; if there are ideas of these, ideas will be compounded of animals.

1082b   And, in general, to make monads to involve a mutual difference of any kind whatsoever would be an absurd and fictitious supposition—now, I mean by fictitious a thing that is forcibly contrived so as to suit a particular hypothesis. For neither according to quantity, nor according to quality, do we see a monad differing from a monad; and it is requisite that every number should be either equal or unequal: but particularly that which is monadic. Wherefore, if it be neither greater nor less it will be equal. But things that are equal, and, in short, devoid of mutual difference, we consider to be the same in numbers.

And, if this be not admitted, neither will there be in this decade dyads that are without a difference, seeing that they are equal; for what cause will one be able to bring forward who makes the assertion that they are devoid of this mutual difference? Moreover, if every monad and another monad make two, a monad which is taken from the dyad itself, and the dyad which is taken from the triad itself, will be derived from monads that are different; and the question may be put as to whether this dyad will be antecedent to the triad, or subsequent to it? But there appears to exist a greater necessity for its being antecedent; for the one subsists along with a triad, and the other along with a dyad of monads.

And we, indeed, in general, are inclined to adopt the supposition that one and one are two, even whether they may be equal or unequal; as, for instance, what is good and what is evil, and man and horse. They who make assertions in this way do not make these assertions of the monads however.

But, if the number belonging to the triad itself be not a greater number than that belonging to the dyad, it is astonishing: or, on the supposition of its being greater, it is evident that there is an equal number, also, in the dyad. Wherefore, this will be without a difference from the dyad itself. This, however, does not admit of taking place if there is a certain first number and a second number; neither will the ideas be numbers. For this very assertion do they correctly make who think that the monads should involve mutual differences, since they will constitute ideas, as has been previously stated; for the subject of both will be one form.

But, if the monads do not involve this difference, both the dyads and the triads will be indifferent likewise. Wherefore, to the authors of this assertion it is necessary to say that in counting one, two, in this way, we must not, beside what is previously existing, make any additional assumption of anything. For neither will there subsist generation from the indefinite dyad, nor is it possible that an idea can exist, for there will be one idea inherent in another, and all forms will be parts of one. Wherefore, consistently, I admit, with their hypothesis do they make their assertions; yet, upon the whole, they do not make their assertions even consistently with their hypothesis. For they overturn many things; since they are likely to say that this itself, at least, involves a certain doubt—namely, whether when we count and say one, two, three, we additionally assume anything in counting, or whether we carry on our reckoning according to parts? We do so, however, in both cases. Wherefore, it would be ridiculous to reduce this into so great a difference of substance.

1083a   8. In the first place, however, above all, it is well that we should come to some final distinctions as to what the difference is between a number and a monad, if there is any difference at all. Now, it is necessary that this difference exist either according to quantity or according to quality; yet neither of these appears to be admissible. But, so far forth as number is concerned, the difference subsists according to quantity.

And, therefore, if monads likewise differ in quantity, one number also would differ from another number, though it may be equal in the multitude of the monads. Further may we ask whether the first monads are greater or less, and whether they may subsequently increase, or the contrary? For all these statements are irrational. But, undoubtedly, neither is it admissible that they should differ according to quality, for it is not possible that there should reside subsequently in them any passive condition; for also they say that there inheres in numbers quality subsequently to quantity. Further, neither would it happen unto them that this should be derived from unity, nor from the dyad; for the one is not quality, whereas the other partakes of the nature of a constituent of quantity, for of the existence of many entities is the actual nature of them a cause.

But if, then, this subsists after a certain manner differently, we must declare that this is the case likewise, in the most eminent degree, with a first principle; and we must come to some final distinction respecting the difference of the monad—namely, that it is especially a necessary one, and why there exists a necessity that this should be the case. If monads, however, do not differ in quantity, nor yet in quality, what difference can speculators assume as existing in them? That, indeed, therefore, on the supposition that ideas are numbers, it is admissible that all the monads neither should be capable of comparison, nor should be incapable of comparison one with another in either of these ways, this point is evident.

But, assuredly, after the manner in which certain other philosophers make statements respecting numbers neither are such assertions made correctly. And these are such as do not consider that there are ideas in existence, neither simply considered, nor as being certain numbers, but lay down the existence of mathematical entities, and contend that numbers are most original amongst entities, and that actual unity constitutes a first principle of them. For it would be absurd to go on the supposition that unity should be something primary amongst the units, as those persons assert it is; but that a dyad should not be something primary amongst dyads, nor the triad amongst triads; for all such points rest on the same reasoning.

If, indeed, therefore, the assertions in regard of number may be viewed after this manner, and if one will seek to establish that mathematical number exists solely, unity, in such a case, does not constitute a first principle of numbers. For it is requisite that unity—such as this is—should differ from the rest of the monads; and, if this be admitted, there will necessarily exist a certain first dyad that is different from the other dyads, and in like manner, also, will it be so with the rest of the numbers—I mean, such as are consecutive. If, however, unity constitute a first principle, there subsists the greater necessity that the case should stand just as Plato used to say the points regarding number were disposed, and that there should exist a certain first dyad and triad, and that numbers should be not capable of comparison with one another. But, on the other hand, if anyone, again, should maintain these assertions, it has been declared that many impossibilities ensue.

But, certainly, it is, at any rate, necessary that the case be either in that way or this way. Wherefore, on the supposition that it be in neither way, it would not be admissible that number should involve a separate subsistence. It is evident, however, 1083b from these statements, that the third mode is expressed even in the worst manner—I mean, that one which makes out that the number which belongs to forms, as well as mathematical number, are the same; for it is necessary that two errors at the same time should concur with one opinion. For neither is it possible that mathematical number should subsist in this manner; but, as regards a person indulging in peculiar hypotheses, it is necessary that he should be prolix; and that he should enumerate the consequences also, whatsoever they are, which ensue unto those who denominate numbers as forms, this is requisite likewise.

But the plan of the Pythagorics partly, no doubt, involves fewer difficulties than the statements that have been previously made; but partly it involves certain different difficulties peculiar to itself. For the constituting number as that which possesses a subsistence not separable from sensibles removes many of the impossibilities; but the assertion that bodies are compounded out of numbers, and that this number is mathematical, is impossible. For neither is it correct to say that it constitutes individual magnitudes; and, in the next place, because in the most eminent degree they are disposed after this mode, the monads, at any rate, do not involve magnitude: and how is it possible that magnitudes should be composed of things indivisible? But, assuredly, mathematical number, at least, in its nature is monadic; yet those persons say that entities constitute number: at any rate, their speculations do they try and harmonize with bodies, as if numbers were derived from those. If, therefore, it is requisite, on the supposition of number being something essentially belonging to entities, that some one of those modes that have been mentioned should exist, but it is not admissible that any one of these should exist, it is evident, then, that there doth not subsist any such nature of numbers as those furnish who constitute number as that which possesses a separate subsistence.

Further, might the question be asked whether does each monad consist from the great and the small equalized; or whether is the one monad from the little and another from the great? If, indeed, therefore, the case stands thus, neither will each number consist from all the elements, nor will the monads be devoid of mutual difference; for in this monad will be inherent the great, and in that the small—being what is in its own nature contrary. Further, how are those resident in the triad itself? For one of them is uneven. But, perhaps, on this account they make actual unity in what is uneven a mean. But if each of the monads arises from both the elements equalized, how will the dyad constitute one certain nature compounded from the great and small? Or what difference will there be in this from the monad? Further, the monad is antecedent to the dyad; for when it is taken away the dyad is taken away. Therefore, it is necessary that this be an idea of an idea, being, at any rate, antecedent to an idea, and that it has been produced prior to such. Of what, then, will it be? For the indefinite dyad would be formative of duality.

Further, it is necessary that, certainly, number be infinite or finite; for speculators make number to be that which involves a separate subsistence, so that it is not possible that the other of these should not subsist.

That, therefore, it is not possible that it should be infinite is 1084a evident, for neither is infinite number odd, nor is it even; but the generation of numbers is invariably either of an odd number or of an even: when unity, in one instance, falls upon an even number, an odd number is produced; and when the dyad, in another case, falls upon the even, that which is from unity is rendered twofold; and when it falls, in a third way, upon the odd numbers, another even number is produced. Further, if every idea belongs to some particular thing—but numbers are ideas— infinite number, also, will be the idea of something, either of sensibles or of something else; although neither does this admit of taking place according to position, nor according to reason; but philosophers arrange the ideas after this manner.

On the supposition, however, that number is finite, how far, in point of quantity, does it extend? For it is requisite that this should be declared—not only that the fact is so, but also why it is so. Undoubtedly, however, if number extends up to the decade, as certain say, in the first place, of course, will forms fail quickly; as, for instance, if the triad constitute ideal man, what number will ideal horse be? For every ideal number reaches up to the decade. Therefore, it is necessary that certain numbers exist of those residing in these, for these are substances and ideas; notwithstanding, however, they will fail, for the species of animal already will be superabundant. At the same time it is, however, evident that, if the triad in this way be ideal man, the rest of the triads likewise will be so, for similar are those that are inherent in the same numbers. Wherefore, will there exist infinite men; if, indeed, every triad constitutes an idea, each man will be an ideal man; but if not, yet, at any rate, men will be so.

And if the smaller belong, as a portion, to the greater—namely, that which is of the monads that are capable of comparison as a portion of those that are in the same number—and if the tetrad itself be an idea of anything, as of a horse or of what is white, man will be a part of horse, if man constitutes a dyad. But absurd, also, is the supposition of there being an idea of the decade, but not of the endecade, nor of the numbers consecutive to this. Further, however, there both exist and are generated certain things of which there are not forms. Wherefore, the question comes to this, on what account are there not forms of those also? In such a case the forms do not constitute causes. Moreover, it would be absurd to imagine that number, as far as the decade, should be a certain entity in a greater degree, and a form of the decade itself, although there is no generation of this, as of an unit, but of that there is.

Philosophers attempt, however, to alter their opinions, as if the supposition were true that number up to the decade were a perfect one. They generate, at any rate, the things thereon following: as, take the case of vacuity, proportion, the odd, and other things of this kind, within the decade; for some things they ascribe to first principles,—for example, motion, rest, good, evil,—but other things to numbers. Wherefore, unity amounts to what is odd; for if it is resident in the triad, how will the pentad constitute what is odd?

Further, how far do magnitudes, and as many such bodies as there are, partake of quantity; for instance, the first indivisible
1084b line, next a dyad, and next those numbers up to a decade?

Further, on the supposition that number involves a separate subsistence, one might feel a doubt as to whether unity were antecedent, or the triad and the dyad. As far forth, therefore, as number is compounded unity is antecedent, but, as far forth as what is universal and is form are prior, number involves an antecedent subsistence; for each of the monads constitutes a portion of number as matter, but the other as form.

And, no doubt, in one way is the right prior to the acute angle, because it has been limited by its definition, and in another way is the acute prior to the right, because it is a part of it, and the right angle is divided into the acute. Undoubtedly, indeed, as matter, the acute angle and the element and the monad are prior; and, again, as in reference to form and substance—such as subsists according to definition—is the right angle prior, and so with the entire, which is compounded of matter and form; for both are more proximate to form and to that which definition belongs unto, but in generation are they subsequent.

How, then, may I ask, is unity a first principle? Because it is not, they say, divisible, but is indivisible, both that which is universal, and that which is particular, and that which is an element; but in another manner is unity partly that which subsists according to definition, and partly that according to duration. In what way, then, does unity constitute a first principle? For, as has been declared, both the right angle seems to be antecedent to the acute, and the acute to the right, and each is one. Therefore, in both ways do speculators constitute unity as a first principle.

But, further, is this impossible; for the one subsists as form and substance, and the other as a part and as matter. For in a manner each one in reality subsists in capacity, if, at least, number is one certain thing and not as an aggregate heap; but different number subsists from different monads, as they say, and each monad does not subsist in actuality.

A cause, however, of the error which ensues is this, that they are accustomed at the same time to pursue their investigations from the mathematical sciences and from universal definitions.

Wherefore, from those, no doubt, as a point, have they established unity, and the first principle; for the monad is a point without position. As, therefore, certain others, also, have compounded entities out of what is least, so do these persons likewise. Wherefore, the monad becomes the matter of numbers, and at the same time is prior to the dyad; and, again, is it subsequent to the dyad existing as a certain whole, and as an unit, and as species. On account, however, of their being engaged in investigating that which has been predicated universally as an unit, they in this way, also, have spoken of it as a part. But it is impossible that these should reside in the same subject at the same time. But, on the supposition of its being necessary that unity itself should subsist merely without position—for in no respect is there a difference, save that it constitutes a first principle, and that the dyad is divisible, whereas that the monad is not so—if this be the case, the monad would be more similar to unity itself; but, if the monad alone be without position, unity will be more similar to the monad than to the dyad: so that, in either case, each monad would be prior to the dyad. These speculators do not say so, however, at least they generate the dyad first. Further, on the supposition that the dyad itself is a certain unit, and the triad itself, both constitute a dyad, from what, then, may I ask, does the dyad itself consist?

1085a

9. But one might also feel perplexed—since contact, likewise, has not an existence in numbers, but that which is consecutive has—in regard of whatsoever monads there is not to be found a medium, as those that are in the dyad or the triad, whether what is consecutive is to be found in unity itself or not; and whether the dyad be antecedent to those things that are consecutive, or anything whatsoever to the monads?

And in like manner, also, concerning the subsequent genera of number do these difficulties ensue, both in the case of a line, and surface and body. For some inquirers make length from the species of the great and the small—for instance, the lengths, as it were, from the long as well as from the short—but surfaces from

wide and narrow, and bulks from what is profound and low; and
these are species of the great and the small. In respect, however,
of the principle that subsists according to unity have different
persons in different ways sought to establish their opinions upon
points of this description: and in these, also, appear innumerable
statements that are both impossible and fictitious, and which are
contrary to all suppositions that are rational. For also it happens
that they are severed in their connection one with another, unless
likewise the first principles are concomitant, so that there should
exist what is broad and narrow, and long and short. And if this be
admitted, the surface will constitute a line, and that which is solid
a surface. Further, however, angles, and figures, and such like,
how will they be assigned? And the same consequence ensues
unto the points respecting numbers; for these are passive states
belonging to magnitude: but magnitude is not a passive condition belonging unto these; as neither is length of straightness and
what is curved, nor solids of what is smooth and rough.

Common, however, to all these assumptions is that which is
allowable as a subject of perplexity in the case of species viewed
in reference to genus, when one may admit the subsistence of
universals—namely, whether animal itself may reside in animal,
or there be something therein that is different from animal
itself? For, on the supposition that this is not separable, it will not
create any doubt; but, on the supposition of its being separable,
as the persons who make these statements affirm, it would not be
easy to decide the question of doubt respecting unity and
respecting numbers; and if such be not easy, it is necessary to say
what is impossible. For when anyone understands unity as
involved in the notion of the dyad, and, in general, in that of
number, the question arises whether does he perceive a certain
actual thing or something else?

Some, therefore, generate magnitudes from matter of this
description, but others from a point; but a point seems to them
not to be an unit, but to involve some similar quality with unity,
and to belong to a different matter—such as multitude belongs
to, but which does not belong to multitude—respecting which

not a whit the less it happens that one feels the same doubts. For if, in fact, the matter is one, the same thing will be a line, and a surface, and a solid, for from the same things will be derived that 1085b which is one and the same thing: but if the matters are many in number, and there will exist one matter of a line, and another of a surface, and another of a solid, assuredly, they will follow one another, or they will not; so that the same consequences will ensue likewise in this view of the case. For either the surface will not involve a line, or it will constitute a line.

Further, how it is admissible that number should subsist from unity and plurality, there is no attempt made to show; yet, howsoever, therefore, they happen to frame their statements, they encounter the same difficulties as those who make number to consist from unity, and from the dyad, which is indefinite. For one, indeed, generates number out of that which is predicated universally, and not out of a certain multitude; but the other from a certain multitude—yet from that which is primary: for they say that the dyad is a certain primary multitude. Wherefore, there is no difference, so to speak, discoverable in all this; but the same doubts will follow whether we assume it to be mixture, or position, or temperament, or generation, and whatever things of this kind there are.

But one might especially inquire—supposing that each monad is one—from what does it subsist? For, undoubtedly, each will not constitute unity itself at least: but it is necessary that it be derived from unity itself, and from plurality, or from a portion of plurality. The assertion, therefore, that the monad constitutes a certain multitude is impossible, since, at least, it is indivisible; but the assertion that a monad is from a portion of multitude involves many other difficulties: for it is necessary, also, that each of the portions be indivisible, or that it constitute multitude, and that the monad should be divisible, and that unity and the multitude should not be an element, for each monad is not from multitude and an unit. Further, the person who puts forward this assertion does nothing else than make another number, for multitude is a number of indivisible things.

Moreover, also, it is worthy of inquiry, in respect of those who make assertions in this way, whether number may be infinite or finite? For, as it appears, the multitude was also finite out of which and unity finite monads were produced, and multitude itself is different from infinite multitude. What sort of multitude, then, and what sort of an element, is unity? And in like manner might one inquire, also, respecting a point and the element, from which they make magnitudes; for there is not merely, at least, one actual point. Therefore, at any rate, one might ask the question from what each of the rest of the points will ensue? For, undoubtedly, it is not from a certain interval, at least, and an actual point. But, assuredly, neither is it admissible that indivisible portions constitute the portions of an interval, as they do of the multitude from which the monads consist, for number is composed of things that are indivisible; but this is not the case with magnitudes.

Now, all these statements, as well as others of this kind, render it evident that it is an impossibility for number and for magnitudes to possess a separable subsistence.

Moreover, the discordancy of the original framers of this theory respecting numbers is an indication that these things, not 1086a being true, are fraught with sources of confusion unto them. For some of this school constituting mathematical natures merely in addition to those that are cognizant by the sense, when they came to perceive the difficulty and fiction attendant upon forms, have withdrawn their assent from the ideal or formal number, and have introduced mathematical number in its stead; but others wishing to make forms to exist at the same time with the numbers, but not discerning in what manner—on the supposition of one's admitting these as first principles—mathematical number will subsist independent of that which is ideal, have constituted ideal and mathematical number as the same in definition; since, in point of fact, at least, mathematical number has been done away with in this hypothesis: for they introduce peculiar theories of their own, and such as are not consistent with mathematical science.

The philosopher, however, who first sought to establish the existence of both forms and numbers, in obedience to the dictates of reason assigns a separate subsistence to forms and mathematical entities. Wherefore, it happens that all of this sect express themselves correctly in a certain respect, no doubt, yet not entirely with correctness. And themselves, likewise, acknowledge so much, as being persons who do not make the same statements at all times, but such as are contrary with one another.

And a cause of this is the following, that their supposition and first principles are false. But it would be difficult from things that are not properly disposed in regard of truth and falsehood to frame an hypothesis with correctness, according to Epicharmus; for in this case, as soon as the assertion is made, immediately also is apparent that which is not properly disposed in the before-mentioned respect.

Regarding numbers, however, let thus much suffice of the questions that have been started, and of the definitions and distinctions that have been framed. For a person who has been brought to a state of acquiescence in a theory would still the more be induced to yield assent from the force of more numerous arguments; but nothing further will prevail towards inducing persuasion in the case of one who has not been prevailed upon to yield his assent already.

With respect, however, to first principles, and first causes, and elements, whatever assertions those persons put forward, who are engaged in framing their distinctions in regard of a substance merely cognizant by the senses, some of these, indeed, have been declared in our treatise on Physics; but the remainder of them are omitted, seeing that they do not belong unto the plan of inquiry proposed to be pursued in our present work. But whatever assertions are made by those who affirm that there exist different substances independent of those that fall under the notice of our senses, this is a subject for investigation consecutive to those statements that have been already made upon this point.

Since, therefore, certain persons affirm that there are such like ideas and numbers, and that the elements of these are elements and first principles of entities, with respect to these we must inquire what it is they say, and how they say it. Those philosophers, then, who are for constituting as such existences numbers only, and such as are mathematical numbers, are to form subjects for examination afterwards.

Of those, however, who affirm the existence of the ideas, one should at the same time be able to preceive both the manner of their existence, and the matter of doubt that is prevalent regarding them; for also do they constitute ideas as existing simultaneously with universal substances, and, again, they view them as involving a separate subsistence even from singulars. But that these statements are not possible has been previously made a matter of doubt. A cause, however, of their connecting these substances into one and the same species—I mean, with those persons who call ideas universals—is because they are not accustomed to constitute them as the same substances with sensibles.

Some singulars, indeed, therefore, that are involved in objects that fall under the notice of our senses they considered 1086b to be in a state of flux, and not one of them to remain in a condition of permanence; but that the universal subsists both beside these and is something that is different from them. But, as we have declared in the foregoing statements, Socrates communicated an impulse, it is true, to this inquiry, by reason of definitions, yet he did not really abstract them, at least, from singulars; and, in thus not assigning them a separate subsistence, he formed his conceptions correctly.

And one could make this assertion evident from the actual occurrence of facts; for without universals, of course, it is not possible to attain unto scientific knowledge: but the abstraction of them from singulars is a cause of the difficulties that ensue in regard of ideas.

But some, as if it were necessary that if there are certain substances beside those that are cognizant by sense and are in a state of flux, they should involve a separate subsistence—some, I say, were not in possession of other natures, but brought forward those that are denominated universals; so that it happens that both universals and singulars are nearly the same natures. This, to be sure, then, would itself amount to a certain essential difficulty to those statements that have been put forward above.

10. What it is, however, that is attended with doubt, both unto those who affirm the existence of ideas, and those who deny their existence, has, likewise, been observed previously, in the doubts enumerated at the beginning of this treatise; let us, however at present, make a repetition of the statements made there. For if, indeed, one will not admit that substances involve a separate subsistence, and that the singulars of entities subsist in that manner as they are declared to do, such a view of things will overturn substance, as we are disposed to allow; yet, should one assume that there are substances possessing a separate subsistence, how will he establish the elements and the first principles of them?

For, supposing them to subsist as a singular, and not as an universal, entities of this kind will be as numerous as elements, and the elements will not be things capable of being made objects of scientific knowledge. For let the syllables in a word be granted to be as substances, and let the elements of them be the elements of substances, in such a case as this it is, therefore, necessary that *BA* be one, and that each of the syllables should be one, if not, in fact, universally and the same in species, yet each must be one in number, and this certain particular thing, and not equivocal; and, further, they regard each one as the very thing itself. If syllables, however, be thus, so also will those things be of which syllables are composed. There will not, accordingly, be more than one letter *A,* nor will any of the rest of the elements be more than one according to the very same mode of reasoning, in accordance with which neither is there any of the other syllables that is the same; but there is one in one word, and another in another. But, certainly, if this be the case, there will not exist any different entities beside the elements; but entities will constitute elements merely. And, further, neither will the elements be objects of scientific knowledge, for they are not universals; but scientific knowledge is conversant about universals as objects of investigation.

Now this is evident both from demonstrations and definitions; for a syllogism is not completed because this particular triangle has angles equal to two right angles, unless every triangle has angles equal to two right angles; nor because this man is an animal, unless every man is an animal.

But, undoubtedly, if first principles are universal, or, also, if substances that are compounds of these are universal, non-substance in such a case will be a thing that is antecedent to 1087a substance; for, what is universal does not constitute substance: whereas the element and the first principle are universal. The element, however, and the first principle are things that are antecedent to those to which a first principle and an element belong. And, therefore, do all these consequences ensue reasonably, when both certain philosophers constitute ideas as out of elements, and when, beside ideas and substances involving the same form, they may be of opinion that there is some one thing that has actually a separate subsistence. If, however, there is no hindrance, but that, as in the case of the elements of speech, there should be a multitude of the letters A and the letters B, and that A itself and B itself should be nothing beside the multitude of these, on this account, at least, there will be infinite similar syllables.

But the fact that all scientific knowledge is conversant about what is universal, so that it is necessary that both the first principles of entities should be universal, and not separable substances— this fact, I say, most especially is attended with doubtfulness above any of the assertions already made. The assertion that is made is, notwithstanding, in a manner true, and in a manner it is not true; for scientific knowledge, as also the act of scientific cognition, is twofold, of which one subsists in capacity, but the other in energy.

Capacity, then, I mean that which subsists as the matter of that which is universal and is indefinite, belongs to what is universal and indefinite. The energy, however, being definite, is likewise this certain particular thing belonging to this certain definite particular thing. But according to accident it is that the power of vision beholds universal color, because this particular color which it beholds is a color; and what the grammarian speculates into as this particular letter A is a letter A; since, if it be necessary that the first principles should be universal, it is also necessary that those things which subsist from these should be universal: as is shown in the instance of demonstrations. And, if this be the case, there will be nothing that involves a separate subsistence, nor will there be in existence actual substance. It is evident, however, that in a manner scientific knowledge is conversant about what is universal as an object of its investigations, but that in a manner this is not the case.

BOOK XIV

1. RESPECTING, indeed, then, this substance let thus much suffice to have been spoken; but that all constitute first principles as contraries—as we have observed in our Physics—this is also the case in like manner respecting immovable substances. If it is not admissible, however, that there should be anything prior to the first principle of all things, it would be impossible that the principle being anything else should be the first principle of all things; as if one should say that a thing that is white was a first principle, not so far forth as it is something else, but so far forth as it is white, and that this, notwithstanding, belonging to its subject is white, and is something different at the same time, for that will be antecedent. But, certainly, all things are generated from contraries as from a certain subject; it is requisite, then, that especially this should take place in contraries. Always, therefore, will all contraries belong to a 1087b subject, and none of them will be separable. But, as also it appears, nothing is contrary to substance, and reason certifies to the truth of this statement. Not one, therefore, of contraries is strictly a first principle of all things, but a principle that is different from these.

Some, however, make one of the contraries as matter; certain of them, on the one hand, constituting the unequal as contrary to unity, that is, to equality, as if this were the nature of multitude; but some, on the other hand, making multitude or plurality contrary to unity. For numbers are generated by some, no doubt, from the unequal dyad—I mean, the great and small; yet a certain philosopher generates them from plurality: by both, however, this is done from the substance of unity. For the person who says that the unequal and the one constitute elements, but that the unequal, as a compound from great and small, constitutes the dyad, speaks of inequality, and greatness, and smallness, as if they were one; and he does not clearly determine that they are so in definition, but not in number. Yet, certainly, even the first principles, which they call elements, they have not correctly furnished an explanation of: some speculators amongst them, introducing along with unity the great and the small, affirm that these three are elements of numbers, the two first, as matter, but unity as form; yet, according to others, the much and the few are elements, because the great and the small are naturally more peculiar properties of magnitude; but, according to the systems of others, elements are things that are more universal in the case of these—I mean, the exceeding and the exceeded.

There is not, after all, any difference, however, between them, so to say, in regard of certain consequences that ensue, unless in respect of logical difficulties merely, which they try to guard against, by themselves introducing logical demonstrations. Nevertheless, it rests on the same mode of reasoning, at any rate—namely, the assertion of the exceeding and the exceeded being first principles, but not the great and the small, and that from the elements number is prior to the dyad, for both are more universal. But now do they make an assertion of the one, but do not make an assertion of the other.

Others, however, have opposed diversity and difference to unity; but some introduce, as principles, plurality and unity. But if entities—as they are disposed that they should be—are generated from contraries, but to unity either nothing is contrary, or if, then, there is likely to be anything, it is plurality; and if the unequal is contrary to the equal, and the diverse to the same, and the different to the same—if all this be the case, most especially are those persons who oppose unity to plurality in possession of a certain opinion that may be urged in their defense; nor, however, have even these speculators adequately proved their hypothesis. For unity will constitute what is fewness; for plurality is opposed to paucity, but the much to the few.

Now, as regards unity, that it signifies a measure is evident: and in everything is there something different that may be classed as a subject—as in harmony the diesis, and in magnitude a finger or foot or something else of this description, but in rhythm the basis or syllable. And in like manner, also, in weight there is a certain definite standard of measure, and according to the same manner, also, it is with all things: in qualities there is found a certain definite quality, but in quantities 1088a a certain definite quantity, and that which is indivisible constitutes the measure; for one sort of measure subsists according to the form, and another according to sense: so that there does not exist any substance that is essentially one.

And this assumption rests on what is in accordance with reason; for unity signifies that it constitutes a measure of a certain plurality or multitude, and number that it is plurality measured, and a multitude of measures. Wherefore, also, it may be concluded, reasonably enough, that unity is not number; for neither is the measure a standard of measure, but a first principle, and the measure, and unity. It is necessary, however, always that measure should subsist as something that is the same in all things: as, for instance, if a horse is the measure, that such should be horses, and if a man, men; but if man, and horse, and a god, are measures, they will perhaps be animal, and the number of them will be animals: but if man, and white, and walking be such, by no means of these will there be number, from the fact of all subsisting in one and the same subject according to number; yet, nevertheless, there will exist a number of the genera of these, or of some other such category.

But those who make the unequal as a certain unity, but the indefinite dyad from great and small, put forward an assertion very far from the truth of things that are apparent and possible; for these are both passions and accidents rather than subjects of numbers and magnitudes. For the much and few constitute passive states of number, and great and small of magnitude, just as even and odd, and smooth and rough, and straight and curved. Moreover, also, in addition to this error, it is necessary, likewise, that the great and the small, and all things of this kind, should be relatives; but relation, least of all the categories, constitutes a certain nature or substance, and is subsequent both to quality and quantity; and is a certain passive condition of quantity which subsists in relation to something, as has been declared, but does not constitute matter or anything else, and, in general, subsists in regard of what is common in relation to something, and in the parts and species of this. For there is nothing that is either great or small, or much or few, and, in short, which subsists as a relative, which is not much or few, or great or small, or a relative, at the same time that it is something else.

That relation, however, in the smallest degree constitutes a certain substance, and a certain entity, is indicated by the fact of there belonging to it alone neither generation, nor corruption, nor motion; just as with respect to quantity there is increase and diminution, with respect to quality, alteration, with respect to place, motion, with respect to substance, generation simply, and corruption. But this is not the case with respect to relation; for, without being put in motion, at one time it will be greater, and at another time less or equal, so far forth as the other is put in motion according to quantity. And it is necessary that the matter of everything should be such as the thing itself in capacity: wherefore, 1088b also, will this be the case with the matter of substance; but relation constitutes substance neither in capacity nor in energy. Therefore, it would be absurd—nay, rather, impossible—the constituting non-substance an element of substance, and a thing that is antecedent to it, for all the categories are what is subsequent.

But, further, elements are not predicated as elements of each of the things of which they are elements; but the much and few, both separately and simultaneously, are predicated of number, and the long and the short of a line, and a surface is both broad and narrow. But if, doubtless, also, there exists a certain multitude of things to which always there belongs something, indeed, that is few—as, for example, the dyad; for, if this were much, unity would constitute fewness, and, if it were much absolutely, it would be much, after the same manner as the decade, and, if this be not the case, it will be more than this, nay even than ten thousand—how, then, will number, on supposition of the foregoing, in this way consist of few and much, for either both ought to be predicated, or neither? But in the present instance only one of these is predicated.

2. But it is necessary absolutely to examine as to whether, then, it is admissible that things which are eternal should be composed from elements, for they will, in such a case, involve matter; for everything that is compounded of elements constitutes a composite nature. If, therefore, it is necessary that a thing be generated from that of which it consists (both if it exists invariably, and if it were invariably generated), but everything is generated from that which subsists in capacity—I mean, the thing which is being generated (for it could not have been produced from that which is impossible, nor had it any existence before it was generated), but that which is possible admits of subsisting in energy, and not of subsisting in this way;—now, if this be the case, that number also, most eminently above all things, always subsists, or anything else that involves matter, it would admit of nonexistence, just as that also which involves the space of one day, and that which possesses any amount of years whatsoever. Now, if this be so, thus much will be true of time also, when it is extended so as to be without limit.

There would not then exist things eternal, since that is not a thing eternal which admits of nonexistence—as it has come in our way to treat of this subject in other portions of our philosophic discourses. If that, however, which is now asserted be true universally, that no one substance is eternal unless it subsist in energy, and that the elements are the matter of substance, there will not exist elements of any eternal substance from which, as inherent, this substance is composed.

But there are some persons who make an indefinite dyad the element, together with unity; but as to the unequal, they reasonably enough encounter difficulties, on account of coincident impossibilities, from whom so many merely of the difficulties are removed as necessarily arise—on account of the making inequality and relation an element—to those who make assertions in this way. As many difficulties, however, as ensue independent of this opinion, these it is necessary should exist for those also both whether they constitute out of them ideal number, and whether they do so with mathematical number likewise.

Many, indeed, therefore, are the sources of the error with respect to these causes; but particularly does this remark apply to the doubt prevalent downwards from Antiquity. For it appeared to the Philosophers of ancient days that all entities will be one— I mean, entity itself—unless one should adduce a solution of the doubt, and at the same time would advance in the investigation in a line parallel with the theory of Parmenides—

1089a

For this would you never know to be 'non-ens';

but there is a necessity for showing, in regard of its existence, that "non-ens" has an existence; for in this way out of entity and something else will entities arise, supposing they are many. Although, in the first place, indeed, will this be true if entity is denominated multifariously; for one entity signifies that a thing constitutes substance, and another that it is quality, and another that it is quantity, and so of the rest of the categories, therefore. What sort of one will all the entities in such a case be, if nonentity will not have an existence—whether will they be substances, or passive conditions, and other things, truly, in like manner; or will they constitute all things, and the one will be this particular thing, and such like, and so much, and such other particulars as signify one certain entity? But absurd—nay, rather, impossible— would be the assertion that one certain nature produced should be a cause, and that of this entity, and of the same entity, something should be this particular thing, and something else should be endued with quality, and that this should belong to quantity, and that to the place where. In such a case, may I ask, from what sort of nonentity and entity will entities subsist? For also multifariously is denominated nonentity, since, likewise, this is the case with entity; and non-man signifies that which is not this, and the non-straight the not being a thing of this description, and the being not-three cubits that which does not possess this particular quality of measure. Of what sort, therefore, of entity and nonentity are many classes of entities?

Now an advocate of this opinion is desirous of asserting what is false, and of calling this nature nonentity out of which and entity arise the many classes of entities that are generated. Wherefore, also, it was said that it is requisite that something that is false be supposed in the same manner as also geometricians allow, hypothetically, that a thing is pedal which is not pedal. And it is impossible that these things be so; for neither do geometricians suppose anything that is false—for that is not what is the object of the proposition in the syllogism—nor are things generated nor corrupted from that which constitutes nonentity after this mode. Since, however, nonentity, according to its declensions, is styled in an equal number of ways with the categories, and besides this that is denominated nonentity which subsists as what is false, and that which subsists according to potentiality, from this generation takes place—from that which is not-man but man in capacity is generated a man, and a thing that is white from that which is not-white in energy but white in capacity; and, in like manner, is it the case whether both one certain thing is generated, and whether many are.

The inquiry, however, appears to be as to how "ens," which is predicated according to substances, should constitute what is plural; for numbers, and lengths, and bodies, are things that are being produced. Now, absurd is the inquiry as to how, indeed, entity which constitutes the nature of some particular thing is plural, and not also to inquire how it possesses either qualities or quantities. For, beyond all doubt, the indefinite dyad is not a cause, nor yet the great and the small, that two things are white,

1089b or that there are many colors, or tastes, or figures, for these would be numbers and monads. But, really supposing that they attended to these inquiries, at least, they would have perceived also in them the cause; for the same thing, and that which is analogous or proportional, would constitute a cause. For the actual deviation is a cause also of the opposition that is under investigation by them, as subsisting between entity and unity, from which and from these such persons seek to generate entities, and have adopted their hypothesis in regard of relation and inequality, because there neither exists a contrary nor negation of these, but one nature of entities as both this particular thing and that particular quality.

And one ought, also, to institute this inquiry, namely, as to how relatives are plural, but not single. In the present case, however, the inquiry is as to how there are numerous monads beside the first one; but they do not also further inquire how there are many unequals beside the unequal. Although they employ and affirm the existence of the great, the small, the much, the few, of which numbers consist—the long, the short, of which length consists—the broad, the narrow, of which the surface is composed—the deep, the low, of which the bulks consist,—and in this way, further, they without doubt affirm the existence of as many species of relatives as they may introduce. What, therefore, let me ask, is the cause with these of their being plural? It is requisite, therefore, indeed, as we have affirmed, that entity in capacity should be supposed as subsisting in each of these; but by one who makes these assertions is this also evinced—namely, that this particular thing constitutes an entity in capacity, and a substance, but nonentity in itself, because it constitutes a relative: just as if he should speak of something of such a quality, which is neither unity nor entity in capacity, nor a negation of unity nor of entity, but one certain thing which is something belonging to entities; and much more will this be the case, as has been declared, if he prosecuted the inquiry as to the manner how entities are plural, not through the investigation as to the mode those things that belong to the same predicamental line constitute many substances, or many things endued with qualities, but how they are many entities; for some things are substances, but some, passive states, and some, relations.

In the case, therefore, of the rest of the categories, the subsistence of plurality involves the matter also of some other investigation; for, on account of their not being separable, as the subject becomes, and is plural, and those things that are endued with qualities and quantities are plural likewise: although, at least, it be necessary that there should subsist a certain matter for every genus, save that it is impossible that it should involve an existence separable from substances. In the case, however, of those things subsisting as a certain particular thing, there is involved some reason in the inquiry how this particular thing is plural, if it will not be something particular, and this very particular thing, and a certain nature of this description. But rather does this doubt originate from hence, how quantities are many substances in energy, but not one. However, without doubt, even though this particular thing is not the same with that which is a certain quantity, it is not expressed how and why entities are plural, but how and why quantities are plural. For every number signifies a certain quantity, and the monad constitutes nothing else than a measure, because it is, according to quantity, what is indivisible. If, therefore, a quantity be different from that which subsists as a definite particular, from what it is that such definite particular results is not declared, nor how plurality subsists; but, if it is the same, the person who makes the 1090a assertion supports many contrarieties.

And one may also prosecute the inquiry, as regards number, whence are we to obtain our confidence as to their existence? For in the doctrine of ideas the Idealists furnish a certain cause of entities, since each one of the numbers constitutes a certain idea; but the idea is the cause of existence to other things, in some way or other, to be sure: for let this be assumed as a supposition of theirs. To one, however, who does not think in this way, on account of discerning inherent difficulties independent of the doctrine of ideas, the case is different; so that on this account, at least, he does not constitute them as numbers: but to one who introduces mathematical number, whence, may I ask, is it necessary even to have confidence in the existence of number of such a description, and in what respect will such be serviceable to other things? For neither does such a one say that it is the cause of anything who affirms its existence; but such a one asserts it as being a certain nature which involves an essential subsistence: nor does it appear that it is a cause, for all the speculations of arithmeticians, as has been stated, will likewise have an existence as conversant with objects cognizant to our senses.

3. Those, therefore, that posit the existence of ideas, and say that these are numbers, should make an attempt to inform us how and why they subsist; since, according to the exposition of each, every idea constitutes one certain thing that is different from what we regard the many as being. Doubtless, however, since these things are neither necessary nor possible, neither is it to be affirmed that mathematical number exists separably, on account of these at least. But the Pythagoreans, on account of their perceiving many passive qualities of numbers as subsisting in bodies cognizant to the senses, made entities to be numbers, I admit, not involving, however, a separable existence; but they regarded entities as compounded from numbers. And why so? Because the passive qualities of numbers subsist in Harmony, and in the Heaven, and in many other things. To those, however, who maintain that mathematical number exists merely, nothing of this kind is it admissible for them to affirm—that is, if they follow their own hypothesis; but it was asserted by them, because of these will there not exist systems of scientific knowledge. We assert, however, that the case stands as we affirmed formerly. And it is evident that mathematical numbers do not possess a separated subsistence; for, if they did, the passive qualities of those that have actually been separated would not have been resident in bodies.

The Pythagoreans, indeed, therefore, as regards a point of this description, are not deserving of reprehension in any way; but so far, however, as they constitute physical or natural bodies out of numbers, or, in other words, from things not possessing gravity nor having lightness, things involving lightness and heaviness,—so far, I say, they seem to speak respecting another heaven, and other bodies, but not of those that fall under the notice of our senses.

Those, however, who constitute number as involving a separable subsistence because axioms will not exist as inherent in objects cognizant to the senses; the assertions, likewise, of the existence of the other, that is, of the mathematical entities, will be true; and these serve to cause a soothing sensation in the soul: and they suppose that numbers exist and involve a separable subsistence; and in like manner is it the case with the magnitudes of the mathematicians. It is evident, therefore, that 1090b also the adverse argument will enunciate things that are contrary, and the point which just now has been declared a matter of doubt must be decided by those who speak in this way—namely, as to why, on the supposition of these things not by any means being inherent in objects cognizant to our senses, the passive qualities of them should be in sensibles.

But there are some who, from the fact of the existence of boundaries, and extremities—viz., from a point being the boundary of a line, and again, a line of a surface, and a surface of a solid—imagine that natures of this description exist necessarily. Therefore one ought also to discover, as regards this reason, whether it may not in reality be very weak; for neither are extremities substances, but rather do all these constitute limits or boundaries, since both of walking, and, in general, of motion, there exists a certain limit. Is, therefore, this limit some particular thing, and a certain substance? But to indulge in such a supposition is absurd. Certainly, however, admitting that they have even an existence, all of them would be found amongst those objects that fall under the notice of our senses, for the argument itself proclaims their existence in these. Why, then, will they involve a separable subsistence?

But, further, would one who was not very credulous investigate respecting, therefore, of course, every number and mathematical natures, as to why such as these as are prior contribute nothing to those that are subsequent; for, according to those who say that mathematical natures merely exist, though number should not have any existence, yet magnitudes will have a subsistence, and though even these were not in existence, yet still would the soul exist, and such bodies as are cognizant to our senses.

It does not, however, appear from the phenomena that Nature is devoid of a connection with herself, just in the way that a vicious tragedy might be. With those, however, who are for establishing the subsistence of ideas, this, no doubt, escapes them; for they constitute magnitudes out of matter and number—from the dyad, indeed, lengths, and from the triad, surfaces, perhaps, and from the tetrad, solids, or also from other numbers, for there is no difference. But whether, one may ask, will these exist, at any rate, as ideas, or what, pray, will be the manner of their subsistence, and in what way are they contributors to entities, as to their being? For, as with mathematical entities, so do these neither contribute anything in that way. But, assuredly, neither of these doth there exist, at least, any theorem, unless one should choose to put in motion mathematical entities, and to create certain peculiar opinions of his own: but it is not difficult for those who put forward any description of hypotheses whatsoever to be able to be prolix, and to speak without ceasing.

Those, therefore, who cement together mathematical entities with ideas are in this way guilty of error; but the earliest amongst these speculators having constituted two numbers, the one of form, and the other of a mathematical nature, by no means either have declared, or would they be able to say, the manner how this is effected, and from what mathematical number will be compounded. For they make it intermediate between formal and sensible number. For, if we suppose that it is composed of the great and small, the same will it be with that which is belonging to the ideas; but if from some other thing that is small and great, this will not be the case, for number produces magnitudes. But if he will speak of anything different, he will affirm the existence of many elements; and if the first principle of each thing constitutes a certain original unity, there will be in the case of these a something that is common—namely, unity. We must likewise investigate how, also, these many are one, and, at the same time, in regard of the fact that it is an impossibility that number should be produced otherwise than from either unity and an indefinite dyad.

Therefore are all these consequences irrational; and they are at variance both themselves with one another, and with those statements that are reasonable, and there appears to be inherent in them the "long discourse" of Simonides. For a long discourse is like that of the slaves, when no wholesome assertion is made. But also they appear with respect to those elements, the great and the small, to bawl out as if they were being dragged away with violence, for by no means are they able to generate number without doubling that which proceeds from unity.

But it is absurd—nay, rather, a certain one of the impossibilities of this system—to introduce generation in the case of entities that are eternal.

As to the Pythagoreans, indeed, therefore, they have no need to labor under doubt whether they do not introduce or do introduce generation; for they manifestly affirm that unity has been established, and that, accordingly, what is immediately nearest to the Infinite, whether from surfaces, or from color, or from seed, or from such things as they are at a loss to declare, is so, because it has been dragged forward, and bounded by a limit or termination. Since, however, they frame Cosmogonies, and wish to express themselves physically, it is just that they should institute some inquiry concerning Nature, but as a departure from the present method of investigation; for we are engaged in the investigation of the first principles belonging to things that are immovable: wherefore, also, we must examine into the generation of numbers of this kind.

4. They do not speak of the generation of the odd number, therefore, as if it were a thing evident that of the even there is in existence a generation; but the even, in the first instance, certain speculators constitute from unequals—I mean, the great and

small equalized. It is, then, with them necessary that inequality should be prior to the equalization of these. If, however, there always existed things in a state of equalization, they would not have been unequal at a prior period; for of that always existing there is not anything prior. Wherefore, it is evident that it is not for the purpose of speculation that they make the generation of numbers.

It involves, however, a doubt, and a subject-matter for reprehension, to one who acquires knowledge judiciously, how disposed in respect of the good and the fair are elements and first principles. The doubt I mean is as follows: namely, whether any of those is such as we are disposed to denominate the good itself and the best, or whether they are not of this sort, but are of subsequent growth? For the difficulty appears to be acknowledged by theologians—by certain amongst those of the present day—who do not actually make an assertion of this description, but who maintain that from the principle of progression found in the nature of entities, the good and the fair make their appearance on the stage of creation. This, however, they do, cautious about falling into a real difficulty which ensues unto the systems of those who affirm, as some do, that unity constitutes a first principle of things.

1091b

But the difficulty to which I allude is not started on account of this—namely, their ascribing "the well" to a first principle as a thing that is implanted in it—but from the fact of their making unity a first principle, and a first principle as an element, and number as consisting from unity. But the poets—those of the early ages—acted in a way similar to this, so far as they assert the dominion and the rule not of these first principles, such as Night, and Heaven, or Chaos, or even Oceanus, but of Jupiter.

Notwithstanding, to these persons does it happen that they assert things of this description on account of their changing the dominative principles of the Universe; because those of these speculators that, at any rate, were for adopting principles of a mingled description, and in respect of their not broaching their theories in a fabulous garb—for example, as Pherecydes and certain others—have, in point of fact, established "the best" as the earliest principle of generation. And this is the case also with the Magi, and with the *Sophoi* or sages of a subsequent period, such as both Empedocles and Anaxagoras; one of whom constituted Harmony as an element, and the other made Mind a first principle of things. Of those Philosophers, however, who asserted the existence of immovable substances, some, I admit, affirm unity to constitute the actual good; they, however, in the most eminent degree regarded unity to constitute the *substance* of the good. The matter of doubt, of course, therefore, comes to this—as to what way scientific men ought to express themselves on this subject.

It would, however, be surprising if in that which is original, and eternal, and most self-sufficient for its own subsistence, this very original attribute—I mean, the self-sufficiency and the conservation of itself—should not be discovered as that which constitutes what is good. But, undoubtedly, not on account of anything else is it incorruptible or sufficient to itself, than on account of its existence or condition of subsistence after an excellent mode. Wherefore, indeed, the assertion of the existence of a first principle of this description appears reasonable, as far as its reality is concerned.

For this, however, to be unity, or, if not unity, both an element and an element of numbers, is impossible; for much difficulty is coincident with an hypothesis of this kind, and certain speculators, in their attempts to avoid this, have lost sight of the point in question, when they acknowledged unity to constitute an original first principle and an element of things, but a principle and an element of number, however—I mean, mathematical number. For, supposing this to be the case, all the monads would become a something that is good, and there would exist a certain fair supply of things which are good.

Further, if forms constitute numbers, all the forms will be such as some certain thing or other that is good. Notwithstanding, let anyone suppose the existence of ideas of any description whatsoever he feels disposed to admit; for, allowing that they are to be classed amongst things that are good merely, ideas will not constitute substances: but if, also, they are to rank amongst substances, all animals and plants are good, and the participants of these likewise.

Now, both do these absurdities concur with this hypothesis, and what is contrary constitutes an element, whether we assume it to be plurality or inequality; and great and small will amount to what is an actual evil. Wherefore, no doubt, a certain philosopher avoided the connection of the good with unity, as if, on this hypothesis, it would be what is contrary, since generation arose from contraries, that the nature of plurality should necessarily be evil. Some, however, affirm the unequal to be of the nature of evil.

Therefore do all these entities happen to have a share in what is evil, except unity—which constitutes actual unity—and we find that numbers participate in a more unmixed state than magnitudes; it also follows that evil is a place of the good, and that it shares in and desires after that which is subject to decay of itself; for one contrary is corruptive of another contrary. And if it is the case, as we have affirmed, that matter constitutes everything that subsists in capacity—as fire in capacity is the matter of fire in energy—evil will constitute the good itself in potentiality.

1092a

Now, all these results concur partly in consequence of their constituting every first principle as an element, and partly in consequence of their making contraries first principles, and partly because they make unity itself a first principle of things, and partly because they regard numbers as first substances, and such as involve a separable subsistence, and because they take the same view of the species or forms.

5. If, therefore, also, the non-positing of the good in the rank of first principles, and the positing it in the way we have alluded to, be what is impossible, it is evident that first principles are not correctly assigned, nor the primary substances. Yet one does not form his opinions correctly, either if he should assimilate the first principles of the Universe to the principle belonging to

animals and plants; because from things that are indefinite and unfinished there arise always things that are more perfect. Wherefore, also, in the case of the Primary Substances, they affirm that it happens in this way, that neither does any particular entity constitute actual unity. For in objects that are here—that is, that fall under the notice of our senses—are the first principles perfect from which these objects derive their original; for man begets man, and the seed is not that which is first. But it would be absurd, also, the making a place along with mathematical solids—for the place of singulars is peculiar to them; wherefore are they topically or locally separable, mathematical solids, however, are not situated in any certain locality; and the assertion that they will be situated, indeed, somewhere, and at the same time not to say what the place is, is absurd.

But it would become those who say that entities are compounded of elements, and that numbers are the first of entities, that they should, by thus making a division as to how one thing derives an existence from another, express themselves in such a way as to make us acquainted after what manner number originates from certain first principles, whether this takes place by means of mixture.

Neither, however, is everything that has undergone mixture different from that which is being produced; and unity will not be a thing that involves a separable subsistence, nor a different nature: but they wish that it should be after this manner. Does number, however, we may ask, subsist through composition as a syllable? But in this case it is requisite that there should be position; and he who employs his understanding thereupon will comprehend unity apart from plurality. Number, then, will constitute this, that is, a monad and plurality, or unity and inequality. And since that body which subsists from certain entities subsists partly as from things that are inherent, and partly that this is not the case, in which, may I ask, will number be found? For those things which do not subsist in this way, as from those that are inherent, are no other than those of which there is generation. Does it, however, then, subsist as from seed? But it is not possible for anything to proceed forth from what is indivisible. Shall we say, however, that it arises from a contrary that does not involve a permanent subsistence? But whatever things subsist in this manner, are also from something else that does possess a permanent subsistence.

Since, therefore, as regards unity, one Philosopher, in fact, posits it as a thing that is contrary to plurality, and another as what is contrary to inequality, employing unity as if it were equality, number should, therefore, subsist as if it were from contraries. There will then be something else from which, as involving a permanent subsistence, a generation of the other is brought about. Further, why then, at all, are the other things of this sort subject to decay, as many as have their existence from contraries, or wherein contraries are to be found?—why, I say, are they subject to decay, even though they may arise from everything, and yet that this be not the case with number? For respecting this nothing is declared, although a contrary, which is both inherent and not inherent, destroys that which is contrary to itself; as, for instance, discord, mixture: and yet, at any rate, such ought not necessarily to be the case; for the former is not contrary to the latter, at least.

There has been, however, no determination arrived at either, as to the mode in which numbers are causative of substances, and of existence, whether as limits, for example, points of magnitudes; and according to the arrangements adopted by Eurytus, that a certain number belongs to a certain thing, as this number belongs to man, and that to horse, just as they who refer numbers to figures, the triangle and the square, thus assimilating the forms of plants to pebbles of calculation? Or, shall we say that this is the case with the ratio or the symphony of numbers? And, in like manner, it is so as regards man, and everything else: but, as regards then the passive states, how, may I ask, are they numbers, such as the white, and sweet, and hot?

That numbers, however, do not constitute substances, and that they are not causes of form, is plain; for reason, that is, the formal principle, constitutes substance, but number constitutes matter, as the number or substance of flesh or bone. In this way are there three of fire, and two of earth: and number, whatsoever it may be, is invariably of certain things, and constitutes either what is fiery or earthy, or of the nature of a monad. Substance, however, is that which consists in being so much with relation to so much, according to mixture; but this no longer constitutes number, but a proportion or ratio of the mixture of corporeal numbers, or certain other things. Neither, therefore, does number constitute a cause in respect of production, nor does it as number exist at all, nor as such number as is of the nature of a monad, nor as matter, nor as the formal principle, and the form itself of things. But, undoubtedly, neither does it constitute that on account of which a thing subsists—I mean, of course, the final cause of things.

6. One, however, might also doubt what "the well" is which originates from numbers, if mixture is to be found in number, either in that which is rational, or in that which is odd. For now would nothing more conducive to health arise from water and honey being thrice three times mingled; but it would be of more service in that way supposing that there were to subsist no proportion in the condiments, but that it be watery, or, in number that which is an unmixed entity. Further, the ratios—I mean those belonging to the mixtures—consequent upon the addition of numbers are not found in numbers themselves, as the ratio between 3 and 2 is that of 3: 2, not thrice two, however, for there ought to be the same genus in the multiplications. Wherefore, it is necessary that both by the *A* should be measured the order in which the *ABG* is to be found, and by the *D,* that which *DEZ* will assume. Wherefore, there must be the same measure in all things. Therefore, there will be of fire *BEGZ,* and of water the number twice three.

But if it be necessary that all things should participate of number, it is requisite, likewise, that there should be a concurrence of many things that are the same, and that there should be the same number for this and for another. Is this thing, therefore, a cause, 1093a and on account of this is there anything that is done, or is it obscure, such, for instance, as is a certain number of the revolutionary movements of the sun; and, again, of those of the moon; and the life and age of each of the animal creation, at least? What obstruction, then, I may ask, is there to some of these being square, but others of them cubical and equal to each other, and others twofold. For there is no hindrance to this: but it is necessary that they be intimately connected with these, if all things are wont to participate in common of number; and if it should be admissible that things which differ from each other should fall under the same number. Wherefore, if the same number happens to be found in certain things, those will be the same with one another, having the same form of number; as sun and moon will be the same, having the same numerical form.

But why are these causes of things? There are seven vowels, no doubt, and seven chords or harmonies, and seven Pleiades, and within seven years some animals cast their teeth—some, at any rate, do so, and some do not—and seven in number were those warriors that undertook the famous expedition against Thebes. Is it, then, the case, because such a particular number is naturally suited for such purposes, that on this account either those chieftains amounted to seven, or that the Pleiades consist of seven stars; or were the "Septem contra Thebas" so on account of the gates of Thebes, or through some other different cause? If, however, we reckon in this manner, and assign twelve stars to Arcturus, at least, yet others agree in assigning a greater number; since *XYZ* they affirm to constitute symphonies, and that because those are three, these also are three. But that there may be ten thousand things of this sort no one in the least feels any concern; for *G* and *R* would be one sign. But if because each of the others is twofold, but another is not so—now the cause is, inasmuch as there being three places, one in each is added to *S*—on this account there subsist three only, but not because there are three symphonies, since there are, at least, more symphonies than three; yet in the present instance there cannot any longer be more than three. Now, these philosophers, also, are not unlike the ancient interpreters of Homer, who discover minute, but fail to observe important, similitudes.

Certain speculators, however, assert that there are many such like particulars; as, for instance, even as regards media, one medium is nine, whereas another is eight, and a verse of seventeen feet is equal in number to these. Now they say that the verse ascends on the right in nine syllables, but in eight on the left, and that the distance is equal, both in letters from A to Z, and in musical instruments from the most grave sound to the most acute, the number of which constitutes an equality in the all-various melody of the Heaven. One ought not, however, to observe things of this kind (for no one would entertain a shadow of doubt as regards them); nor ought we to make any assertions concerning them, nor to attempt to discover them in things that are eternal; since, also, they are to be discovered in things that are subject to corruption.

Those natures, however, in numbers that are the subjects of applause, and the things contrary to these, and in general those that fall under our notice in the mathematical sciences—as some, in fact, affirm them to be, and constitute them as causes of Nature—appear to persons, at least, who view the matter in this light, to escape their notice; for according to no one of the modes of those that are defined respecting first principles is any of them causative. And yet they *do* make manifest that point, namely, that "the well" has a subsistence, and that to the coordination in the case of the fair belong the odd, the straight, the equal, the powers of certain numbers. For at the same time subsist seasons, and such a particular number, and other things, therefore, of this sort— such as they gather from mathematical theorems—these all involve this power or capacity. Wherefore, also, they seem like unto casual coincidences; for they are accidents, no doubt, yet all are appropriate to one another, the analogical, however, is one. For in each category of entity is there the analogical; as the straight in length is analogous to the even in superficies, to, perhaps, the odd in number, and in color to the white.

Further, numbers which are in the species do not constitute causes of things harmonic, and the like; for those that are equals in the species differ from each other, for likewise do the monads differ. Wherefore, on account of these things, at least, we must not constitute them species. As regards the consequences, indeed, then, that ensue, both these, and even still more than these, can be collected. They appear, however, to furnish a proof of the fact that the supporters of the Ideal Hypothesis fall into many errors respecting the generation of them, and that in no way can a connection be traced in their systems; inasmuch as mathematical species do not involve a subsistence separable from sensibles, as some affirm; nor do these constitute the first principles of things.

ENDNOTES

INTRODUCTION

[1] W. D. Ross. *Aristotle*. London: Methuen, 1949, 5th rev. edition., 154. See his chapter on the *Metaphysics*, 154-185.

[2] Treddenick, 1935: ix.

[3] See John Worthington's preface to W. D. Ross' (1956) translation of the *Metaphysics* and Ross' introduction.

[4] Some matter allows only spatial motion; some also allow alteration; increase or decrease; and generation and destruction. "Sensible matter implies intelligible matter [if it can be senses it can be conceived of or understood], and each grade of sensible matter implies all the previous grades." Treddinick, 1935: xxvii.

BOOK II

[1] This book is titled "Book I the Less" by McMahon. Scholars argue that it may not belong to *The Metaphysics* but be an insertion from another work of Aristotle, possibly *The Physics*. In numbering these books sequentially, I follow the order of McKeon's edition. (Ed.)

SUGGESTED READING

AQUINAS, THOMAS. *Commentary on the Metaphysics of Aristotle.* Trans. J. P. Rowan. Chicago: Henry Regnery Co., 1961.

RADICE, ROBERTO, AND RICHARD DAVIES. *Aristotle's Metaphysics: Annotated Bibliography of the Twentieth Century Literature.* Foreword by Giovanni Reale, in Collaboration with Matteo Andolfi [et al.], New York: E. J. Brill, 1997.

ROSS, W. D. *Aristotle.* London: Methuen, 1949, 5th rev. edn.

WEDIN, MICHAEL V. *Aristotle's theory of substance: the Categories and Metaphysics Zeta.* New York: Oxford University Press, 2000.